Dora and Hubert Foss in 1943 at a Musical Summer School
at Knebworth House, Hertfordshire

Music in Their Time

Music in Their Time

*The Memoirs and Letters
of Dora and Hubert Foss*

Edited by

Stephen Lloyd, Diana Sparkes and Brian Sparkes

With an introduction by

Simon Wright

THE BOYDELL PRESS

First published 2019
The Boydell Press, Woodbridge

ISBN 978-1-78327-413-0

The Boydell Press is an imprint of Boydell & Brewer Ltd
PO Box 9, Woodbridge, Suffolk IP12 3DF, UK
and of Boydell & Brewer Inc.
668 Mt Hope Avenue, Rochester, NY 14620–2731, USA
website: www.boydellandbrewer.com

A catalogue record of this publication is available
from the British Library

This publication is printed on acid-free paper

Text designed and set by BBR Design, Sheffield

Contents

Illustrations

Frontispiece

Dora and Hubert Foss in 1943 at a Musical Summer School at Knebworth House, Hertfordshire. By kind permission of the Hon. Henry Lytton Cobbold.

Text figures

Plates

Preface

AFTER THE DEATH OF MY MOTHER DORA in early 1978, I discovered, amongst her effects, a number of chapters she had completed about various musicians and writers with whom she had come into contact between the wars. As the wife of my father, Hubert James Foss, the founder-manager in 1923 of the Music Department of the Oxford University Press, she rejoiced in entertaining a wide range of distinguished men and women at Nightingale Corner, their house in Rickmansworth, and later in the Hampstead Garden Suburb. When my father died in 1953, aged only fifty-four, my mother inherited the huge tomes which were familiarly known to us as the 'Commonplace Books'; they were filled with correspondence, articles, letters, programmes, newspaper cuttings of reviews, etc., and there were also dozens of files containing hundreds of individual letters. During her twenty-five years of widowhood, my mother researched deeply into all these and, as a result, was able to compile the memoirs within this book, together with her many lively reminiscences, which add a vital personal touch to the chapters. A few of her memoirs are more sketchy, but the correspondence in them is extremely valuable. What is written here by my mother gives us a unique and witty picture of the renaissance of English music in the 1920s and 1930s.

Over the past decades – in fact forty years – in which I myself have grown old, I have tried to discover a way forward to publish these remarkable memoirs, together with a selection of the huge mass of letters to and from my father, 'his' composers and noted literary figures of the time. In the 1990s I had the pleasure of assisting Stephen Lloyd when he was writing his book on William Walton. He found our archive invaluable. More recently, I became, for Stephen's Constant Lambert book, virtually a copy-editor; and, of course, through these contacts, we became good friends. Later, I had a sudden thought that maybe he could be my editor for this volume, which I am so keen to publish before it is too late. What a relief I felt when he accepted my invitation! He is the perfect editor. He is experienced about publishing and knows the period of English music in the 1920s and 1930s extremely well. I owe him a huge debt of gratitude for all that he has done for my parents and for me. In addition, I must thank my husband Brian, also very experienced in the skills of publishing, for all that he has done to prepare this volume for the printers. The book's title was suggested by him. In 1933, my father published a book entitled *Music in My Time*, which he dedicated to me. The present book centres on both my parents, so the borrowed and adapted title *Music in Their Time* is very apposite. I must also thank Simon Wright of the Music Department of the Oxford University Press for so willingly agreeing to write the Introduction. His knowledge of the history of the Music Department is unparalleled. Finally, I am extremely grateful to Michael Middeke of Boydell & Brewer for accepting this book for publication.

My mother's memoirs are the substance of the first part of this book (pp. 19–175). The second part (pp. 177–237) contains correspondence within the wider circle of musicians and literary figures who were closely connected with my parents' lives. The book concludes with the many tributes paid to my father after his death in 1953, a selection of his poetry and the eulogy to my mother given in 1978 by Sir Henry Wood's daughter, Avril.

I hope this book gives a lively picture of the joys and trials of the fascinating musical world between the wars, and I am very proud of the parts which both my parents played during this period.

Diana Sparkes (née Foss)
July 2018

Acknowledgements

T HE EDITORS ARE MOST GRATEFUL to the following for granting permission to reproduce certain letters that are still in copyright: Peters Fraser & Dunlop on behalf of the estates of Margery Allingham and Dame Edith Sitwell; Keith Chapman on behalf of the estate of Michael Ayrton; the Bax Estate; the Bliss Trust and the Bliss family; the Britten–Pears Foundation; Jane Craxton, the granddaughter of Harold Craxton; the copyright holder of E.J. Dent; Emily Gardner, daughter of John Gardner; Jennie Goossens on behalf of her father Léon Goossens; the estate of George Percy Grainger; Nigel Hess for the correspondence of Dame Myra Hess; the Literary Executors of the Herbert Howells Trust; the John Ireland Charitable Trust; Margaret Jacob Hyatt (the widow of Gordon Jacob) for letters by Gordon and Sydney Jacob; Oxford University Press on behalf of John Johnson; the Literary Trustees of Walter de la Mare and The Society of Authors as their Representative for the correspondence of Walter de la Mare; the Milford family on behalf of Sir Humphrey Milford; Daniel Woodgate for the estate of Roger Quilter; Sylvia Darley on behalf of the estate of Sir Malcolm Sargent; Justine Hopkins on behalf of Evelyn Sharp; Edward Johnson on behalf of the Leopold Stokowski Estate; the Tertis Foundation; the Vaughan Williams Charitable Trust; and the Trustees of the William Walton and La Mortella Trust. The editors and Boydell & Brewer are grateful to the Will Trustees of the Michael Tippett Estate for their kind permission to include the letter from Michael Tippett. Thanks are also due to Eve Thynne, Sarah Thomas and Rowena Cardew, the surviving granddaughters of Sir Henry and Lady Wood and nieces of Avril Wood, for their permission to include Avril Wood's eulogy and Henry and Muriel Wood's correspondence. The editors wish to acknowledge the assistance of Judith Curthoys, Christ Church, Oxford, Dr Valerie Langfield and Martin Maw, archivist of the OUP.

All the photographs are from the Hubert Foss Archive. Figure 8 and Plate 17 are reproduced by permission of the Secretary to the Delegates of Oxford University Press, and the frontispiece taken at Knebworth House (www.knebworthhouse. com) is reproduced by permission of the Hon. Henry Lytton Cobbold.

Every effort has been made to trace all owners of copyright material, and in the event of any relevant oversight sincere apologies are offered and amendments will be made in any reprint of this book if either the editors or the publishers are made aware of any such omissions.

Finally, the editors would particularly like to acknowledge the generous financial support of the Vaughan Williams Charitable Trust and the Trustees of the William Walton and La Mortella Trust towards the publication of this book.

The Hubert Foss Archive

THE HUBERT FOSS ARCHIVE, the property of Diana Sparkes (née Foss), is a collection of books, correspondence, programmes, invitations, menus, press cuttings, articles and other papers collected by Dora and Hubert Foss during the 1920s, 1930s and 1940s. The majority of these items are housed in various extremely large Dickensian-type ledgers. It is not known whether these volumes were kept in the Oxford University Press office or at home. These 'Commonplace Books', as they were always called in the Foss family, are now at the home of Diana and Brian Sparkes in Southampton, and have been willed by Diana to the OUP on her death. Soon after the books' arrival in Southampton in the late 1980s, a catalogue was made of all the entries in each volume, and this exists in hard copy, on CD, and on USB.

Also in the Archive Room there is a complete collection in box files of Hubert Foss's programme notes, and Dora Foss kept all the letters Hubert had written to her from his many visits abroad for the OUP or when she was in a sanatorium, and these she boxed in chronological order. There is also correspondence from many distinguished composers and writers of all kinds, including William Walton (32), Vaughan Williams (44), Benjamin Britten (3), Edith Sitwell (7), Henry Wood and his wife Muriel Wood (41). The present state of the letters is variable. Some are a little torn, or slightly faded. Occasionally a page is missing, but, for the most part, the condition is good considering their age. Over the past thirty years a number of scholars have visited the Archive to research the following musicians and writers: Hamilton Harty, Charles Williams, Charles Kennedy Scott, William Walton, Constant Lambert, W.G. Whittaker, Ivor Gurney, John Ireland, John Goss, Thomas Pitfield, Percy Turnbull, Peter Warlock, Ethel Bartlett and Ray Robertson.

The contents of the main files, all labelled, indexed and numbered, are as follows:

1. Correspondence 1 (1917–1934): 1–277
2. Correspondence 2 (1933–1941): 1–483
3. Correspondence 3 (1935–1937): 1–98

4. Correspondence 4 (1933–1938): 1–28
5. Miscellaneous (programmes, invitations, cards, music, menus, etc.): 1–236
6. Programmes (1923–1938): 1–246
7. Press cuttings 1 (1923–1933): 1–740
8. Press cuttings 2 (1930–1938): 1–432
9. Articles 1 (1923–1938): 1–237
10. Articles 2 (1922–1938): 238–278

The letters chosen by Dora, and included in this book, are those which she thought complementary to her memoirs. (One should perhaps add that those included which she received from Hubert represent only a small percentage of their surviving correspondence.) When one considers that she was a widow from the age of fifty-nine until her death at eighty-four, twenty-five years later, one can realise that she had a considerable amount of time to research and write about what she felt and remembered. She clearly wanted her memories to be open to everyone. Neither Diana nor her brother, Christopher, had any knowledge of these writings until they were found in the boxes of papers taken from the Foss family home after Dora's death. Some were in manuscript, but a major part had been roughly typed; some entries had not been completed. The memoirs are unique, and it has been Diana's ambition since then, for forty years, to publish them.

The other items in this book, including further letters, programmes, poetry, eulogies, etc., have been chosen by the Editors. The majority of the letters are unpublished, although a number of those from Vaughan Williams and Walton were published respectively in *Letters of Ralph Vaughan Williams 1895–1958*, edited by Hugh Cobbe (OUP, 2008) and *The Selected Letters of William Walton*, edited by Malcolm Hayes (Faber & Faber, 2002). All the correspondence in 'The Wider Circle' can be found in the Archive.

All the letters are original, some of them extracted here. The majority were handwritten, and when this is not the case, 'typed' has been inserted after the recipient's name. They have been published as they were written, preserving any idiosyncrasies and vagaries of spelling and punctuation (most noticeable in the Walton correspondence), with any necessary amendments or clarifications made either in square brackets or in a footnote. Any missing, torn or unclear sections have been similarly indicated.

A Chronology

19 December 1893	Birth of Dora Maria Stevens
2 May 1899	Birth of Hubert James Foss (hereafter HJF)
1913	HJF entered Bradfield College
30 December 1918	Discharged from the Army
1919–20	Assistant editor *Land and Water*
1921	Joined OUP as education sales representative
1923	Appointed first head of the OUP Music Department
1924	Joint founder of 'The Double Crown Club'
20 July 1927	Wedding of Dora Stevens (hereafter DMF) and Hubert Foss
1927	*The Heritage of Music* (ed.)
21 May 1928	Birth of Christopher Foss
1928	Hadow's *Collected Essays* (ed.)
20 September 1933	Birth of Diana Foss
October 1933	*Music in My Time*
1934	*The Heritage of Music* (ed.; 2nd series)
1935–39	Tovey's *Essays in Musical Analysis* vols 1–6 (ed.)
1941	Resigned from OUP
1941–53	Freelance journalist and broadcaster
1950	*Ralph Vaughan Williams: A Study*
27 May 1953	Death of Hubert Foss
6 February 1978	Death of Dora Foss
3 February 2003	Death of Christopher Foss

Introduction

Simon Wright

Head of Rights & Contracts, Music, Oxford University Press

IN 1933 THE PUBLISHER RICH & COWAN LTD, of Maiden Lane in Covent Garden, London (their list was primarily of literary books) launched a series of monographs exploring varied aspects of the contemporary scene: art, the theatre, and the press, for example, were covered, the books unified by an 'In My Time' series title, at once proclaiming that they were both personal and up to date. The novelist Compton Mackenzie contributed *Literature in My Time*, and *The Theatre* volume was written by the Belfast-born dramatist and critic St John Greer Irvine. The little series opened windows on carefully chosen themes considered important to the enquiring mind at the time, and as it developed came to reflect the preoccupations, perhaps the anxieties, of the decade: *The Navy in My Time* (1933) was delivered by Admiral Mark Kerr, *London in My Time* (1934) by the prolific chronicler and imaginer of that city, Thomas Burke, and *Marriage in My Time* (1935) by Marie Stopes. The topic of music, not unnaturally, found an early place in the list: *Music in My Time* was published in October 1933, and its author was Hubert James Foss.

Foss, in 1933, was at the apex (one might say) of his work as a music publisher. Ten years earlier he had been appointed as the founding editor and manager of a brand-new music publishing department at Oxford University Press. The Press's scholarly books (under the Clarendon Press imprint) were then published at Oxford, but the publisher's trade, educational, and children's books were managed from London, as were its increasingly important overseas operations. The Publisher to the University, Humphrey Milford, was in charge at London, presiding from the elegant (now demolished) Amen House in Warwick Square. At the suggestion of the writer Percy Scholes it was Milford who had personally commissioned Foss, already working at OUP as a sales representative, to 'dip a toe' into issuing sheet music (conditional upon a haircut and a general tidying-up of his bohemian image, of which Milford did not approve). Milford, always one to grasp an unusual opportunity (OUP remains today the only major university press with a music publishing operation), expected, perhaps, a desultory trickle of choral music and piano music, and a continuation of the existing hymn book portfolio (the Press had published *The English Hymnal* in 1906). Foss, being Foss, threw not just a toe but his whole body into the operation, creating in just a few years a vast, diverse, and modern list which embraced instrumental and orchestral music, opera and ballet, songs, sacred and secular choral works, school music materials, carol and folk song collections, a journal, music appreciation and text books, and treatises, a list firmly supported by intricate international distribution and representation arrangements. By 1933, with OUP's music catalogue running to hundreds of pages listing thousands of items, and its publicity strapline 'A Gateway to Music' speaking an almost literal truth, other London music publishers could only stand back, gazing in awe at what Foss had achieved. 'There was', said Foss in the year of his book, 'a big job to be done and the Press, seeing the opportunity, decided to take it.'

Oxford University Press's first music publications (a sequence of short choral works published as 'leaflets' in the Oxford Choral Songs series) appeared in June 1923; Foss had celebrated his twenty-fourth birthday just one month earlier. When, ten years later, he wrote *Music in My Time*, he was thus still a young man, much younger indeed than any of his fellow authors in the Rich & Cowan series (Admiral Kerr had been born in 1864, Irvine and Mackenzie in 1883). The frame of Foss's 'time', then, was far narrower than theirs: the boundaries of his book scarcely embraced thirty years. But, the vision was intense. For Foss was not merely a music publisher, but was involved with every single aspect of music: its composition; its look and layout on the printed page; the developing technologies of sound recording, broadcasting, and reproducing piano, each facilitating the delivery of music in novel ways, to massed and distant audiences; the performance and criticism of music; its history, teaching, and appreciation; and the relationship of music to other performing arts, to literature, to painting. *Music in My Time* is no collection of programme notes, and it is certainly not a narrative musical history (Foss manages a provoking, virtuoso, and blindingly original ten-page discussion of Debussy's music without mentioning a single one of that composer's works). Instead, Foss draws on the rich experience of all aspects of music that his work as a publisher had enabled, and writes a determined, opinionated, philosophical, and occasionally polemical discourse on the role and position of music (in all its manifestations and branches) 'in his time'. Pioneering as always, Foss, in *Music in My Time*, practically invented a genre (it is a personal musical manifesto), and pre-empted what were to become more celebrated examples of it: *Music Ho!*, Constant Lambert's study of music 'in decline', published just one year after Foss's book, or *Musical Chairs*, Cecil Gray's musical memoirs, which came out in 1948. The publisher Victor Gollancz's *Journey Towards Music* (published in 1964 and called by the author 'a memoir') was more substantial (and autobiographical) than any of these books, but was clearly cut from Foss's cloth: Gollancz's assessment of Debussy, for example, has clear echoes of Foss's, made thirty years earlier. Foss possessed an encyclopaedic grasp and instinctive understanding of the music of his time (and of other times, too), how it worked, and who was in it: his 'young man's' book instinctively sets all that down as a matter of record, but in many ways looks as much to the future as it does to either past or present.

Following the publication of *Music in My Time*, Hubert Foss continued to work at Oxford University Press for a further eight years. While Foss poured his energies into his work unabated (these years saw the publication of Vaughan Williams's Symphony No. 4, Walton's Symphony No. 1, and Percy Scholes's *The Oxford Companion to Music*, all of which were major projects closely supervised by Foss), clouds increasingly loomed on his horizon. Humphrey Milford regularly called Foss to heel over apparent extravagance in his expenditure and the unplanned and uncontrolled nature of his publishing (Foss characteristically rebuffed all criticism, presciently claiming that his catalogue was being 'built not for immediate sales only but for a long history of usefulness'), there was a motor accident, and Foss began to suffer ill health and depression. He resigned from OUP in November 1941, and devoted his next decade to broadcasting and writing (his book *Ralph Vaughan Williams* (1950) was the first major survey of the composer and his music). The critic of *Musical Opinion* had, in 1937, labelled Foss 'a human comet, blazing a brilliant trail here, there, and everywhere' but, like all comets, Foss was destined to burn out and disappear from the scene: he died in 1953, just weeks after his fifty-fourth birthday, having recently accepted the editorship of *The Musical Times*, a post he was never to take up.

Hubert Foss had married the singer Dora Stevens in 1927 and their marriage and subsequent family life were characterized by an intense sociability which, crucially, seemed to interact seamlessly with the various branches of Foss's work. The *Musical Opinion* had enumerated these as: 'Hubert Foss, composer and arranger; Hubert Foss, conductor; Hubert Foss, accompanist; Hubert Foss, lecturer and debater; Hubert Foss, author of innumerable articles, and writer of books; Hubert Foss, educationist, both in this country and America; Hubert Foss, *litterateur*; Hubert Foss, authority on the fine art of printing and engraving.' Hubert and Dora moved within and amongst a vast social network growing on these 'branches' or disciplines: friends, acquaintances, and composers and executants. In most cases, any expected boundaries between professionalism and intimacy were, for Foss, blurred or non-existent. 'Willie comes to tea tomorrow with Symphony' was the excited message that Hubert sent to Dora on 2 September 1935, as Walton neared the completion of his first symphony, exemplifying succinctly an easy-going, mutually trusting relationship between a composer and his publisher. There were many others, and into them all Dora was drawn, at concerts and post-concert parties, but often in the setting of the Fosses' Rickmansworth house, Nightingale Corner, with its lawns extensive enough for deck tennis: Walton, Bax, Britten, Lambert, Moeran, Henry and Muriel Wood and their daughters Tania and Avril were all visitors there, with Dora as hostess. The Fosses' sociability was not simply ephemeral. This was music in their time and Dora, perhaps with an eye to a longer game, was careful to preserve as much of record as she could: concert programmes, photographs, and ledgers into which were pasted letters, articles, press cuttings, and correspondence (these books were known in the family by the charming, now old-fashioned, term 'commonplace books'). These she supplemented with her own typescript reminiscences and memoirs of the major (and sometimes minor) figures from her and Hubert's network, recalling incidents, conversations, and jokes which would otherwise have been lost to time, and drawing intimate pen-portraits of those who passed through the door at Nightingale Corner. The content of these papers and memoirs (which form a significant and extensive collection in their entirety) form, as it were, the DNA of *Music in My Time*, recording the people, the events, the music, which led to the firmly held opinions distilled in that book. The scene from which 'Hubert Foss, comet' early disappeared in 1953 was one largely of his own making, and the 'in their time' archive represents its record. It is from material in that archive that Hubert and Dora's daughter Diana, Brian, her husband, and the chief editor Stephen Lloyd have shaped the current book.

'Hubert's creation of the musical department of the Oxford Press was nothing short of epoch-making in English music. Before that, the young English composer met with no encouragement from the old-established music publishers who were interested only in oratorios, church & organ music of the conventional kind, or in drawing-room ballads and military band music ... the OUP was the only hope for young composers, and for a good many young composers in foreign countries too. The modern English school could never have made headway without Hubert's understanding, encouragement & practical help.' Edward Dent's tribute forms a letter to Dora sent immediately following Hubert's death, and accurately pinpoints Foss's achievement as a music publisher, while simultaneously placing it in historical context. There was barely a composer active in Britain during the 1920s and 1930s that did not have at least one work represented in Foss's catalogue; and several of those he published then offered the majority, or all, of their works to OUP. Hubert Foss signed to Oxford University Press both leading and well-established composers (for example, Ralph Vaughan Williams who, under a 'gentlemen's agreement', offered the large majority of his pieces written after 1923), and, with considerable risk but undeniable foresight, those altogether untried at the time: Constant Lambert (whose *Rio Grande* (1928) became a best-seller) and William Walton (Walton published the entirety of his works with OUP under a 'retainer agreement'). Oxford University Press became distributors for the dense and difficult works of Kaikhosru Shapurji Sorabji, and success-fully handled the early works of Benjamin Britten (but the letters included in this book show how their relationship eventually deteriorated). Overseas composers, too, played a small but significant part in the list (for example, Foss published a lavish English-language edition of Bartók's *Hungarian Folk Music*, and with the Russian State Publishing Department a co-edition of Mussorgsky's *Boris Godunov*).

Foss had been a co-founder in 1926 of the Bach Cantata Club, and through the Press's publications of editions of music by J.S. Bach he ensured that OUP was at the forefront (was even driving) the incipient 'early music' movement. Donald Francis Tovey produced a pioneering modern edition of *The Art of Fugue*, and William Gillies Whittaker became Foss's editor for a series of Bach cantatas (Foss's letter to Dora of 14 November 1938, following a visit to Whittaker and complaining of the messy food, a table always cluttered with nut cutlets and bananas, and his 'awful anthracite stove' but no hot water, adds a colourful human dimension). The piano (or two-piano) transcription of Bach's music reached a peak in popularity during the 1930s, and Foss ensured that his catalogue was well populated with examples (*A Bach Book for Harriet Cohen*, published by Foss in 1932, is the archetype). English church music of the sixteenth and seventeenth centuries also featured strongly in Foss's early lists – he had inherited the Tudor Church Music volumes (which the Press was publishing for the Carnegie United Kingdom Trust) and this he developed into a major series of offprints and related publications. Speaking of the various editors working on the 'early music' aspects of his catalogue, Foss, in *Music in My Time* and using characteristically vivid imagery, wrote, 'by their scholarly and practical labours, they have opened up this new continent of sound'. In a very real sense, the OUP catalogue of the Foss years provides a panoramic 'motion film' of the music of his time (including the revival of music of former times), with Foss both directing and recording the production.

Music publishing involves not only the printing and sale of sheet music (although to many a Tin Pan Alley publisher at the time that was the main concern), but embraces a range of other supporting responsibilities. Foss, as a modern publisher, in a sense codified these. He went, for example, to Siena in September 1928, with Walton, Lambert and the Sitwells, for that year's International Society for Contemporary Music's World Music Days, at which Walton's *Façade* (which OUP was to publish) was performed. As the documents included in this book attest, Foss was on hand to give all manner of support, fixing everything from copying music to changing light bulbs.

The *Musical Opinion* critic of 1937 (enlarging on his 'Foss as comet' metaphor) remembered, as a child, watching the lamplighter passing down his road each evening, 'changing a spark into a series of fairy glows'. He likened this to Foss's achievement: 'Hubert Foss has been lighting lamps ever since he burst into the world of music, and it would be a dull world without his incandescent spirit'. Many of the lamps that Hubert Foss lit as publisher shine to this day, with the copyrights he acquired continuing to bring both inestimable value to his old company and enjoyment to many; the vast catalogue he created continues to form the bedrock of OUP's modern music publishing.

Music, as notated on the printed page, is not music at all, but merely its analogue, a mechanical manifestation: metal, tools, ink, paper, binding. Under Foss's purview, the printed music formed an essential bridge, the pathway, between the composer's concept and the performer's performance. Only at the point of aural realization did printed music really become 'music'. The quality of the notes on the printed page and their layout, the tone of the paper, the binding, the information on the cover – all of these, Foss maintained, directly shaped the quality of the performance. Inferior printed product resulted in a poorer live performance. As a shaper and influencer of music in his time, Foss made a significant contribution to improving the quality of printed music and therefore, as he believed, to its performance. 'The Plight of Music Printing' was the title given by Foss to an article in *The Music Review* in 1941, suggesting that music printing was something that needed rescuing. Using characteristically vivid imagery, Foss, in that article, cut to the heart of the matter: 'Music-printing offers nothing to the success of a concert, save a means of attainment of an object. It affects the sound of a Beethoven symphony only in so far as it provides a method of informing the players of that work what they should do at a special moment with a special instrument ... It is the hand-maiden of an emotional art ... But indubitably music-printing is on the decline, and soon, if the musicians continue to take no interest in this necessary "department of supply", will cease to exist except in the position of a very ill-paid servant in a very badly-run commercial hotel. We do not want wet sheets and dirty bedrooms in the house of music; that is why I direct attention to this urgent problem.'

Foss directed much of his energy to enacting the rescue, primarily through his work in ensuring the quality of OUP's music publications which, under his direction, quickly developed a distinctive style that soon came to be appreciated by his composers and customers alike. In an adroit piece of strategy, Foss commissioned the London firm of Henderson & Spalding to print the majority of his OUP titles, while simultaneously becoming engaged as their typographical adviser for music. He was thus able to set down a series of dashing new standards which became the 'house style' of his publications. Deploring the jigsaw-style effect of typeset music notation, as used often by Victorian music publishers in the production of vocal scores, Foss insisted on rigorously proportioned engraving. Clarity was of the essence, and he bravely abandoned whole-bar rests in orchestral scores, instantly giving the pages a light, clean feel. Rehearsal numbers were placed discreetly in small circles at top and bottom of the page, the use of italic was limited, and borders were generous. Creamy off-white paper reduced glare and show-through in performance. To covers, equal attention was given – for the major composers and series in his lists Foss developed specific design styles, frequently commissioning artists to provide appropriate images, the most celebrated of which was a green and black modernist 'cartouche' comprising stylized flowers and musical instruments designed by Gino Severini, for the scores of William Walton.

'Every paper that leaves your house with printing on it', wrote Foss in a Henderson & Spalding prospectus entitled *Good Printing* (c. 1926), 'is an advertisement for you. It may be an attraction; it may be a handicap, a barrier. If it is worth money to print anything, it is worth getting that printing done well – for the same money.' The elegant, immediately recognizable OUP house style developed by Foss through Henderson & Spalding marked a turning point in British printed music, but it did not materialize in isolation. Other individuals and organizations, during the 1920s and beyond, realized the truth in Foss's dictum that printed material 'is an advertisement for you', and therefore the fundamental importance of good design, fine illustration, and uncluttered typography, both for leading the customer to a product or service, and for its appreciation. The London Underground paid obsessive attention to the typography and detail of its signage, route diagrams, and printed publicity (the result was an early example of successful 'corporate identity'); Ordnance Survey transformed its plain standard small-scale map covers by employing skilled in-house artists to create illustration and design appropriate to content and location – a deliberate popularization of essentially 'military' and official products; and, above all, the 'Big Four' railway companies (following their 'grouping' in 1923), and the Shell Oil Company became de facto art patrons through their wholesale commissioning of posters advertising travel facilities and destinations from top-rank artists. Foss's triumphs with page image and cover design for printed music simply provide further exemplars. He was working in parallel with these organizations, and in some cases using the same artists (John Banting drew Foss's Constant Lambert covers, and designed for Shell). Regarding covers, the services of Henderson & Spalding, wrote Foss in *Good Printing*, 'include the provision of ideas, the work of the best artists, the true reproduction of their pictures'. Like the railway companies and the map-makers, Foss's focus was on an integrated product, a corporate identity for both his company and his composers.

It was on *The Joyce Book* (1933, a privately printed and published collection of thirteen settings of poems by James Joyce by various composers) that Foss concentrated his greatest typographical skill and care (it is remarkable to note that he designed and supervised this book in the same year that he made the concentrated effort of *Music in My Time*). Dora's 'Music in Their Time' archive preserves some of the tributes. 'It is indeed lovely, surely the loveliest thing that has come out of an English Press', wrote its editor, Herbert Hughes, to Foss. 'As regards the paper and the cover, the type and the proportions, my heart swells with fulsome praise', said Bernard van Dieren. The bibliophile and publisher Holbrook Jackson praised Foss's design skills over and above the book's musical content: 'you as a typographer have risen to the occasion'.

The collection, published by Henderson & Spalding under their private Sylvan Press imprint, was intended as a gift to the then-impecunious James Joyce, who wrote to Foss noting his trouble and painstaking zeal in making the book what it was. Copies of *The Joyce Book* are now rare and most eagerly sought after. The many OUP music publications issued according to Foss's standards, in the sense of having provided an ideal and aesthetically pleasing product for practitioners, are his real typographical memorial; but *The Joyce Book* is his pièce de résistance.

In April 1923, just two months ahead of Foss's earliest Oxford University Press music publications, the first number of a new journal, *The Gramophone*, appeared on London's newsstands. 'An apology is due to the public for inflicting upon it another review', ran the opening Editorial in a headmasterly tone redolent of the day, 'but I should not be doing so unless I were persuaded that many of the numerous possessors of gramophones will welcome an organ of candid opinion ... I have received many kind promises of support from distinguished writers; and if I find that the sales warrant me in supposing that gramophone enthusiasts want the kind of review THE GRAMOPHONE will set out to be, I can promise them that I will do my best to ensure their obtaining the finest opinions procurable ... Our policy will be to encourage the recording companies to build up for generations to come a great library of music.' The writer was *The Gramophone*'s founding editor, Compton Mackenzie, Hubert Foss's Rich & Cowan fellow author-to-be. In establishing the journal, Mackenzie was acknowledging and responding to the increasing popularity of sound recording as a means of access to music, and his vision of a vast library of music for future generations uncannily foresees Foss's own later assessment of the OUP music catalogue as built not only for immediate consumption, but for 'a long history of usefulness'. 'We shall have nothing to do with Wireless in these columns', puffed Mackenzie and, largely speaking, *The Gramophone* (which remains in publication today) never did. But there was soon widespread acceptance that the one medium (recorded music) directly fed the other (broadcasting). The British Broadcasting Company (formed on 18 October 1922, and four years later to become the British Broadcasting Corporation) rapidly became a nationally recognized consumer and broadcaster of recorded music, the means by which a vast range of commercially manufactured 'records' became accessible, not yet to the man-in-the-street or even to him on the Clapham omnibus (that would, of course, follow), but certainly to the listener in the home and in the workplace – which is not to overlook the BBC's critical and equally important role in promulgating and broadcasting live performance, which developed in parallel with its attention to recorded music. The two technologies were, in fact, intertwined, and during the 1920s and 1930s broadcast and recorded music became widely known under the generic and aptly descriptive label of 'mechanical music'.

Foss, both as publisher, and in his work elsewhere, embraced the new technologies – 'mechanical music' – with vigour and optimism, though never recklessly and without caution. He wished to embrace their power, their potential, without acquiescing to their novelty or possible ephemerality. Dora (as Dora Stevens) had recorded as early as 1914 – on 19 May of that year she set down, at the Hayes Gallery, songs by Haydn Wood, R. Coningsby Clarke, and Beatrice Parkyns, and that recording survives as a poignant reminder of the freshness and crisp diction of her singing at the time. Foss, with Dora, once they had married, together made several sound recordings for Decca (one of which, from 1940, was of Walton's *Three Songs* to poems by Edith Sitwell, of which the couple was the dedicatee – a gift from Walton, thanking them for their professional and personal support); and Foss would attend recording sessions along with his composers (he was in the studio for the first recording of Walton's Symphony No. 1, in December 1935). But, as ever with Foss, he was to ruminate on the whole topic over many years, considering it carefully from all its angles. Even ten or so years after the BBC's and *The Gramophone*'s launches, and the huge rise since then in the ubiquity of mechanical music, Foss (in *Music in My Time*) was writing, 'It is too soon, after ten years of broadcasting and twenty-five of the gramophone, to form any judgement of the eventual place of the mechanical methods of music distribution in the life of the people, or to assess the part they have played in the age of their introduction. The waves have not settled down from the disturbance after the first plunge'. Foss was worrying that the set times of radio broadcasts imposed artificial limits on their audience (in his mind, was he nurturing the idea of today's 'time-shift' and 'mobile' technologies, or at least seeing a need for them?): 'The times of the programmes matter considerably. A good programme broadcast at a time when men and women workers are in the train or at work will have a poor audience: a bad programme put out at a time of general leisure will be listened to irrespective of its merit.' And, as he had with printed music, he recognized that mechanical music was not really music at all. 'One thing must not be forgotten', he concludes his chapter on recording and broadcast, 'that the mechanical aids to music have given us not music itself, but a reproduction of music in a new medium of sound.

That is inevitable, to whatever pitch of perfection the scientists develop their instruments'. These, and other considerations, found fuller and more extensive treatment one year later in Constant Lambert's *Music Ho!*, in which Lambert, tongue edging impishly towards cheek, laid the blame for what he called 'the appalling popularity of music' at mechanical music's feet.

Under copyright legislation (the United Kingdom's 1911 Copyright Act recognized the economic value of 'mechanical music' for the first time), income will automatically flow from the broadcast and recording of copyright music, and Foss's Music Department at OUP thus immediately enjoyed a monetary stream not available to his book publishing colleagues. But he was also eager to deploy the technologies directly, or to work alongside them, as a means of publishing or as an adjunct to it. Foss saw a symbiosis between print and mechanical music, and used this to publish materials designed to guide the listener into 'music appreciation' by these means. In this he supported his leading author, Percy Scholes. Scholes set the scene in his *The First Book of the Gramophone Record*, which Foss published in 1924. 'A very few years ago', Scholes proclaimed, 'fine music was the private preserve of a few people living in the largest cities. The Gramophone, the Pianola, and Broadcasting have changed all that ... By means of the Gramophone people everywhere can enjoy the Queen's Hall Orchestra, or Chaliapin, or the London String Quartet, or Sammons, or Samuel, or Busoni. No other agency of musical reproduction for years to come is likely to reduce the popularity of the Gramophone ... But people, I find, are crying out for a guide ... So in this little book I have tried to be helpful. After days and weeks of careful testing of hundreds of Records by various makers, I have settled upon a choice of fifty, which I have here listed, arranged, so far as convenient, in historical order, explained and quoted in the form of music-type illustrations.' This might have been Foss speaking, for at this time he and Scholes thought and worked in close partnership (acknowledged years later by Scholes in *The Oxford Companion to Music*), resulting in a remarkable series of publications embracing the new media, and delivering a new type of musical education and appreciation. Although Scholes airily further supposed 'that all Arctic explorers nowadays take Gramophones; in fact we may be sure that they do', *The First Book of the Gramophone Record* was designed to guide the general (warmer, armchair-bound) listener towards the 'top' fifty classical music records then available, in repertoire ranging from the madrigalists, through Rameau, Bach, and Handel, to Beethoven and Schubert. Its grey binding was impressively embossed with a blue design featuring a stylized gramophone with an extremely large horn, facing the reader, as if to say: 'listen!' The *First Book* was chatty and informal, and Scholes's comments on the chosen recordings covered sound quality and performance, distilling the requirement of all subsequent gramophone criticism to its essentials; in prescient recognition, Scholes's book was dedicated to Compton Mackenzie.

As the technology for the mechanical reproduction of music developed and improved, so Foss and the Press kept up with it. Scholes was one of the earliest to give broadcast talks on music, becoming in the summer of 1923 'the BBC Music Critic', a role which also involved writing music appreciation articles for *Radio Times*. He rapidly became the catalyst in the relationship between the broadcaster and Oxford University Press. For *Everybody's Guide to Broadcast Music* (1925), with a foreword by John Reith, then General Manager of the British Broadcasting Company, Scholes adapted features of his earlier *The Listener's Guide to Music* (published in 1919, a simple guide to repertoire and terminology) for the radiophile. *The 'Radio Times' Dictionary of Musical Terms* came out in 1930, a collaborative effort, published by OUP using BBC branding, to provide a glossary of terms enabling the common listener to unpick, from 'the Broadcasting programmes', erudite radio announcements concerning 'highbrow' music (such deliveries were early criticized for being almost incomprehensible, and it took many years before they settled into what became the comfortable and familiar Third Programme style). It was, though, *The Columbia History of Music Through Ear and Eye*, launched in 1930, which formed Oxford University Press's first 'multi-media' project. In association with the Columbia Gramophone Company, the Press provided a series of 70-page booklets, written by Scholes, to accompany the five sets of eight specially produced double-sided gramophone records, embracing music through time. The sets were each conveniently, if laboriously, labelled by 'period': 'Period II. From the Beginning of the Opera to the Death of Bach and Handel', for example. For the first time, it became possible to listen to, and to read about, the whole gamut of musical history from the comfort of the home: the ear and the eye were equally engaged.

Foss, along with Scholes, was one of the earliest and most regular exponents of what became known as 'radio talks', short spoken features, often broadcast live, introducing or following broadcasts of music, or exploring aspects of a particular composer, work, or topic. At the time of his retirement from OUP Foss had already given around fifty radio talks, and through the war years and into the 1950s he maintained an intensive schedule of preparing and delivering broadcasts, sometimes giving as many as six in a month. Eleanor Geller, in her Southampton University MA dissertation on Foss as a broadcaster, has identified 547 broadcast talks given by Foss for the BBC between 1933 and 1953 – an average of about twenty-eight talks in each year. William Walton remarked 'how clear and resonant' was Foss's airwave manner, 'really what a "broad-casting" voice should be', and surviving sound recordings of a handful of his talks bear this out. Foss covered a wide, multi-hued spectrum, with composers from Debussy, Liszt, and Purcell to Stravinsky, and Sullivan (with Gilbert), and artists such as Wanda Landowska, Alfred Cortot, and Kirsten Flagstad coming under his inspection. Foss talked on music theory, and 'the use and abuse of the miniature score', and contributed regularly to Julian Herbage's popular *Music Magazine* programme, after its launch in 1944. Vaughan Williams and his music became a strong and recurring theme, and in his twenty years as a broadcaster, Foss gave approximately twenty-one talks on this composer.

As with his broadcasts, the breadth and scope of Foss's work as an author directly reflect both the world in which he worked and a great deal about his multi-faceted personality and interests. Foss's authorship extended to books, and to both music criticism and programme notes (for works that he had published personally, and others too); he was heavily in demand in all genres. Throughout his life, Foss issued forth, as of some inner biological necessity, a stream of music criticism and articles, as well as pieces on music printing and typography, for reviews, newspapers, and journals, including for *The Dominant* (his own short-lived OUP journal, flourishing briefly at the end of the 1920s under the editorship of Edwin Evans), for J. & W. Chester's more senior equivalent, *The Chesterian*, for the BBC's *The Listener*, and, after the War, for *The Gramophone*. Foss also wrote for the *Penguin Music Magazine*, an occasional publication launched by Penguin Books in 1947 under the editorship of Ralph Hill, running for just nine issues before becoming an annual review. Foss's contributions to the *Penguin* magazine included his fine and beauti-fully illustrated 'Romance of Music Printing' (February 1948) and one side of the story in the deliberately provocative dual-author 'To Start An Argument' pieces, in which pertinent themes were aired and discussed from opposing perspectives: Foss, in the 'What is the Place of the Performer?' debate with the Italian-born composer and *Daily Telegraph* critic Ferruccio Bonavia (September 1947), characteristically hoists his colours in statements such as 'Any form of personal intrusion in the performance of music is an insult to the composer and a barrier between composer and listener', and 'Who can imagine William Byrd fussing about "interpretation" when a motet by him was performed at

Lincoln Cathedral or the Chapel Royal?'. 'Vaughan Williams and the Orchestra', which appeared in the final *Penguin Music Magazine* (July 1949), was a serious attempt by Foss to distil and marshal his thoughts on this composer ahead of his full-length study of Vaughan Williams of the following year: his *Penguin* article sows the seeds of themes which come to full flower in the book. Foss leaves no doubt as to the originality of his thinking. 'Yet even at a near distance, and from aural reception only', Foss wrote of the recently premiered but as then unpublished sixth symphony, for example, 'one was able to see that it is this sixth symphonic utterance which brings the diverse previous five into one massive whole. It is a complete integer, yet it is a focal point where the far rays of the other planets gather in one brilliant stream of light.'

The eloquent eulogy given by Herbert Howells at Foss's funeral, included in this book, specifically singles out Foss's programme notes, which Howells calls 'the reflection not merely of a rich mind but of a warm humanity' – apart from crisply summing up the qualities of the man in those few words, which other programme note writer has ever received quite such a tribute from a composer? Foss's technique in his programme notes was immediately to immerse the reader into the sound world of the composer and work concerned, setting listeners up for an immediate acceptance and appreciation of the music. Foss provided, for example, the note for the first London performance of Walton's *Belshazzar's Feast*, given by the BBC Symphony Orchestra and 'The National Chorus' under Adrian Boult, on 25 November 1931 at the Queen's Hall. 'William Walton does not give a descriptive sub-title to his first choral work, and rightly, for it is not cantata, oratorio, or dramatic scena. There is no exact term in the musical vocabulary to cover adequately a work which presents a dramatic picture by choral narrative, with a strong sense of the historical connotations of the scene. Before our eyes (and ears) this music lays the vision of the Jews in captivity, of the prophets' warnings against Babylon's wickedness, of the false Gods, the writing finger, the fall and death of Belshazzar, the joyful liberation of the captive race, and their thanks to the God to whom they have returned. The picture, self-contained as it is, in Walton as in Daniel, is really a type of Old Testament History.' There could be little better way of setting the scene than the epic, almost cinematographic approach adopted here by Foss.

Music in My Time was Foss's first book, and a further four were to follow during his last two decades, with a sixth, final volume published the year following his death. A concertgoer's handbook, a guide to books about music, the study of Vaughan Williams, a short biography of Modest Mussorgsky for Novello &

Co., and a 'portrait' of the London Symphony Orchestra were his themes. His untimely death halted two further projects: books on Constant Lambert, and William Walton had been planned and started. Foss edited, introduced, or contributed to a stream of other books, notably the volumes of *The Heritage of Music* (1927, 1934, 1951) into which he had commissioned and assembled a collection of essays by distinguished writers (many of them his OUP collaborators such as Richard Runciman Terry, Donald Tovey, Michel-Dimitri Calvocoressi, and Gustav Holst) on the work of composers as diverse as Palestrina, Alessandro and Domenico Scarlatti, Liszt, Verdi, and Ravel – Foss himself contributed the essay on Mendelssohn. Each essay (or rather, the fact that the essay is there) demonstrates an awareness by Foss of a contemporaneous reawakening of interest in a particular composer or school, or of the need for a reassessment, or of an opportunity to put a leading living composer under scrutiny.

Of his own books, *Ralph Vaughan Williams* (subtitled 'A Study' and bearing on its wrapper a striking photograph of Epstein's bronze bust of Vaughan Williams) was probably Foss's most significant, it being the first full-scale assessment of that composer's works published under one cover (Foss had already published three slim surveys of 'early', 'late', and 'dramatic' Vaughan Williams in his OUP 'The Musical Pilgrim' series in 1928 and 1937, much material from which was later included in Frank Howes's *The Music of Ralph Vaughan Williams*, following a few years after Foss's book, in 1954). It is up to date, and positions expressed in articles as recently as the previous year's *Penguin Music Magazine* contribution were subtly reassessed. The score of Symphony No. 6, for example, was by now published – 'handsomely printed' said Foss – and his earlier assessment of that work is strikingly re-focussed: 'I have not yet made up my mind about the weight of this work. At present it appears to me to be less perfect as a work of art, less successful in the fusion of matter and manner, than Three, Four, or Five'. *Ralph Vaughan Williams* is the result, the distillation, of the personal working relationship between the composer and Foss, as his music publisher, spanning more than fifteen years, and as his advocate for a further decade. The book evidences another instance of Foss both directing the music of his time, and recording it. Foss's Prologue uses the script of a BBC radio talk given by him in 1942 on the occasion of Vaughan Williams's seventieth birthday, and it contains two substantial contributions by Vaughan Williams himself: 'Musical Autobiography', a present, Foss says, from the composer; and Vaughan Williams's 1912 *Royal College of Music Magazine* essay '"Who wants the English Composer?"'. There is a neat sense of fulfilment as the book (a full-scale account and review of all the composer's major works to date, and also an exploration of what Foss calls 'The English Background') is read and finished, the eye then alighting on the opening sentence of the 1912 piece, which forms an appendix. 'It is reported', Vaughan Williams had written nearly forty years before Foss's appraisal, 'that the head of a famous publishing firm once said, "Why do you young Englishmen go on composing? Nobody wants you."'. The inclusion of his essay here, at the close of a book by another (former) head of a famous publishing firm, is simply now Foss's way of saying, to Vaughan Williams and to all composers, 'Yes, go on composing! I want you!' – a summation of his life and work.

It is not only the eclectic (encyclopaedic, even) range of subjects upon which Foss writes, but the way in which he does it which distinguishes him as a writer. Foss's prose, tending towards the analytical and occasionally inclining to a light shade of purple, never descends to rhetoric or hollow verbosity. He is forthright, and his sometimes complex and tightly constructed sentences unfailingly move with unutterable logic, inexorably hitting their target. His imagery and metaphor are rich, and always original. Examples of Foss's verbal virtuosity abound within the material now collected in this book. Women singers, it seems, excited the fantastical in him. 'Dame Clara', he wrote, describing in his own memoir an early encounter with Clara Butt singing the Angel in *The Dream of Gerontius*, 'both looked and sounded massive and almost architectural'; Odette de Foras singing Turandot, he writes to Dora from Edinburgh in 1929, 'comes through positively dowdy with no sex charm at all ... She stood for whole scenes with her hands stretched out as if she were a clothes horse'. Elsewhere, in Foss's professional and published writings, however occasional their purpose, memorable verbal images abound. In a radio talk given shortly before his death, immediately following the first performance of Vaughan Williams's *Sinfonia Antartica*, Foss observes that today, in that composer's output, 'we reach the Antarctic wastes, the plateaux of untenanted snow' – just ten words, two obvious phrases, but deliciously coupled in a way that instantly conjures a vast and chilling, majestic landscape gained after long journeying, an image achieved so succinctly by no other writer on the work since, and a true encapsulation both of the whole score's underlying meaning, and its place in the Vaughan Williams canon. 'The engineer's drawing of a motor-car and its parts is no less a terrifying object to a conductor than a modern full score, with all its instrumental lines, to an inventor', wrote Foss in *Music in My Time*, using the brash and (in 1933) strikingly modern image of the inner workings of an automobile as an analogy for the intricacy of music written in his time – equally frightening for some. The material concerning the composition of *Music in My Time* itself included here (letters to Foss from Sir Henry Hadow, who was given a draft to critique) gives some idea of the inner workings of Foss's mind as he wrote. Hadow calls the book 'provocative and convincing' (and he points up that excellent section on Debussy), and Havergal Brian is surprised by its 'downright concentrated thinking'.

It is material by Dora Foss which provides the substantive thread of *Music in Their Time*. In contrast to Hubert's 'downright concentrated' style, Dora's seems direct, homely even. Her heart is often, though never conspicuously, on her sleeve. Unlike Hubert, Dora was never published as a writer, and reading her memoirs, and the letters that she left, therefore gives the sensation of glancing at a personal diary, with the occasional twinges of guilt at having inadvertently seen something intimate which doing that inevitably brings. Dora 'tried my best to be intelligent' with Edith Sitwell, the poet 'consciously anointing my wounded susceptibilities'; Hubert she finds 'white and exhausted' following a gruelling meeting with the inexorable Donald Tovey; Dora recalls the Muscat grapes required for a fruit cocktail at a party, 'endlessly peeling them and feeling I should never get them done in time'; and the receipt of 'armsful and armsful of the most superb chrysanthemums and dahlias' from Sir Henry Wood's wife, Lady Muriel, was 'a sweet and generous gesture to a newly-married woman'. Dora's writing adroitly records aspects of Hubert's associates overlooked by others (even by Hubert himself), and its publication here is of prime historical importance: it illuminates, and adds invaluable extra detail to, that which is already known and published about those who shaped and made music in Britain during the interwar years.

An anecdote recorded by a keen observer of the 1930s London musical scene, the critic Felix Aprahamian (his musical diaries have recently been published in an edition by Lewis and Susan Foreman), underlines not only how central to the propagation of music Hubert Foss became in that decade, but also how he managed to float above it all in the role of independent arbiter, seer, and prophet. The occasion was the long-awaited first performance of Paul Hindemith's colossal oratorio *Das Unaufhörliche*, on 22 March 1933 at the Queen's Hall, conducted by Henry Wood. 'On the steps after it was over', wrote Aprahamian in his diary, 'Hubert Foss was announcing to the world in general & Ralph Vaughan Williams in particular that he had given the broadcast talk on it [the oratorio] that evening & that he was awfully glad RVW liked it as most people didn't. RVW signified his approval & like of the work by several noddings and gruntings.' Wherever new music was happening, in his time, Foss seemed to be there, on this occasion hearing 'a new language forged out of the old ... the rightful tongue being spoken in a way that made the previous language sound like a rather tentative slang', as in short order he summed up *Das Unaufhörliche* in *Music in My Time*, at the close of a longer discussion there about the work and its performance. My essay has considered the Fosses 'in their time', but in reality Hubert Foss thought outside of time's limits. He was as at home striding the sixteenth-century polyphonists' new continent of sound and Vaughan Williams's plateaux of untenanted snow as he was looking into a future written in the syntax of a Hindemith. Between all of these, Foss saw no essential differences.

Music in My Time was published, in October, just seven months after that concert in March 1933, and one month after the birth of Hubert and Dora's daughter, Diana. It was to her that Hubert touchingly dedicated the book. Now, more than eighty years later, Diana neatly returns that compliment, by offering here vivid glimpses of her parents' world and the personalities that passed through it, viewed, as it were, from within, and related through first-hand memoir, reminiscence, and document. *Music in Their Time* tells the inside story of *Music in My Time*.

Simon Wright

Moreton-in-Marsh, October 2017

Dora Foss's Memoirs

Dora Maria Stevens was born in London in 1893, the eldest child of Alfred Stevens, a wealthy businessman, and Maria Enrriqueta Stevens (née Welton), a young woman of British descent, from Bogotá (Colombia). The family first lived at 35 Hillfield Road, West Hampstead, and then in 1898 moved to 47 Aberdare Gardens, before settling down at 13 (later 25) Redington Road, Hampstead, which became the final family home.

Dora remembers being taught music and singing by her mother, and then at the age of eight attending Threave House School, Hampstead. She later boarded at Wycombe Abbey School. She never forgot the names of many of her music teachers, but particularly Miss Arch at Wycombe Abbey, who, she recalled, had a strong, pure soprano voice of very lovely quality.

WHEN I LEFT SCHOOL, I went to the Hampstead Conservatoire and had piano lessons first from Hilda Weber, and later from her father, Carl Weber, then one of the foremost pianoforte teachers of the day. I adored my lessons and practised for hours daily, but never reached anything approaching a professional standard. My mother then insisted on my halving my piano lessons – 'You will never be anything but second rate,' she said, 'but you HAVE got a voice' – and taking singing lessons from Henry Beauchamp. At that time I considered that playing the piano was 'real' music and that singing was just a social accomplishment. I was definitely unhappy at this enforced change in my musical education.

My mother was right. With first-class training I progressed very rapidly and at nineteen won the gold medal at the London Academy of Music – an institution long defunct.

The years of the war interrupted concentrated work and during the last two years I was a full-time VAD.[1] I had many opportunities for singing 'in public' – though I had to sing 'popular' songs. Even so, I tried to book a lesson from Mr Beauchamp whenever I could find time.

After the war I felt I wanted to broaden my very conventional outlook, and early in 1920 I deserted Mr Beauchamp for a time and paid for two courses of lessons with Signor Manlio di Veroli, the well-known teacher in London. On many points we disagreed. He tried to turn me into a real 'mezzo'. I lost my

---

1   Voluntary Aid Detachment – voluntary nurses without full professional training who served mainly in hospitals. In WW1, military authorities did not accept them on the front line. See plate 4.

high notes, and I felt strained and unhappy with the heavier, thicker voice he tried to produce, and I left him before the courses were finished. However, strangely enough, it was to him, an Italian, that I owed my introduction to modern English songs. Before this happened, he taught me a small repertoire of contemporary Italian songs – Malipiero, Castelnuovo-Tedesco and Pizzetti. I enjoyed learning these, but many of them I felt were not suited to my voice.

The day came when he told me to bring some Bax songs. They enthralled me with their atmosphere of Celtic mystery, their poignancy, and sheer beauty. I bought volumes of them and literally wept as I learned them. Then Frank Bridge – di Veroli admired his songs very much, but although I sang several of them for years, they did not appeal to me as much as the Bax songs.

During this year (1920) I went through a personal emotional crisis. (I had been engaged to a young Naval officer, and this engagement came to an end in disillusioning circumstances which caused me intense unhappiness at the time.) To sing at this period of my life seemed impossible. I stopped attending singing lessons, so there was no magisterial incentive to work. I was miserable and hurt, and in any case, to sing with my voice in its present condition was an effort. So for about six months I was more or less silent. At the end of this time I metaphorically kicked myself and decided to go back to Henry Beauchamp and make myself sing once more. Before doing so, I began to practise again and, to my great joy, my voice in a very short time returned naturally to its original production and ease, but I was troubled by a 'nervous throat' which lasted for many months. During this time I continued to practise, as my doctor told me there was nothing radically wrong with my throat. It felt constricted and yet I wanted to tie it up with scarves in the summer. I then thought I would try other fields of singing and went to the Carl Rosa Opera School. My doctor painted my throat with nitrate of silver before I went for an audition and interview with Madame Tietjens, and I sang 'Ah lo so' better than I had ever sung it before or, for that matter, since! Madame Tietjens called her husband to hear me and they accepted me as a pupil immediately. However, instead of coaching me in Mozartian soprano roles, I was made to learn 'Elsa'. At first I was stimulated by the change to Wagner, but as the weeks went on, I found that to sing such a strenuous and dramatic part was physically exhausting and I reluctantly decided that *Lohengrin* was not for me.

At this period I went not only to hear opera, but to many song recitals, and I began to realise that my voice and musical proclivities were leading me to this latter field of work. I went to song recitals by Gerhardt,[2] Frieda Hempel,[3] Vladimir Rosny, d'Alvarez, Anne Thursfield, Megan Foster, John Armstrong, Dorothy Silk, John Goss[4] and hosts of others. From all the aforementioned, and, of course, others, I learned a great deal, but there were many other song recitals to which I went, and I came away knowing, quite objectively, and without conceit, that I could give one equally well, if not better. I loved the variety that could be encompassed by a single programme. I was fascinated by the artistic power that could emanate from one person – for so many of the 'recital' singers at that time had the Ruth Draper[5] like gift of filling the room with multitudes of people of all kinds, or projecting the whole gamut of emotions while maintaining the maximum of reticence in their demeanour. The ability to express every kind of emotion, the tenderest tenderness, the most bitter sorrow, the sinister, the calm of a summer evening, the gaiety or the tragedy of youth, by the conscious use of one voice, seemed to me the most marvellous and enviable gift, and this virtue I strove to gain.

Under Henry Beauchamp I had acquired a very adequate technique. 'It takes eight years to make a singer' he used to say, and I had worked my eight years. I had to learn to use my voice in the way I wanted. I had enough money in the Post Office Savings Bank to pay for a recital and I took my courage and my programme in both hands to Henry Beauchamp. He was damping in the extreme: 'Do you think you can do it?' He may have been testing my confidence, but he did not, at any time, give me any at all. However, he insisted that I should have Harold Craxton[6] as my accompanist. Craxton was the greatest accompanist of that period. He played for the finest artists and I felt absolutely terrified. 'Oh no!' I said to Henry Beauchamp. 'He'll never take any interest in me.' Beauchamp was adamant and one autumn afternoon I went to the Craxton house at 5 Grove End Road and, with my throat again nervously sore, sang through part of my proposed programme. Harold was calm and sweet and gently encouraging. He treated me as an artist, which was flattering. I had four

2   Elena Gerhardt (1883–1961), German soprano and a renowned recitalist, especially of German lieder.
3   Frieda Hempel (1885–1955), German soprano, known particularly for her operatic roles in Mozart.
4   John Goss, singer. See p. 207.
5   Ruth Draper, American actress. See p. 200.
6   Harold Craxton (1885–1971), English pianist and teacher, student of Tobias Matthay.

rehearsals with him before my first recital and at the last one he made some very kind remarks about my singing, and finished up by saying 'and what I like too about your singing is that you're absolutely professional'.

My parents and family could not believe that I was good enough to 'sing in public' and my mother thought that Harold's compliments on my singing, which were modestly retailed to her, were conventionally paid as 'part of the service'. She hadn't then met Harold or she would have known that he was the last person on earth to say what he did not mean.

Up to this time, I had only one musical 'contact' – Martin Shaw.[7] I had met him through the Charles Brands[8] of Fellows Road who were worshippers at St Mary the Virgin, Primrose Hill, where Martin Shaw was organist and choirmaster. Through him I was asked to sing at some of the Sunday afternoon services at the Guildhouse, Eccleston Square, where Percy Dearmer[9] and Maud Royden held unconventional 'services', though that is hardly the name for these hours of poetry, reading, and music. I was attracted to Martin Shaw's songs but not completely enthralled by them. I learned and sang them, as in many ways they appealed to me, and a large number of them suited my voice very well. In retrospect, I think I was subconsciously looking for something in them which I hoped to find, but did not find in them, charming as they were. However, they were a definite landmark in my search for English songs.

At my first recital, 17 April 1923, I sang a conventional 'mixed' programme – early Italian songs, two Mozart arias, a group of Schumann, Brahms, Strauss, a group of songs in French, ending this group with two of Arnold Bax's settings of traditional *Songs of France*. In the final English group I included Parry, Rootham,[10] Martin Shaw, Bax again, and for the benefit of kind but middlebrow and even low-brow friends, Huntington Woodman's *A Birthday* – a song which I shed from my programme later – though in fairness to it, I must say it is great fun to sing.

7   Martin Shaw (1875–1958), English composer and organist. Co-editor with Vaughan Williams of *Songs of Praise*, OUP, 1925.

8   Family friends and neighbours of Dora's parents. Their son Neville was Christopher's godfather.

9   The Rev. Percy Dearmer was editor of *The English Hymnal* (1906), *Songs of Praise* (1925) and the *Oxford Book of Carols* (1928), for each of which Vaughan Williams was music editor (with Martin Shaw for the last two publications).

10 Cyril Rootham (1875–1938), English organist and composer.

I had an unexpected success and my press notices were more than kind. I had started a career, I felt. I gave another recital in early July, and sang more Bax and Shaw, and that autumn I broadcast for the first time – two old English songs and the ubiquitous *A Birthday* accompanied by Stanton Jeffries. All that autumn Bax, Martin Shaw and Frank Bridge formed the mainstay of my English 'groups'. During the autumn and winter of 1923–24 I sang groups of modern English songs at Victoria and Albert concerts, BBC and various provincial concerts. At the V and A I sang two long groups which included songs by Bax, Rootham, Ireland, Craxton, Shaw, Parry, Gibbs, Rowley and Bridge.

In March 1924 I sang eight of Martin Shaw's songs in a broadcast – part of a series called 'Hours of Music with living British Composers'. I gave another recital – Bax and Shaw again – but I was learning to sing old English songs, the Elizabethans, influenced by Harold Craxton, and I had discovered Hugo Wolf. The first time I heard Wolf sung was at a concert given by Dorothy Silk and John Goss, and Hubert accompanied them. It proved to be a momentous day for me. It was the first time I saw Hubert. I was very impressed with him. He accompanied the singers most beautifully, he was modest in demeanour and he had an air of freshness and enthusiasm which was indescribably beguiling. (I knew nothing whatever about him, but I heard him play for John Goss and a quartet at the Wigmore Hall and at the Coliseum later.)

Sometime during the autumn of 1924, the Oxford University Press announced on the music page of the *Daily Telegraph* that it had published a number of songs by modern British composers and stated that these were on sale at Messrs Chappell's and at Murdoch's, etc. And the paragraph ended with 'Hubert J. Foss, Musical Editor'. I was very interested thus to discover who this accompanist was. I went to Murdoch's where I usually bought my music and, to my disappointment, found they had not yet received any OUP songs. I therefore wrote a short letter to H.J. Foss informing him that, in spite of the announcement in the *Daily Telegraph*, the songs were not obtainable at Murdoch's. By return of post I received a postcard from him apologising and saying that he was sure I would find them at Murdoch's now. I did, but only in the three-penny edition for schools. I bought several and again wrote to H.J. Foss saying I could only buy the little 'schools' edition, but I had played through the songs and was entranced with several of them, including Warlock's setting of 'Sleep', and Hubert's two exquisite miniatures, *As I walked forth* and *Infant Joy*, to Blake's words. (I told him in my letter of complaint how much I liked them.) In reply he asked if he could send me another of his songs, *Clouds*, which was published by

Boosey's. This he did, and a very Vaughan Williams-ish song it is – uneven and amateurish, but quite beautiful in parts. I might add that the OUP songs in their later famous coloured covers were on sale the next time I went into Murdoch's.

The previous autumn (1923) I had joined the Guild of Singers and Players. This society, which flourished for a number of years under Mrs Lily Henkel's[11] enthusiastic leadership, was formed to encourage and help the young professional musician. A certain standard was demanded and before a member was accepted, he or she had to perform at one of the Guild's Musical Evenings held in a house in Grosvenor Street, and, so to speak, prove themselves worthy and suitable.

The Guild helped young artists to give recitals either singly or, more often, in conjunction with one or two others, finding in some cases inexpensive halls and employing an excellent out-of-London printer. All this was an advantage to musical aspirants, but, in addition, there were the monthly evenings where not only those on trial but accepted members played and sang and met each other informally. I applied for membership and was asked to audition.

Through the kind interest of Martin Shaw, I had been engaged by Messrs Cramer's to sing at one of their Ballad concerts at the Aeolian Hall that night (where I sang, amongst other songs, Martin Shaw's *At Columbine's Grove*), so that when I arrived, rather late, to sing at Grosvenor Street, I was no longer nervous. I knew my voice was good, and I sang my best. I had taken some Wolf and I sang from the Italienisches Liederbuch *Erstes Liebeslied eines Mädchens*. Reginald Paul, the most accomplished sight-reader of all the accompanists, played for me. It was a momentous evening for me, as from that time I was accepted as a fellow musician by other musicians. John Barbirolli was there, Rae Robertson and Ethel Bartlett,[12] and many others whom I was to know well later.

By the autumn of 1924 I had added [Arthur] Bliss and [Eugene] Goossens to my repertoire of English songs, and, among many other appearances, I gave a joint recital under the auspices of the Guild at Bath. Later I was asked to join Evelyn Ruegg and Jean Buchanan in a recital also sponsored by the Guild, at the now-demolished Court House in Marylebone Lane.[13] I told Lily Henkel that

11   English pianist who studied in England and, under Clara Schumann, at Frankfurt.
12   Rae Robertson (1893–1978) and Ethel Bartlett (1896–1978), a renowned married two-piano duo. Both were students of Tobias Matthay.
13   1 April 1925.

I wanted to sing Hubert Foss's three songs. She at once said, 'But you MUST get him to play for you; he is a beautiful accompanist and is going to do a lot for English music, and we want him to join the Guild.' I hedged at once, 'I don't know him, and I have several accompanists whom I work with. Anyhow, I don't like asking favours of someone I've never met.' Madame Henkel insisted that it was a wonderful opportunity for getting him to join the Guild, so rather reluctantly I wrote and asked him if he would care to play for me on the date proposed if he was free as I was singing his songs. His reply was modest and ingenuous. He was quite free and only had two dates booked. I was impressed by his lack of conceit. So many people would have implied that they were booked up practically every night. Hubert came to rehearse at my parents' house. My later programmes show that Warlock, Peterkin,[14] Arthur Benjamin[15] and Moeran had been added to my English song composers, as well as Foss.

1.   *7th April 1924   Harold Craxton to Dora Stevens*
                           Acomb Lodge, 8 Grove End Road, London NW8
Dear Miss Stevens,
    Ever so many thanks for your very kind letter & enclosed cheque.
    I congratulate you on your notices – how splendid *The Times* is – I was delighted for I feel you deserved every bit of it. Your concert[16] & the rehearsals were a joy to me & I love playing for you. It was your best performance so far & you will do even better next time I'm sure.
    Keep on as you are going now and – well I'll tell you something when we meet. Essie joins me in sending our warmest feeling to you & your family.
    Yours sincerely,
    Harold Craxton

Gerhardt is singing in two groups tomorrow & I'm playing in two groups on my own to save her as she has a bit of a cold.
    H C

14 Norman Peterkin, composer, sales manager of OUP Music Department, and godfather to Diana Sparkes (née Foss). See plate 17.
15 Arthur Benjamin (1893–1960), Australian pianist and composer who won a scholarship to the Royal College of Music in 1911. After war service in the Royal Fusiliers and the Royal Flying Corps, when he was shot down and taken prisoner, he returned to England in 1921 to become professor of piano at the RCM. Benjamin Britten was one of his pupils.
16 Wigmore Hall, 2 April 1924.

WIGMORE HALL,
Wigmore Street, W.1.

Tuesday Evening, October 27th, at 8.15

DORA STEVENS

VOCAL
RECITAL

ASSISTED BY

LEON GOOSSENS
(Oboe)

HAROLD CRAXTON
(Pianoforte)

CHARLES WOODHOUSE
(Violin Obligato)

BÖSENDORFER GRAND PIANOFORTE

TICKETS (Including Tax): Reserved, 8/6 & 5/9; Unreserved, 3/-
May be obtained from the Box Office, Wigmore Hall, usual Ticket Offices,
DORA STEVENS, 25 Kellington Road, Hampstead, N.W.3, and of
IBBS & TILLETT, 124 Wigmore Street, W.1.
Telephone: 4180 Mayfair. Telegrams "Organisl, Wesdo, London."

For Programme P.T.O.

Fig. 1: Publicity leaflet for Dora's recital, October 1925

2.   *[n.d.]   Geoffrey Shaw[17] to Dora Stevens*

34 Elsworthy Road, NW3

Dear Miss Stevens,

Will you and Reginald Paul come to us at the Victoria and Albert on Saturday Jan 26th? I wish I could offer more than six guineas, but I haven't more than that to spend on each concert.

I think a programme of Modern English Music would be just right.

May I see it soon? And forgive me if I make suggestions after I have seen it. I know my audience so well by now. 'Good and Attractive' is the idea.

Yours

Geoffrey Shaw

17   Geoffrey Shaw (1879–1943), English composer, singer and HM Inspector of Music. Brother of Martin Shaw (1875–1958). Associated especially with church music.

3.   *3ʳᵈ November 1925   Leon Goossens*[18] *to Dora Stevens*

70 Edith Road, West Kensington, W14

Dear Miss Stevens,

Thank you so much for your letter and the cheque for seven guineas.[19] I shall hope for the pleasure of playing for you again some day.

With kind regards

Yours sincerely,

Leon Goossens

4.   *5ᵗʰ October 1926   Patrick Hadley*[20] *to Dora Stevens*

28 Comeragh Road, W14

Dear Miss Stevens,

Thank you so much for sending me the ticket for your recital. I shall do my best to be there, but may be prevented by having to conduct a rehearsal that night, in which case I shall send you back the ticket. That tune of mine should be taken very slowly & if possible never above a whisper. But I expect you have your own ideas which are just as good as mine. Have you got the necessary instruments[21] or just with piano alone? I see you have a flute.

Yours truly,

Patrick Hadley

5.   *21ˢᵗ October 1926   Patrick Hadley to Dora Stevens*

28 Comeragh Road, W14

Dear Miss Stevens,

I must write to tell you that I thought you sang that setting of mine most beautifully the other night. It is the way exactly that I have always wished to hear it sung, and so far never have, interesting as the versions have been that I have heard. I was agreeably surprised too that it could go so well with piano alone. I enjoyed in fact the whole evening though I was very sorry to miss the Bach. What I particularly liked about the way you sang my thing was, not only the mezzo voice and slow tempo you were able to sustain all the way through

18 Leon Goossens (1897–1988), renowned oboist and brother of composer Eugene and harpists Marie and Sidonie Goossens.

19 Wigmore Hall, 27 October 1925, with Harold Craxton, Charles Woodhouse (violin obbligato) and Leon Goossens. See publicity leaflet, fig. 1, p. 27.

20 Patrick ('Paddy') Hadley. See p. 211.

21 Patrick Hadley, *Scene from 'The Woodlanders'* (Hardy), for soprano, flute, violin, viola and piano, OUP 1925. Wigmore Hall, 19 October 1926, with Harold Craxton.

(and I know how difficult it is to get that), but the very moving simplicity you got into it; I feel you must have read the book and absorbed Marty South's character most faithfully.

Many thanks for such a delightful evening.

Ys sincerely

P Hadley

Eventually in 1927, after an entirely musical friendship into which our common interest in Wolf – for Hubert was a devout admirer – and modern English songs had led us, and after Hubert had spent two months in America, we found, on his return, that our friendship had matured into something deeper, and we became engaged. We married in July that year,[22] and from that time I entered a musical world of which I then knew little, the world of composers, not only of songs, but of chamber music, of symphonies, even of operas, of school music, and writers of books on music, and to me Hubert appeared to be the keystone of this growing edifice of British music – and not only to me, but to many young and not so young writers and composers. There seemed to be no side of musical activity in which he was not interested.

Hubert was in a unique position: he had sympathy, he had understanding and, owing to Milford's[23] faith in him, he had power. He was courted by most of the blossoming and blooming composers of the day – not only the composers but all the writers on and about music. 'Courted' is a misleading word. Every writer, whether it be of music or words, wants to give something to the world, to his fellow creatures; the urge to give the thing that is in him can almost be a physical ache. Composers and writers came to him as to a gateway to release. Hubert was a musician himself, he understood the longing for fulfilment and he had the power and the means to give them what they wanted, and in giving them fulfilment he gave England a musical rebirth.

Our lives were filled with constant excitement and speculation. How was this or that composer developing? How was this or that work progressing? Was there a jewel among the pile of manuscripts Hubert had brought home with him? Then the thrill of first performances: Queen's Hall – would it be full? Would all the critics be there? Would everyone who mattered in the world of music be

---

22   See plate 7.

23   Humphrey Milford, publisher to Oxford University Press, who appointed Foss head of the music department. See p. 221.

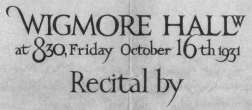

WIGMORE HALL^w
at 8.30, Friday October 16th 1931
Recital by

DORA STEVENS
of Modern English
Songs

accompanist Hubert Foss

Tickets 8/6, 5/9 & unreserved 2/4 including tax
from the Hall; The Oxford University Press;
Aeolian Hall, New Bond Street, W. (Mayfair 1442)
The Usual Agents, and Miss Stevens
Nightingale Corner, Rickmansworth (Rickmansworth 73)

Fig. 2: An example of Hubert's typography

there? Would the performance be good? Good enough at any rate to show the audience how fine (we hoped) the work was? I myself sat invisibly divided. One part of me was drowning in the surge and beauty of orchestral sound reaching out and holding on to the melodic spars which I knew in their piano versions, and almost unbearably moved by their transformation. Simultaneously, the rest of me felt aloof and objective and I listened attentively to orchestra, choir or soloist, and judged and criticised whether I was competent to do so or not. As the finale drew to its close, I fused into one entity again, experiencing one emotion. It was sometimes awe for the sublime, exhilaration for the magnificent, heartbreak for the soul-revealing, mystification for the incomprehensible, and sometimes too, irritation for the boring.

I had had an intermittent cough for some time, and three or four months after our son Christopher's birth I was found to have pulmonary tuberculosis, so in the autumn of 1928 I had to go to the sanatorium in Mundesley[24] for six months. In 1933 our daughter Diana was born. The end of 1934 brought anxiety and tragedy to us. Our son Christopher was operated on for a sudden attack of appendicitis; two days later my sister died, to me, unexpectedly. Later that autumn my father had a major operation and an old man died a week after literally walking into Hubert's car. In the midst of all this misery, my chesty symptoms, which were increasing, seemed an intrusion, and I took little care of myself. In the early spring of 1935 an x-ray showed my other lung to have several cavities, and after some weeks in bed at home I again went to Mundesley. I was there for some months and then had a six weeks' 'holiday' at home, returning to the Sanatorium before Christmas to stay till the spring of 1936, when the family moved to the Hampstead Garden Suburb.

DORA'S POEM: SANATORIUM TREATMENT[25]

I went to a house on a wooded hill
When I was ill.
I cried aloud 'O give me health!'
But they gave me wealth.

24   Situated on the north coast of Norfolk near Cromer, it was the first large establishment to be built in England (1899) specifically for the open-air treatment of tuberculosis.
25   This poem was written by Dora in January 1936. The gold she refers to is the gold treatment she underwent: very painful injections, for her tuberculosis.

I opened my arms and lo! their fold
Was filled with gold.

I went to a place near a lonely shore
I could face no more.
Unuttered thoughts said 'Give me rest!'
But they pierced my breast.
I longed for peace with a dull despair
As they gave me air.

Time stumbled on. Day after day
Passed. As I lay
I whispered a prayer 'O make me whole!'
And my fainting soul
Yearned for the dark cool depths of night
But they gave me light!

Thus Hubert's and my hopes for a singing career – or rather a joint partnership as singer and accompanist – were more or less killed. I had given two recitals in 1931–32 and had sung at a number of small concerts, but I never felt 'safe' enough to concentrate on my singing and, indeed, I found the ordinary round of domestic life was as much as I could cope with, until in 1938 when I had a major operation – an extra-pleural pneumothorax was induced most successfully by Tudor Edwards – and from that time I have been well. It was a great grief to me to have to limit my singing so drastically and it was equally so for Hubert who loved it so dearly. It added to my own sadness that I had somehow 'let him down'. After the Second World War, my voice was as good as it had ever been, though I think, perhaps, my breath control was not. We sang and played together at our Silver Wedding Anniversary Party in [July] 1952 as if we were both soaring on wings – but within a year, he had gone.

Hubert Foss

Dora left only a few notes on what she had in mind to write about Hubert. Other
material has been added by the editors to enlarge the picture. Naturally there is
much in her account of her own life that covers the time after they met. So this
mini-biography expands on the earlier years. In the last few months of his life
Hubert dictated some reminiscences of people he had met and places he had
visited, beginning with his childhood. These are indented from the main text.

HUBERT FOSS WAS BORN ON 2 MAY 1899, the thirteenth and last child of Annie
and Frederick, solicitor and one-time mayor of Croydon. His three eldest
sisters, Agnes, Muriel and Rose, were more or less twenty-one, twenty and
nineteen when he was born. Two brothers, Edward and Kenelm, followed on,
then another girl Josephine, then William and Henry (Harry), again a girl Renée,
then Hugh who died at a year old, Bernard, Robert who died as a baby, and then
Hubert. There were four years between Hubert and the next surviving brother
Bernard, and another four years between Bernard and Renée. Hubert was very
much the Benjamin of the family, and although he was only nine when his father
died, he had been treated as a sensible companion to him for some years. A family
friend told Dora that at the age of three, Hubert could converse like a man of
twenty-seven! This was, of course, an exaggeration, but it is understandable that
the youngest child of a large and mostly grown-up or nearly grown-up family, and
made very much of by his father, should become adult, superficially at any rate,
before his time. Hubert went to a kindergarten at Woodford House School in East
Croydon in 1904. He had singing lessons from an early age from Dr Stanley Roper[26]
at his home in Norbury, and was accepted for Westminster Abbey Choir. This was
after his father's death in 1908, but Mrs Foss was advised that the education at
the Choir School was not first-rate, so she did not allow Hubert to join.

After a few years at Woodford House School, in 1909 he went to his prepar-
atory school at St Anselm's in Park Lane, Croydon, which had a good record
of scholarships to public schools, and from there in 1913 he won a Foundation
Scholarship to Bradfield College in Berkshire.

---

26   Stanley Roper, CVO (1878–1953), organist Chapels Royal, who later wrote of Hubert that
     he had 'known him for nearly 50 years – since he first came along & sang his little songs
     to us'.

As a small boy I lived in Surrey and at one time used to haunt the river Mole above Dorking. As I paddled my toes it made me think how odd and interesting it was that so near to Box Hill lived a great novelist [George Meredith], one whose name in the library shelves and textbooks stood alongside those of the remote giants Dickens and Thackeray. Little did I realise then that I should not by the age of fifty succeed in reading completely from cover to cover a single one of his novels.

I did not hear the sound of an orchestra in my childhood until I was about eleven years old. Such an experience would be impossible for a child of today's generation. I remember the occasion. I was taken (it seems to me rather unsuitably) to the Public Hall at Croydon in broad daylight – it was a rehearsal of a part of *Hiawatha* conducted by my fellow townsman Coleridge-Taylor [1875–1912]. The composer-conductor, I recall, was dressed in a real old-style frock-coat, and with his dark face and black hair he looked extremely funereal, quite unlike the music, which was very gay and bright. The next orchestral occasion in my life was one of those remarkable concerts which Clara Butt organised with the London Symphony Orchestra in aid of the Red Cross, Elgar's *The Dream of Gerontius* with Dame Clara singing the Angel. This was an experience indeed. The concert I heard was given in Reading, and Dame Clara both looked and sounded massive and almost architectural.

The awakening experience orchestrally was for me, as it must have been for thousands of others, a Henry Wood Promenade Concert. At my first Prom, I recall [Henry] Wood played Delius's *Brigg Fair* and I had then heard no music by Delius nor any other music in the least like it. I saw a completely new view of musical expression, brought up as I had been so very largely on Anglican Church Music.

Hubert attended Bradfield College from 1913 until the end of 1917. He was a Senior Classical Entrance Scholar at the start and Stevens Classical Leaving Scholar at the end. His time was well spent studying subjects such as English literature, creative writing, piano playing, and he took part in the 1914 Greek play, Euripides' *Alcestis*, in the open-air theatre.

At my public school in 1914, the music-master suffered from a distaste for, as well as a lack of ability in, his chosen subject.[27] No composer himself, he was

---

27   As Hubert Foss wrote in *Music in My Time*, p. 205, 'Music in my own time at Bradfield flew no further for my first three years than the heights of singing Stanford's *Revenge* and Elgar's *Banner of St George*, with piano lessons as an extra.'

the last person likely to encourage a boy-beginner. After some terms, his place was taken by an elderly man, who had retreated from the busy life of a cathedral town to this peaceful country school. During the holidays on one occasion I received at home from him a letter saying, 'Do let me know what you are writing during the holidays. I am (he continued) working on so-and-so.' So, I found, he takes me seriously as a composer, and he, I knew from service lists and advertisements, was famous and successful. That was the greatest encouragement I ever received as a budding writer. The wise encourager was in fact Bertram Luard-Selby.[28]

The Reverend Thomas Banks Strong[29] held, among other eminent positions, those of Dean of Christ Church, Oxford, Bishop of Ripon, and Lord Bishop of Oxford [also, a Delegate of the OUP]. I first met him when I was invited during my schooldays to the Deanery at Christ Church. I was a private guest, not even a prospective undergraduate. The warning was given me that the Dean liked to hide his love and gifts for music, which I later found to be equally profound and broad, to such a degree that he had arranged for the piano in his study to be so cased as to look like any other piece of furniture. I was more or less challenged to make him open it. I got the talk around to former organists of the Cathedral, of whom I had heard something from the then organist, Dr Henry Ley. In his enthusiasm to expound to me their ways and personalities, the Dean opened his piano and played a chord or two à la Dr William Corfe.

Hubert won a scholarship to Pembroke College, Oxford but for financial reasons was unable to accept it. After leaving school at the end of 1917 he found himself in the 5th Middlesex Regiment as a second lieutenant. Special remarks on the 'Qualifications of a Cadet on leaving Bradfield College' state: 'He is an able boy, with quite good powers of command. As a prefect he has shown himself to be a good disciplinarian and a good organiser. He is very musical, and has some of the defects of the musical temperament, such as excitability and a tendency to long hair.'

On discharge from the army at the end of 1918 he spent a short time as an assistant master at Harrow View School in Ealing but showed an interest in journalism. He was quick to capitalise on a previous encounter at school:

---

28   Bertram Luard-Selby (1853–1918), English composer and organist of Rochester Cathedral until 1916, when he joined the staff of Bradfield College.
29   Dr Thomas Strong (1861–1944) did much to encourage Walton's progress when he was a student at Christ Church, Oxford.

At my public school during the First World War, as voluntary war-work, C.L. Graves of *Punch* and *The Spectator* used to journey down once a week to teach us in the Upper Sixth about English Literature. After war-service I was looking for a job and wrote to C.L. Graves for advice and help as I wanted to go into journalism. CLG invited me to go to see him at the Athenæum. I remember the occasion (so terrifying to me at the time), and I never enter that august hall, hardly changed in thirty years, without the picture vividly coming back into my mind. I was asked to sit on one of those backless and armless sofas which stood inside the main door, and eventually C.L. Graves, who, like Ajax, walked delicately, gently walked down the immense staircase. The interview, I am happy to report, successfully launched me into the main stream of the Street of Ink.

The position in journalism that ensued was assistant editor on the weekly journal *Land and Water*.[30] He held this position for just over a year (October 1919 to November 1920). It was during this time that he encountered Hilaire Belloc:

In 1919 I was working in the office of a weekly newspaper in Bream's Buildings, off Chancery Lane, London. A regular contributor of ours and a frequent visitor was Mr Hilaire Belloc. I say 'regular', but he was in fact a little erratic. I remember wondering where his usual 'copy' was and when I was to get it for the printer, when in he walked and demanded to use a secretary for dictating, saying, 'I am not writing you an article this week. I will dictate you a poem.' So that, thought young and innocent I, is how poets work. I remember him perched on a chair, half-chanting rhythmic phrases with hand-movements to suit, in a sing-song voice – the poem was 'Do you remember an inn, Miranda?'

Hubert came into contact with Vere Collins, the Educational Manager at OUP, through his first wife, Kate Carter Page (whom Hubert married in March 1920 and divorced in 1925). Kate was a friend of Bronwen Thomas, and Vere Collins was at the time living at Forge House in Otford, the home of Bronwen's mother, Helen Thomas, widow of Edward Thomas, not far from Eynsford, where 'The Warlock Gang'[31] was in residence. Hubert and Kate originally lived at Eynsford but later rented Forge House. Collins was taken with Hubert, whom he found amusing and vivacious, extraordinarily mature and with an

30   A weekly journal, edited by Hilaire Belloc, that ran from 1914 to 1920.
31   See pp. 62–7.

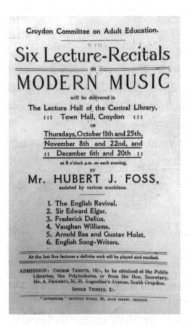

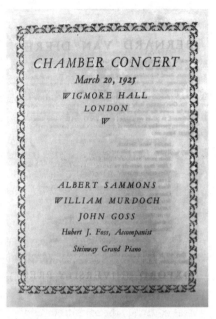

Fig. 3: A series of lectures on
English music that Hubert Foss
gave in Croydon in 1923

Fig. 4: Programme of Hubert Foss as
accompanist, Wigmore Hall, March 1925

amazing knowledge of English literature. Collins told Hubert that the OUP were short-staffed as a consequence of the war, explained that as a result of H.A.L. Fisher's Education Act of 1918 the school-leaving age was to be raised and further education expanded, and asked Hubert if he would mind 'travelling' to the public schools to see what they wanted, to take what he thought they might want and to look out for new talent. Apparently, Collins was slightly nervous of suggesting Hubert directly to Humphrey Milford, the Publisher to the university, and advised him to approach the Master of Pembroke with whom Hubert had kept in touch despite his inability to take up the scholarship. Collins even offered to pay Hubert's fare to Oxford. The Master recommended him to C. Cannan, Secretary to the Delegates, who passed on the recommendation to Milford. So in April 1921 Hubert was appointed as senior assistant to the Educational Manager, with the position of educational sales representative to public schools.

Although the OUP had previously published books on various aspects of music, it was unusual for them to publish sheet music. However, change was afoot. Milford was anxious to extend the range of publications and in 1923 had in mind to open a music department in London with its offices at Amen House, Warwick Square. He chose Hubert to be the head as Musical Editor. Printing, publishing and music were treated to, what Sutcliffe has called, a 'virtuoso performance' by which Hubert 'astonished not only his employers but the whole musical world'.[32] For the next twenty years he attracted young and old composers to the OUP banner and worked tirelessly for the cause of music. He had an aptitude for friendship – from a duke to a dustman – but he particularly favoured those who impressed him with an unpretentious and pragmatic approach to life.

In the 1920s one of the most interesting musical provisions in London was that of Sir Richard Terry[33] at Westminster Cathedral, where daily at the offices the works of English and other polyphonic masters were sung as a matter of course. What, one wondered, was this man like who knew these remote works so well not merely as library pieces but as practical daily music for use? Terry was editing at the same time a little paper called *The Musical News and Herald*. I sought an opening for my pen in its columns, and indeed long contributed to it a regular column called 'The Drum'. So I met the great Terry, and found him no remote theoretician but a very simple and ordinary musical journalist with a wide knowledge of life and affairs.

Of all the able men I have ever met, Sir Henry Hadow[34] was the one most able to inspire in his interlocutors a sense that they were his equals. He seemed always to speak up to rather than down from his great knowledge. On one occasion I was staying at his house at Ecclesall, at a time when he was Vice-Chancellor of Sheffield University (1919–30). Sir Percy Buck was also staying there, and was to lecture at the University. Hadow and I went. Buck, who had been an undergraduate under Hadow at Worcester College, Oxford, told me how nervous he was at speaking in front of Hadow. But after the lecture, a fine piece of work, Hadow's comment to me was 'I always like listening to Buck. I always learn something from him'.

32   P. Sutcliffe, *The Oxford University Press: an Informal History*, Oxford: Clarendon Press, 1978, p. 211.
33   Sir Richard Runciman Terry (1865–1938), English organist, conductor and composer, and director of music at Westminster Cathedral 1901–24. Terry was knighted in 1930.
34   Sir William Henry Hadow (1859–1937), educator, writer and composer, and general editor from 1896 of the *Oxford History of Music*. Hadow was knighted in 1918.

My first meeting with Sir Henry Wood occurred when he invited me and my then fiancée to lunch one Sunday at Appletree Farm House, Chorleywood. When we arrived at an appropriate hour, Sir Henry was perched up a ladder dressed in his roughest working clothes. In his home Sir Henry was the most domestic and informal of hosts, and like many great-minded men I have met, was intensely interested in other people and in outside events. This visit is memorable to me for another reason, in that another guest at lunch that day was that wonderful, if somewhat formidable, woman Dame Ethel Smyth.

Dora has already written of her first meeting with Hubert and of the flowering of their relationship, and the letters quoted in her following account, together with those in the second part of this book, present a vivid picture of the frenetic pace at which Hubert lived his life.

Marriage to Dora in 1927 provided Hubert with a secure antidote to the worldwide career he had already created – she was the personification of calm. In 1930 the family moved from a flat in 24 Belsize Park Gardens, where their son Christopher had been born, to Nightingale Corner[35] at Rickmansworth, which furnished a perfect refuge from the hectic life in London.

In the 1930s I lived at Rickmansworth, on the border of Herts, Middlesex and Bucks, in a house designed by a doctor for his own use. He had a liking and an eye for sun, so South aspects were predominant. The garden had a lawn planned for tennis in the days before that game became so expensive and energetic. Lacking room and equally desirous of tennis, I imported from ships to land the game of deck tennis which, played on a full-sized badminton court, is an energetic game. It is also inelegant, unprofessional and lacking in apparatus, and so one found that the inexpert who had good will could try their hand at a game without feeling that they look too ridiculous a ninny. Among those who played deck tennis in my garden were Sir Henry Wood, Sir William Walton – and once, Sir Hamilton Harty consented to endanger his beautiful hands in a trial game. The antics of the players were photographically entertaining, if not pretty.

Life at full tilt for twenty years took its toll on Hubert. His drinking and smoking, together with the financial problems that the Music Department was causing the OUP, added to the effect that work had on his health. He was

---

35   See plate 10. For further details about the house's history, see Lewis Foreman and Susan Foreman, *London – A Musical Gazetteer*, Yale University Press, 2005, pp. 189–90.

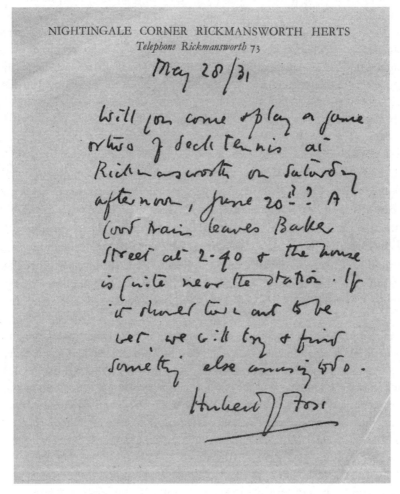

Fig. 5: Hubert Foss's invitation to deck tennis, 1931 [see plate 11]

prepared to resign in 1932 but stayed on. In 1933, when Milford was called to account by the Delegates for the scale of the losses, he defended Foss, claiming that 'it had under Foss done more for British music in ten years than the rest of the London music publishers had in thirty'.[36] Handwritten notes suggest

36   Sutcliffe, p. 211.

that Foss was proposing to apply for another position; whether he did or not is unclear, but in 1936 a breakdown followed. For three months in late 1938/early 1939 Foss took an extensive tour for the OUP of Canada and America (he had been before to the USA in 1926–27 and 1930). It was an exhausting but successful visit that included Montreal, Ottawa, Toronto and Seattle, San Francisco, Los Angeles and New York. He was back in his customary top gear.

When war came, the department was moved, for the duration of the phoney war, to Oxford and late in life Hubert recreated an ironically idyllic tableau of the working conditions he experienced there together with his colleagues:

> The scene is a charming square solid country house [Southfield House] on the outskirts of Oxford towards Cowley, bordering in fact upon the golf links. On the first floor a spacious bathroom. In 1940 we observe in the darker part a man in his early fifties writing, in pencil on a pad, verses about the Arthurian legend. At the table by the wide window overlooking a handsome and well-kept rose-garden sits a slightly younger man dictating letters and handling papers about music. The third occupant of the room is a bright-eyed young girl with red hair who is typing away as if for dear life. The poet is Charles Williams,[37] the musician is the writer of this paper. A few minutes before our entry to view the scene, the two men were standing at the window planning in imagination an amateur production in the rose-garden of the Malvolio scenes from *Twelfth Night*. Nearly all traces of the room's original ablutionary functions have been covered up by shelves of rough wood, and in their place we see files of papers, MSS and stationery, for wartime has decreed that this is no longer a bathroom but a publisher's office. At any moment tall, grey Sir Humphrey Milford may join the company and ask his incisive questions.

In 1941, after a period of sick leave, Foss resigned from his position at the OUP.[38] The remaining years of his life were devoted to as many freelance tasks as he could find. He worked for ENSA (the Entertainments National Service Organisation), for CEMA (Council for the Encouragement of Music and the Arts) and for SAME (the Society for the Advancement of Music in Education).

---

37   Charles Williams (1886–1945) was an Oxford University Press editor and a close friend of Hubert Foss. In the 1920s he wrote three short plays (masques) celebrating the work of the Press, two of which he performed with fellow workers for the entertainment of the OUP staff, with music by Foss. See pp. 150–8.

38   He was succeeded by Norman Peterkin, and later Alan Frank; see plate 17.

These contacts involved him in travel in England to conduct music summer schools and abroad to entertain British troops. He was particularly delighted and amused by the invitation he received soon after the war ended, to give a series of illustrated lectures on the operettas of Gilbert and Sullivan in Italy and Malta. He thought little of Sullivan's music but appreciated that it suited Gilbert's words, which he admired for their vocabulary, rhythms and clever allusions. He enjoyed sitting at the piano and singing the songs, accompanying himself. He was fitted out with a uniform and given the Honorary Rank of Captain; in many of the naval messes he was often the most senior officer, and everyone had to salute him – he who had been a Second Lieutenant in WW1 and a Sergeant in the Home Guard in WW2!

Recent research into his broadcasting shows how popular he was and how he was able to adapt the words he had written to a spoken style that proved most effective. He was a born communicator whether in lecture halls or in concert venues, but his particular strength was at the microphone, whether the subject was music, travel or even food, though he was notoriously incompetent in a real kitchen. He assisted in the week of broadcasts to mark the 70th birthday celebrations for Vaughan Williams in October 1942, and in the later 1940s he worked on a study of the composer.[39]

Illness still plagued him. In March 1950 a group of fellow musicians and musicologists subscribed to a fund that enabled him to take a convalescent holiday at Buckfast Abbey in Devon.

6.   *5th April 1950   Stanley Roper to HJF*

41 Thornton Avenue, London SW2

My dear Hubert,

I know you have been feeling rather exhausted lately but you will understand why I have not written sooner when I tell you that many of your dearest friends wanted a little plan of theirs to mature before we got into touch with you personally. Now I think all is arranged for you to settle for a few months in some quiet spot that attracts you so that you can plan your new book without undue interruption and I feel sure that if you are happy there and need an extension eventually, all needs will be forthcoming. It is very long since we met & I was sorry not to be able to do so in Dec last, but Charles does know that I still do not like to go near Trin[ity] Coll[ege] & the place he chose was almost

---

39   *Ralph Vaughan Williams: A Study* by Hubert Foss, George Harrap, 1950.

on its doorstep. Now you are not to write to anyone unless you feel like it and we would not interfere with your work for worlds but if you can spare time for two or three words on a card at any time just to say you are enjoying the change I shall of course be delighted to have them. I am not going to talk to you like a father, altho' I might, but you do know that your lively intellect & imagination has run away with you – this is not surprising for you were working far too much – so you must take your tasks more easily in future – perhaps even more leisurely. I know all about anxieties, in fact you helped me wonderfully when they almost overwhelmed me, indeed you helped me much more than even you knew at the time, so let this grateful remembrance help to sweep away your worries and replace your former confidence in yourself.

Love and thoughts & wishes

Yours aff[ectionate]ly

S

Convalescence subscriptions

7.   *30th March 1950*

Dear Hubert Foss,

We, whose names are signed below, want to tell you what we believe and hope you know already of our affection for you and our admiration for your work.

Thomas Armstrong, Arnold Bax, Arthur Bliss, E.J. Dent, P.A.S. Hadley, Gordon Jacob, Maud Karpeles, J. McKay Martin, Sydney Northcote, Stanley Roper, R. Vaughan Williams, Herbert Wiseman, Thomas Wood

In 1951 Hubert had an operation for a tumour on the lung, but in July 1952 he was well enough to prepare an application for the position of Controller of the BBC Third Programme. For references, apart from names at the BBC, he quoted Vaughan Williams, Geoffrey Cumberlege of the OUP, Harold Vesey Strong and Ronald Staples. Later the same year he was appointed editor of *The Musical Times*, a position that he was sadly unable to take up, as in early 1953 he had a serious stroke from which he seemed to recover but in May suffered a second, more serious stroke from which he died almost immediately, just before the Coronation of Queen Elizabeth, which he had hoped to watch on the family's newly acquired television set. Sadly, it was not to be.

Hubert Foss was a polymath: composer, conductor, pianist, accompanist, enthusiastic judge at local music competitions, author, editor, publisher, designer, typographer, printer, lecturer, journalist, music critic, and a frequent broadcaster with a keen interest in the promotion of serious music on the air. There were few aspects of the cultural scene in the period between the two World Wars to which he failed to make a valuable contribution. He had boundless energy and a gift for friendship that was second to none.

John Barbirolli

MY FIRST MEETING WITH JOHN BARBIROLLI was on 1 October 1924. The occasion was the monthly musical evening of the Guild of Singers and Players in Grosvenor Street, that remarkably helpful organisation, which, under the guidance of Madame Lily Henkel, did so much to encourage young artists. I was to sing that night, and my acceptance as a member of the Guild depended on my reaching a certain standard of artistry and technique. Earlier that evening, as I have already related, I had sung at the Cramer concert at the Aeolian Hall, so I had recovered from any initial nervousness, and when I had to sing in Grosvenor Street, I was not only calm, but elated. John, with Rae Robertson and Ethel Bartlett, his wife, were amongst members present. I sang the few songs by Hugo Wolf that I had brought with me and then I had recourse to the Cramer publications which included Martin Shaw's *At Columbine's Grove*, as the audience asked for more. It was a happy evening. The knowledge that I was singing well and that it was obviously liked by artists of the calibre of John and the Robertsons and many others, was inspiring – almost intoxicating.

This meeting led to a friendship between myself and Ethel Bartlett. In March 1925 Ethel and John, who were giving many sonata recitals together, played at a musical evening given by my mother at 25 Redington Road, Hampstead. They played the first movement from Boëllmann's Sonata in A minor and Debussy's beautiful sonata in the same key. I had met Hubert shortly before this and I sang his two song settings of Blake's *Infant Joy* and *As I walked forth*, amongst others that evening. This may well have been the first time Hubert and John met. Later that night John and Ethel played Delius's Sonata to an enchanted residue of guests.

In March of the following year, I went to Reading with Ethel and John, where we gave a Delius-Debussy recital. (We had come by train, third class, from London early, and were hoping for, rather expecting, some refreshments.) As soon as the concert was over, the Music Club Secretary bounced into the artists' room in a state of great excitement. 'We're all going to a champagne supper,' he said – and for a moment I thought we were included, but my hopes were squashed when he continued, 'so I must say goodbye now'. Very disconsolately we trudged to the station hotel, where we had glasses of port while we waited for the train. In the dingy, rather badly lit third-class carriage, John sent us into the most abandoned fits of laughter by his wildly funny imitations of a common-to-all-of-us friend who had asked his advice on marriage! Luckily we had the compartment to ourselves as we literally rolled helplessly on the seats. It was the most superb performance – and there was nothing unkind or malicious in it – just the faint underlining of idiosyncrasies and mannerisms, and done with a feeling of affection rather than of mockery.

Later that week, on the Saturday, John went with the Music Society String Quartet to Sevenoaks (André Mangeot, Boris Pecker, Henry J. Berly) at Hubert's invitation. They played the G minor Quartet of Vaughan Williams, and Dohnanyi's Quartet in D flat major. Between these quartets John and Hubert played the Delius Sonata.

Extracts of letters from Hubert Foss to Dora Foss

8. *21ˢᵗ October 1929 HJF to DMF*

Edinburgh

> I found Tito[40] in the theatre rehearsing, with the usual operatic difficulties about him – Percy Heming ill and William Michael taking the part of Figaro at a moment's notice. Tomorrow they do Turandot[41] which I've never seen, so I shall go.

40 The diminutive 'Tita' was the name by which John (Giovanni) Barbirolli (1899–1970) was known to his family, varied by English friends to 'Tito' (Michael Kennedy, *Barbirolli, Conductor Laureate. The authorised biography*, MacGibbon & Kee, 1971, p. 17).

41 With the newly formed Covent Garden Opera Company, Barbirolli conducted the first performance of *Turandot* in English at Halifax on 27 September 1929 (Michael Kennedy, *Barbirolli*, p. 63).

9.   *22ⁿᵈ October [1929]   HJF to DMF*

***The Caledonian**, Edinburgh*

   We're going to hear Turandot, Tito having given us seats; he's coming back
to supper afterwards. I look forward to it greatly; I've not seen Puccini on the
stage for a long time, as I usually hate the music so much; but all my most
similarly-minded friends have recanted over T. We saw an act of Barber last
night – quite enough for me. I hate the music anyhow and the comedy was
so badly produced that it hardly came through. Finally everyone accepts the
Rossini tradition without believing in it and the result was most half-hearted
– Noel Eadie poor in the extreme and neither Michael nor Nash counting for
a penny. But there were two exceptions to this attitude of faithful insincerity
– Tito and an Italian who played Don Basilio, named Auton. He has a fine big
voice and a good sense of comedy, though his producer lets him overact. A
good round performance.

10.   *23ʳᵈ October [1929]   HJF to DMF*

   I was latish (about 2!) last night with Tito (of which more later).

11.   *24ᵗʰ October [1929]   HJF to DMF*

   At the hotel I ran into Octave Dua, the tenor from the Monnaie [opera house]
at Brussels with whom I and John B had spent much time talking on the previous
night. We had a longish chat about opera in general and John's Company in
particular, which delayed us a bit.

   In a separate envelope you'll find the programme of Turandot. It was a really
thrilling show: the only Puccini opera I've ever been able to stand! Tito kept
everyone up to absolutely top pitch, and made with his 43 players and 40 chorus
a noise far more resonant and splendid than ever I heard at Covent Garden itself.
The secret of the show was easy to spot. Tito knows one very fundamental thing,
that the only way to get over the badness of the only available principals is by
swinging the music along and not letting them mess it about. His tempo was
perfectly marvellous – everything kept going red hot the whole time. The one
really good performance was the Emperor – a very old man who has to sit still
all up near the flies in the most distressing position for singing, and be pathetic
and dignified and never sentimental. Parry Jones was just a joke, and, except
for one good moment, so was William Michael: Dua alone kept Ping Pang Pong
together. Staging as stupid as usual but it looked better because of the gold and
bright colours.

I was interested to see Odette de Foras [Turandot]. It's a good voice, with lots of endurance – the part needs it, for it hangs about interminably on long A's and B's fortissimo. But she's incredibly amateur and like all people who act off the stage, she can't act at all ON and comes through positively dowdy with no sex charm at all. A marvellous part – easy to play if difficult to sing. Full of sympathy and nothing to do most of the time except look marvellous and remote and dignified. She can't even walk! She almost tripped up, and as for turning, why, it's absurd to ask her to! She stood for whole scenes with her hands stretched out as if she were a clothes horse. [Francis] Russell [Calaf] was singing better than usual, a little less strain, but he was a miserable lover-prince: he looked so like an English clerk that one wondered why he'd forgotten to put on his glasses.

Yet the show was splendid – all Tito of course. He carried them through and made the house thrill with excitement.

12.   *29ᵗʰ January 1939   DMF to HJF* **(America)**

60 Corringham Road, NW11[42]

She [Helen Sandeman][43] is very intrigued at the thought of Barbirolli's possibly marrying Evelyn Rothwell,[44] which I told her in confidence. She tells me she heard that Toscanini's only remark at Glyndebourne was to ask who the oboe player was, and when told it was Evelyn Rothwell, he was much surprised and said words to the effect that he could hardly believe that such marvellous playing could be done by a woman!

Bernard van Dieren

BERNARD VAN DIEREN[45] WAS UNIQUE. The model for Epstein's 'Christ', he could on occasion appear Machiavellian. A man in constant pain due to kidney trouble, so Hubert told me, he was able to obtain drugs for its relief. He could drink gin like water – and Hubert many times told me he had seen him do so – but it had apparently no ill effect on him whatsoever. There was an aura of mystery surrounding van Dieren. He had a vast knowledge of many subjects

---

42   The London address in Golders Green to which Dora and Hubert moved in September 1936.
43   Close Glaswegian friend of Dora and Hubert Foss. Helen and her sister Dorothy met Hubert and Dora on a music cruise organised by Hubert.
44   They were married at Holborn Register Office on 5 July 1939.
45   Bernard van Dieren (1884–1936), Dutch composer who settled in London in 1909.

other than music. He was a fascinating talker, but Hubert never felt at ease with him, and came back very exhausted.[46] He once said to me that he never knew if Bernard was God or the Devil. Hubert had a very great admiration for his music, and the OUP published many of his songs and other compositions.

My own meetings with van Dieren were few, but two incidents are, I think, interesting. One was at a party given by Dorothy and Robert Mayer[47] at their house at Harefield, Middlesex in October 1930. There must have been twenty at dinner, mostly musicians. When we went into the drawing-room for coffee, van Dieren sat on a sofa by the fireside. He looked very pale and uncomfortable and must have been suffering immensely. I was standing facing the fire, with others. Suddenly, out of the blue, he addressed me in a very distinct, sharp voice. 'Mrs Foss, do you believe in God?' I said, 'Yes. I do', but I was, not unnaturally, rather shaken by being questioned thus in public. 'Then why,' Bernard continued, 'do you not go down on your knees here' (indicating the rug in front of the fire) 'and pray "Dear Jesus, please take away Bernard's pain."' Alas, I cannot recollect with accuracy exactly what happened next. I remember feeling dizzy with embarrassment, and I know that somehow Hubert rescued me from a situation which overwhelmed me. To my regret, I know that I did not go down on my knees. When I was older, I should, I believe, have had the moral courage to do so, but I was not brave enough then.

The second incident took place during a party given by Herbert and Suzanne Hughes[48] at their fine Chelsea Studio. Hubert and I were standing in a group with van Dieren and his wife Freda. I remember watching Conchita Supervia[49] talking to Harriet Cohen.[50] Conchita, auburn-haired, dressed entirely in white, smothered in white fox fur; Harriet, pale and dark, in black from head to foot,

---

46   A Kettner's restaurant menu dated 20 October 1928 bears the signatures of Hubert Foss, Herbert Howells, van Dieren, Vaughan Williams, Calvocoressi, Maurice Bird, Norman Peterkin, Arthur Benjamin and Edwin Evans.

47   Robert Mayer (1879–1985), German-born patron of music later Anglicised, remembered especially for the children's concerts which he founded and which bore his name. Knighted in 1939.

48   Herbert Hughes (1882–1937), Irish composer and critic, known especially for the many Irish folk songs he arranged. Suzanne was his second wife, and Patrick 'Spike' Hughes his son from his first marriage.

49   Conchita Supervia (1895–1936), renowned Spanish opera singer.

50   Harriet Cohen (1895–1967), English pianist and dedicatee of works by Vaughan Williams, John Ireland, Lambert and Bax, who was her lover.

but an animated black, for it had lots of little silk bobbles. It was an unforgettable picture which I can visualise now: these two strikingly handsome women, in the foreground in complete white and complete black, stately and still, against a moving background of colour. Eventually Conchita glided away and Hubert went off to talk to someone else, so he was not with me to hear the following passages:

Harriet attacked van Dieren – 'Will you write something for my Bach Book? You must.'

Harriet was then persuading well-known composers to arrange chorales or arias by Bach for the piano for her to play. These were subsequently published as a collection entitled 'Harriet Cohen's Bach Book'.[51]

Van Dieren at once hedged and more or less refused. 'Oh, but you must,' Harriet repeated. 'Everybody is doing it; you needn't do anything yourself: I'll arrange it and you can put your name to it.' Van Dieren smiled enigmatically (the only word for it) and Harriet continued, 'I want you to do "Bist du bei mir"', then, rather coyly, 'I don't know what it means.' 'It means "Will you lie with me?"' said Bernard. Inwardly, I could not help laughing, as, indeed, Bernard was, quite openly. Harriet, nettled, said, 'Don't be silly,' and then the various groups in the party kaleidoscoped and I was drawn into another group.

13.   *4th April 1932   Bernard van Dieren to HJF*
                              35a St George's Road, West Hampstead, NW6
My dear Hubert,

It was very good of you and the Duchess to think of me for your party on the 9th, and most thoughtful to give me all the particulars about how to reach your present abode. I am so sorry that I shall not be able to hear the new music, as it happens that the whole of that particular evening had been given away weeks ago. I do hope that you will have a great success with your [Violin] Sonata, of which I hope to see a copy as soon as it is published.

Our very kindest regards to you both,

Yours sincerely,

Bernard Van Dieren

---

51   *A Bach Book for Harriet Cohen*, Oxford University Press, 1932, reissued 2013 with an introduction by David Owen Norris.

*Two other musicians unable to attend, Frank Bridge and Lionel Tertis,[52] also
replied:*

14.   *[n.d.]   Frank Bridge to HJF*
       Friston Field, near Eastbourne, Sussex [printed], 4 Bedford Gardens, W8

My dear Foss,

   Thank you so much for your kind invitation for April 9th. We should have
been delighted to come if we had been in town but we are down here until the
middle of April. So sorry not to be with you & hear the new works.

   With greetings to you & Mrs Foss,

   Yours sincerely

   Frank Bridge

15.   *20th March 1932   Lionel Tertis to HJF*
                                    Smalldown, Belmont, Sutton, Surrey

Dear Mr Foss,

   How very kind of you to ask me for April 9th. Thank you very much, I shall
much hope to come. It will depend on my condition of health. I have been
fighting 'flu' on and off for a month or more and I have a lot on just now but I
should be disappointed to miss such a delightful evening.

   With kind regards

   Yours sincerely

   Lionel Tertis

16.   *[1935]   Bernard van Dieren to HJF[53]*

   I cannot tell you how pained I am to think things are not going better than
you described to me. I know too well what it all means and my sympathy and
concern are as far as they could be from formality. Let us hope that the intensity
of good wishes may have some occult effect.

---

52   See p. 233.
53   Regarding Dora Foss's illness.

Henry Hadow

HUBERT HAD A GREAT LIKING for older and old people, not necessarily VERY old, but the senior generation. He never felt or caused them to feel that he was the new generation which knew better. He was never obsequious, though always respectful – he felt he could learn so much from them. They, in their turn, loved him for his enthusiasm, his interest in them and his willingness to learn from them. He took endless trouble to please them and to help them whenever and wherever he could, and it was not only the well-known or famous 'old' that he tried to help. With some he carried on a voluminous correspondence, others he would help as far as he could with their legal affairs, or he would visit them or be really glad to see them. Naturally there were many who crossed his path in his publisher's life and to these he was literally a guardian. Indeed, it was this very word which was used by an eminent musician and conductor more than old enough to be Hubert's father who said to a friend after Hubert had died, 'I feel as if I had lost a close relative.'

Among Hubert's elderly friends in the 1920s and 1930s was Sir Henry Hadow, a friendship dating from 1924. Sir Henry was then sixty, and Hubert twenty-five.[54]

The first letter Hubert had from Hadow is dated 14 November 1924:

17.

> ... Many thanks for the delightful collection of songs which I found awaiting me here. May I say how specially I have been struck with your two contributions!
> Yours ever,
> W H Hadow

The songs referred to were Hubert's settings of Blake's *As I walked forth*, and *Infant Joy*.

In 1926–27 Hubert was thinking of publishing a collection of Hadow's essays and wrote to me from SS *Olympia* on his way to the USA.

---

54   Hubert Foss contributed a personal memoir, 'William Henry Hadow', to *Music and Letters*, vol. xviii no. 3, July 1937, pp. 236–38.

18.   *1927   HJF (SS Olympia) to DMF*

In the middle of all this mixture [Tom Jones and Joseph Vance] I read a proposed book of collected essays by Hadow[55] – very brilliant and including a new-old one on Iago as a real live human being, cunning, opportunist, but unimaginative. I was quite thrilled.

19.   *17ᵗʰ February 1929   HJF to DMF*

Did you see A[rnold] Bennett's crack-up of Hadow? I send it in case you didn't. I invented that book and collected the essays as well as designing the page, binding etc.!!

Sir Henry Hadow married in 1930, at the age of seventy-one, a Miss Troutbeck. Hubert was very touched at the thought of the elderly couple finding romance in the late autumn of their lives and arranged a little celebration: luncheon at the Berkeley Hotel. It was like taking out two children: every course, every mouthful almost was enjoyed to the utmost, Lady Hadow uttering little cries of appreciation and delight. The Berkeley restaurant staff, who had been informed by Hubert that it was a more or less bridal party, looked after our table with tact and tenderness. In retrospect I see us surrounded by benign and smiling waiters. There was an excellent small orchestra which entranced the newly-married couple. We eventually finished our luncheon and were leaving the Restaurant when the band began to play *The Blue Danube*. This was the crowning moment. Lady Hadow stopped at once. She listened as if in a happy dream, then in ecstasy she clapped her hands and said to the conductor in a voice literally thrilling with emotion, 'Oh, I danced to that when I was a girl'. He was delighted with her outspoken appreciation and beamed at her. We all stood there till the Waltz finished, gazed on, so I felt, by the entire room, and egotistically I was glad I had on an impeccable dress and hat. Lady Hadow thanked the conductor with fervour, and her dream lasted till we were in the lobby outside when she, so to speak, woke up. Sir Henry and she thanked us warmly, then, as we were about to part, the dream came back into her eyes for a moment and she added, 'Oh, it has been a LARK!!'

55   W.H. Hadow, *Collected Essays*, OUP, 1928, edited by Hubert Foss.

20. *28ᵗʰ April 1930   Henry Hadow to HJF*
The Vice Chancellor, The University, Sheffield

Dear Foss,

I have just found your kind letter. Many thanks for it and for all the words of congratulation and good will which it contains. My wife has, I think, had the pleasure of meeting you at the Bach Cantata Club:[56] in any case we both look forward to the pleasure of future meetings.

I am much interested in your account of Chicago. America is a problem of some of which we became aware last August at Lausanne.

Very sincerely,

W H Hadow

In the chapter on Sir Henry Wood is an account of the dinner party at Nightingale Corner with Hadow in April 1931.[57] When Hubert wrote *Music in My Time* he sent each chapter to Sir Henry Hadow as it was written and Sir Henry replied with shrewd and detailed comments and criticism, showing an amazing understanding of Hubert's musical outlook, yet not hesitating to query or even occasionally to condemn parts of which he did not approve.

21. *23ʳᵈ May 1931   Henry Hadow to HJF*

13 Belgrave Road, SW1

Dear Foss,

I have been going through the catalogue[58] with great admiration. It is a model of order and arrangement and will, I think, be the pioneer of a new method.

But I have grave misgivings about writing its introduction. My name occurs some half a dozen times, and to commend it would seem like drawing attention to a tutti in which my own trumpet is not unheard. Can I come and talk it over with you? If so, can you give me a time either on Tuesday (for choice) or on Wednesday morning?

---

56 The Bach Cantata Club was founded in 1926 by Hubert Foss, Charles Kennedy Scott and Stanley Roper. The select choir, conducted by Kennedy Scott, usually performed in either St Margaret's Church, Westminster or Westminster Abbey. It was disbanded in 1935.

57 See pp. 165–6.

58 *Catalogue of Oxford Music and Books on Music Published by the Oxford University Press, London*, July 1931, which was published without any introduction by a specific personality.

Meanwhile, might I suggest Herbert Thompson?[59] He stands sufficiently clear of it, and of other publishers, and he is a good man of letters who knows his job thoroughly, and his name would carry weight in the North of England. The difficulty is that you have included among your contributors almost every English musician who matters.

Let me come to canvass possibilities. I should like to help if I could but you see the obstacle.

Yours ever,

W H Hadow

22.   11th June 1931   Henry Hadow to HJF

13 Belgrave Road, SW1

Dear Foss,

I have not the least doubt about the suitability of the essay.[60] It is, if I may say so, a really fine piece of work, well-balanced in judgement, and clear in expression. It will certainly enhance the value of the new volume.

For completeness' sake, it wants a considerable section on the vocal works which you hardly mention: not only the oratorios, which are a compendium both of his strength and of his weakness – I do not think he ever wrote anything worse than O rest in the Lord or better than He that shall endure – but even his songs which opened in England a hesitating door for the Romantics. They are mostly trivial, but they struck a new note to us, and one of them at any rate (By Celia's Arbour) is beautiful.

Anyhow, if you write this section it should be interpolated so that you close on your three selected works. They are exactly typical, and I entirely agree with your treatment of them.

All congratulations

Yours ever,

WHH

---

59   Herbert Thompson (1856–1945), music critic of the *Yorkshire Post*.

60   'Felix Mendelssohn-Bartholdy' by HJF in *The Heritage of Music*, vol. 2, OUP, 1934. Hadow contributed an article on Handel. Much earlier, Foss had written a three-part article entitled 'A Commentary upon Mendelssohn' for *The Musical Times*, May, June and July 1924.

Music in My Time

Music in My Time by Hubert J. Foss, Rich & Cowan Ltd, October 1933, was a personal survey of the development of music and its place in society, discussing contemporary music and also covering such aspects as broadcasting, education and, briefly, popular music and jazz, with which Foss was not in sympathy. It bore the dedication 'For Diana Foss', his daughter, born in September 1933. Hadow's numbering presumably refers to a final draft of the book before publication. The numbers in italics in square brackets correspond to the pagination of the published version.

Pre-publication comments by Sir Henry Hadow

23.   *14th August 1933   Henry Hadow to HJF*

King's Head, Wrexham

Dear Foss,

Many congratulations on a very notable book. It is both provocative and convincing which is a rare combination, and it is very well written.

There are a few tiny roughnesses of style which I have mostly left unmarked – they lie on the surface and are of no more account than misprints in a typescript. And the phrases 'As I have shown' and 'as I shall show later' are familiar pieces of deadwood which I am always having to cut out of my own work. Is 'necrophilous' right on p. 68? It doesn't seem to have exactly the meaning that you want.

Substantial points – not for criticism but for discussion:

1. American School Orchestra (p. 29 seq.) [*34*]. I once had the opportunity of inspecting a dozen competing school orchestras at an Educational Festival in Bangor [Maine]. They played very well, good tone and good attack – but the programme was a nightmare. The least intolerable thing was a light song of Gounod. One of the other battle-horses was a school march entitled 'Stabat Mater' and adapted from Rossini's 'Cujus animam'. I hinted that in England we paid a good deal of attention to standard of selection. 'Quite right' said the superintendent. 'So do we.'
2. Death of the craftsman (p. 36) [*39*]. Overstated like Mark Twain's death. Lamentable if true, but is it so? There is surely a great revival of craftsmanship in Village Industries – Newlyn, Grasmere, Yattendon and many others. Much encouraged in school e.g. lettering.

3. Amateur-weak professional (p. 45) [*48*]. Very good. I am particularly struck with the phrase 'dismissed from the stage to his rightful place in the stalls' [*51*] because that gives him a positive and not dishonourable part to sustain.

4. Novelty in art (p. 50) [*52*] isn't part of the reason that a great many 'cultured' people feel that they have a responsibility to express some opinion about art and that they don't understand enough about it au fond to express that opinion in temperate terms? Nearly all bad criticism is a criss-cross of alternating superlatives and it's easier to be abusive. The French say 'il est fou' of a man who goes down the street with an unusual coloured tie.

5. Society of Contemporary Musicians [*56*]. You might strengthen this. They are very unduly neglected and consequently a little defiant.

6. Caravaggio (p. 65) [*66*]. I have long wanted to see a study of his work which compared it mutatis mutandis with the monastic movement in music. Light concentrated on a single point instead of being diffused contrapuntally over the whole surface. Won't you do this? Or am I overstating the parallel.

7. Performance and tuition for the composer (pp. 88 seq.) [*ch. v*]. Excellent. Should be further emphasised.

8. The clarinet (p. 107) [*105*] counted in Handel's time & for nearly a century afterwards among the brass instruments. The detailed history wants looking up. I believe that the reedy tone came in with Gossec.[61]

9. Nationalism depends on a breakaway [*111*]. Is this so? Isn't it rather a primitive instinct which for a time was forced into a common scholastic uniform but retained its inherent differences underneath. The 'Cosmopolitan' movement in turn [unclear] is comparatively modern.

10. Stravinsky, Mendelssohn [*126*]. This will want even further elucidation, otherwise the reader will think it's a paradox.

11. Bartok's 'passionate expression' (p. 154) [*148*]. Is passionate the right idea? All of his work that I know seems to be the result of calculation.

12. Quartertones (pp. 167–8) [*160*]. Isn't the main difficulty that they are used so far rather timidly – an appoggiatura followed by chromatic or diatonic principal notes instead of constituting a scale by themselves traversing slantwise that of the ordinary gamut? I don't think that anything like enough has been made of their possibilities. They never seem to venture out of reach of shore.

Your criticisms of contemporary musicians are excellent, especially Debussy.
Yours ever
W H Hadow

---

61   François Gossec (1734–1829), Belgian composer.

24.   *17ᵗʰ August 1933   Henry Hadow to HJF*

Burlington Hotel, Sheringham

Batch VIII

The main part of the reason is, I think, that we are suffering from an attack of nimiety. There is too much of everything – too much cricket, too much aeronauting, far too much record-breaking, too many words, too much news in general. I don't mean that the quality of each example is worse because they are so frequent, but there is less time to attend to them and consequently we don't study enough to detect the outstanding names. And then there is a common tradition of technique which tends to obliterate distinction. But this is difficult to say here because it might be misunderstood as if it depreciated the spread of musical education about which you speak in the next section. It doesn't, of course, mean that but it might be misinterpreted to involve it.

So on the whole I should pass over it lightly until the time comes when it can make a volume by itself.

Batch X

Your sentences on Standards in the choice of school music (England and America) answer the point which I raised in Chapter 1. A single reference to it is sufficient: it might be enlarged or emphasised.

25.   *22ⁿᵈ August 1933   Henry Hadow to HJF*

Burlington Hotel, Sheringham

Dear Foss

I should quite agree to ending quietly and unrhetorically. The overture to Egmont is a good precedent.

Batch XI

I should be inclined to omit Proust. Rockstro [222] gives you everything that you want and makes by himself a better antithesis to Morris. Besides, Proust, for all his egregiousness, did try to draw from the living world. He was often wrong but he was not (like Rockstro) an [unreadable]. See his book on orchestration which is really inductive.

I doubt about the phrase 'At Random', not because it isn't often appropriate, but because it is never credible. When a man says 'to take two instances at random', I always suspect that he has chosen them with special care.

Batch XIII

? Omit the opening sentence. You begin better 'It is the supreme paradox ...'
[238]

Batch XIV
A little too negative in [unreadable], but it does not want emphasising.

Yours ever
W H Hadow

Comment by Havergal Brian:[62]

26.   *18th October 1933   Havergal Brian to HJF*

1 Jasper Road, SE19

Congratulations on your book. I had no idea you had any time for such downright concentrated thinking. A great surprise. ...

Hamilton Harty

HUBERT HAD A VERY DEEP, even emotional friendship for Hamilton Harty.[63] He says of him: 'I can see Hay Harty standing before me. Tall, almost unbearably good-looking, shy, quiet of speech, silent, indeed, until he had something to say worth saying, and then how good it was.' Harty was 'aware' mentally and aesthetically, always perceptive. He had the penetrating eyes of the poet and the prophet and the pure artist. In those years after I became Harty's friend, I always used to sit up at the back of the orchestra so as to watch those wonderful eyes in action with the music. He hated intellectual music – eccentric modernisms and theoretical experiments in mere sound. He would say of new music, 'It can't be any good unless it comes from here' and point to his heart. That is why the music of William Walton and Constant Lambert touched him – it has emotional appeal. He championed both those composers

62   Havergal Brian (1876–1972), English composer of thirty-two symphonies, of which *The Gothic* is best known, chiefly for its size. With his music largely unplayed during most of his lifetime, he earned his living through journalism, two volumes of which have been published by Toccata Press. From 1927 to 1940 he was a regular contributor to *Musical Opinion* and the majority of his literary output was written for that journal.

63   Hamilton Harty (1879–1941), Irish composer, pianist and conductor, of the Hallé Orchestra (1920–33) and the London Symphony Orchestra (1933–34). Knighted 1925.

when they were young: in Lambert's *Rio Grande* he played the piano part and gave up his stick to the newcomer; he conducted Walton's Symphony, both incomplete (that historic occasion!) and then complete; he urged Moeran to write a Symphony and went over it bar by bar with him. You see, he was 'quick to understand'.

I always say that I loved him – it's the only word. Harty inspired love, from his players as well as his friends. Harty came to see us at Rickmansworth and I well remember his first visit. He sat on a sofa in the drawing-room and looked all round the room as if he was listening for something. It was almost uncanny. He was silent for a few moments, then he said, 'This is a good house, a good house.' I felt as if I had been blessed by him.

Hubert sat up all night with him once after dining with him in order to win him over to Walton. At first Harty very much 'sat on the fence'. Hubert was determined he should like Willie's music. As everyone knows, when he accepted it, he was one of its greatest champions and exponents.

Hubert's friendship with Harty lasted until Harty's death (in 1941).

27.   *23rd March 1929   Hamilton Harty to HJF*
                              Devonshire Club, St James's, SW1

My dear Foss,

A few lines to put things in a clearer way than perhaps I did last night. I agree in principle with all your ideas regarding the BBC but, though I have no official connection or understanding with them, they have treated the Hallé Society with some attempt at fairness.[64]

My first duty is to the Hallé people, while I am their conductor, and therefore my hands are tied by what I am sure you will consider honourable motives.

You were in good form last night and I thought you put your case very eloquently. If only composers were as good as their champions!

Yours ever

Hamilton Harty

64   Contentious issues at the time between the BBC and the Hallé concerned broadcasting fees, the formation in 1930 of the BBC Symphony Orchestra, which it was felt might tempt away players, and the abandonment by the BBC of a four-week season of Proms in the North that involved Harty and the Hallé.

28.   *11ᵗʰ December 1931   HJF (Manchester) to DMF (Nightingale Corner, Rickmansworth)*

The concert was really marvellous – Harty at his best and Myra [Hess] playing better than I ever knew she could. The best performance of Beethoven Concerto I've ever heard. What a superb work the Sibelius is! I stayed out for 'get your hair cut' [*Symphonic Variations*] by César Franck and found the Mussorgsky too long.[65]

Harty was kind but for some mysterious reason would not stop and chat. [Alfred] Barker[66] could not imagine why but says he's been quite funny and like this all season. He looks so old now. I feel quite sad about it.

29.   *22ⁿᵈ February 1933   Hamilton Harty to HJF*

Ballinderry, Ellesmere Park, Eccles, Manchester

My dear Hubert,

I am so sorry you are having anxiety as to your wife's health, and hope that the news is better now. You know, as soon as I finish here,[67] I shall have much more leisure to see my friends, of which you are certainly a foremost one. Thanks for Shepherd's kind remarks.

I don't know what to do about 'Horizons',[68] because, very privately, I was a bit disappointed with it when he played it for me in a duet arrangement.

But he is such a nice fellow, and the work, anyway, is respectable and on a large scale, so I'll try to find a good opportunity for its première here. Why don't you go over to Switzerland and wrest poor WW's Baroness[69] away from him so that he can stop making overtures to her and do a symphony for me instead! (Rather a good joke!)

Yours ever

HH

---

65   Beethoven Piano Concerto No. 4 (Myra Hess), Sibelius Symphony No. 7, Mussorgsky-Ravel *Pictures at an Exhibition*.

66   Alfred Barker, leader of the Hallé Orchestra.

67   Harty resigned as principal conductor of the Hallé Orchestra in 1933.

68   Symphony No. 1 *Horizons* by Arthur Shepherd (1880–1958), an American composer with whom Foss was in correspondence in July 1930 about the work.

69   Baroness Imma von Doernberg, with whom by 1931 Walton was living in Switzerland. Their intense affair was largely the cause of the delays with the First Symphony.

30.   *30th March 1934   Hamilton Harty to HJF*
                                    1 Norfolk Road, St John's Wood, London NW8

My dear Hubert,

I never wrote to thank you for the books (at least I don't think so). I shall read them with great pleasure on my voyage.[70] I shall be back in August and let us meet then.

Tell Walton that next season's dates are being arranged and I hope the symphony will be one of our chief exhibits – good luck to him.

And the best of good wishes to restless Hubert. (But it is so much better to be restless than dead – like so many people are who think they are alive.)

Yours ever

Hay

31.   *11th December 1934   HJF* **(Liverpool)** *to DMF* **(Rickmansworth)**

Hay Harty is here so we are all going to the Damnation of Faust tonight. I've seen him for a few minutes. 7.45 what an hour!

32.   *15th June 1937   Hamilton Harty to HJF*
                                    1 Norfolk Road, St John's Wood, London NW8

My dear Hubert,

I am being sent abroad for some weeks' change, but I shall be back again after that, and most pleased if you could give me a ring on the telephone and we could arrange to have a chat. I well understand how sick you must be of the 'Toshcanimics' of the semi-musical critics and the like. All that will die away in time but never the extremely bloody stupidity which make such things possible.

Yours always

Hay

Four more letters from Hamilton Harty are included in the Walton section: no. 111, p. 122 and nos. 121–3 pp. 130–2.

---

70   In April, Harty sailed for Australia for a two-months' engagement with the Australian Broadcasting Commission.

Philip Heseltine/Peter Warlock[71] and 'The Warlock Gang'

H UBERT FIRST MET PHILIP HESELTINE in February 1923 at one of Lady Dean's
Concerts Intimes[72] at the Hyde Park Hotel. At this concert John Goss sang the
Warlock-Yeats song-cycle *The Curlew* which was later published by the Carnegie
Trust. The friendship which began that day between Hubert and Philip lasted a
comparatively short time. The quarrel which ended it was a personal affair and
had nothing to do with the musical interests of either of them. Hubert had the
very highest opinion of Warlock's song-writing, an opinion which never wavered
with the years. He always did everything in his power for Warlock's songs. He
published them, Norman Peterkin conducting all the business affairs, wrote
about them, lectured on them and knew them all backwards. There is only one
letter from Philip in Hubert's commonplace book. I am quite ignorant of what it is
about, this mysterious missive written in the tiniest, neatest writing imaginable.

33.   *Tuesday night [Nov./Dec. 1924]   Philip Heseltine to HJF*[73]

113 Cheyne Walk, SW10

My dear Hubert,

I am really so very sorry about this absurd business with Gray.[74] You probably
won't believe me when I say so – it is so obvious to construct a conspiracy out of
the facts. All the same I feel I must write and assure you on my word of honour
– if indeed you can still believe me capable of possessing such a thing – that I

---

71   'Peter Warlock' was the pseudonym under which the music of Philip Heseltine (1894–1930)
      was published.

72   A series of chamber concerts presented by Lady Dean Paul (1880–1932), Belgian composer,
      née Irene Regine Wieniawska, known professionally as Poldowski. The concert was
      actually on 31 January 1923.

73   See plates 18–19.

74   Cecil Gray (1895–1951), Scottish composer, critic, author and first biographer of Philip
      Heseltine (*Peter Warlock*, Jonathan Cape, 1934). This controversy arose out of comments
      Gray had made about Holst in the draft of his *Survey of Contemporary Music*, to which
      OUP had objected. (See Heseltine-Gray correspondence, May 1924, in *The Collected Letters
      of Peter Warlock Volume 4*, ed. Barry Smith, Boydell Press, 2005, fn. 1 p. 97.) Heseltine
      had suggested to Gray that rather than finding a new publisher he should replace the
      offending paragraph with a footnote stating that a section had been 'deleted at the demand
      of the publisher'. When the book was published by OUP in October 1924 it still contained

had no intention whatever of pursuing this matter without your consent – and I am most truly sorry that you should have been worried by it this afternoon and evening. I tried to find you to-night at the Aeolian Hall – I waited from 8 till 8.25 but you were either before or after me. Anyway – I saw Gray again this evening and persuaded him to drop any further action for at least a month – and even then he will do nothing without consulting both of us – between you and me (though I feel I have no right to use that phrase at all) he will cool down in that time, no doubt, so that virtually there is no question of the matter cropping up again at all.

Only I feel so ashamed of having caused you even this temporary anxiety – and of having broken so pleasant a confidence. After all that you have done for me, it is a very sorry thing to let you in for worry of this kind.

Ever yours

Philip Heseltine

One of the last lectures I heard Hubert give was on Warlock's songs at the Arts Council in St James's Square, with Sinclair Logan singing the illustrations. The room was packed and the audience enthralled by the magic of the music. However, during the short time that the friendship lasted and particularly when Hubert lived at Otford and Heseltine at Eynsford, they saw a good deal of each other. Hubert was as intrigued as Cecil Gray was, by the original ménage there, and he hoped to write his impressions of it if and when he wrote

---

some damning comments on Holst, inferring that he had no 'originality of outlook' but a style which was 'a compendium or *pastiche* of the styles of nearly all representative modern composers which he has equally failed to make his own' (p. 252). Heseltine's involvement in this matter, which seems to have taken more serious developments with legal threats, was quite likely as peace-maker between his friend Gray and Foss, especially since in January Heseltine was to move into the cottage at Eynsford, Kent, rented by Foss. Ironically, Heseltine had an almost pathological dislike of Holst, especially *The Planets*. (Foss had himself only recently written an assessment, 'Gustav Holst: will he be permanent in music?', in *Cassell's Weekly*, 26 September 1923, pp. 35–36; in *Music in My Time* (1933) he makes hardly any comment on Holst.) This was not the only occasion when Gray's strongly expressed opinions nearly got him in trouble in print. Review copies of his autobiographical *Musical Chairs* (Home & Van Thal, 1948) were about to be sent out when its co-editor pointed out 'a grave and serious libel' against Sir Thomas Beecham, including mention of an 'enobled dynasty of pill-makers', that was removed just in time (Pauline Gray, *Cecil Gray – his life and Notebooks*, Thames Publishing, 1989, p. 79).

an autobiography. He hints at the atmosphere there in his article 'The Warlock Gang.'

I, myself, never met Heseltine, though I saw him at various concerts – he was a fascinating and magnetic personality from whom it was hard to turn one's eyes. He wrote to me once to tell me that I was giving the first public performance of his song *Consider,* of which I was unaware, and also to tell me that he did not like his early song *Romance,* which I was singing at the same concert. This setting of RLS[tevenson]'s *I will make you brooches* Hubert and I thought was the epitome of freshness and charm.

PHASES OF THE MOON – THE WARLOCK GANG
by HJF[75]

Modern time moves swiftly. In keeping with up-to-date inventions, it literally is still a-flying. Clocks tick faster than Alice ran in the Looking-Glass: 'time gallops withal'; the successive moons chivvy each other across the neon-lit sky. For young people now, twenty years ago – 'before the war' – represent the dark ages of 'the bad old days', thirty are fit only for a greybeard's droolings. This was not always true; when the great English public discovered the *Enigma Variations* twenty-five years after they were written, they were regarded as fashionable, not *passé*. Those naughty 'twenties seem like the dark backward and abysm of time: the 'nineties have become almost nearer. But, as Prospero asked Miranda, 'What seest thou else there?' For one thing, the profession of music has become incredibly, almost insufferably respectable; positively lady-like (and not always in the best sense). Parry endowed us with the worthy legacy that it was possible to be a musician and an English gentleman, but Parry himself was a full-blooded man. We seem to have taken his message the wrong way; we are so nice we have forgotten how to swear, much less how to begin to drink. We are such good girls now.

The recent deaths of Cecil Gray and Constant Lambert, too near together with that of E J Moeran[76] under a year ago, have caused a physical gap, not only one of

---

75   *London Symphony Observer*, November 1952, pp. 98–100. Written by Hubert Foss only six months before he died.

76   E.J. Moeran (b. 1894) died on 1 December 1950, falling into the water from Kenmare pier during a heavy storm possibly as the result of a heart attack; Constant Lambert (b. 1905) died on 21 August 1951 from broncho-pneumonia and undiagnosed diabetes mellitus; and Cecil Gray (b. 1895) died from cirrhosis of the liver on 9 September 1951. In all three cases, poor health had been much aggravated by heavy drinking.

semi-oblivion, between ourselves and that roisterous, vivid group of musicians who were associated with Peter Warlock in the nineteen twenties. They lived, in truth, so near to us in date as to be remote, like the stars in modern velocity. While we catch up on our own rapidity and find ourselves, as Alice did, in the same place, one or two memories from an old inhabitant may help us form a reasoned and objective judgment on that remarkable gathering of artists. I am writing no threnody; those people were too good at writing threnodies themselves; when their jovial masks were laid aside, they were passionately sad.

About 1921 or so, I happened to see a vacant cottage at the village of Eynsford in Kent, in the then beautiful Darenth valley. At the twenty-mile range from London, it was still a village – I used to join in folk-singing at a pub on the hills outside; a village of odd character, but individual, with a resident tradition of hand-made paper of supreme quality. The cottage was once a bakery, with an eighteenth century bow shop-front, and a built-in oven. The former I kept, the latter I had removed to convert into my study-bedroom. Though a bath was installed, it was fairly primitive. While living there, I was offered an Elizabethan cottage five or so miles further south [at Otford] and took it. Heseltine-Warlock had been restlessly lodging in Chelsea for two or three years; when he consulted me about a rustic *pied-à-terre*, I suggested and rented to him my cottage at Eynsford. It was not long before I made him principal tenant.

That house and the Warlock régime therein has been richly described by Cecil Gray in his *Peter Warlock* (a splendid book); even so, the author left out much that might have been added in the way of picturesque detail, nor do I propose to amplify, with physical incident, his sufficiently vivid pictures. A few words about the spirit of the *ménage*, and a few more about its comers and goers, are my contribution.

It was not an orderly house: the habits were in no sense regular. On the other hand, it was acutely, sometimes insanely, alive; each day it blossomed into a new unpredictable, semi-exotic flower. It was not exemplary, but it contained genius. The inmates and many visitors were joined in a pursuit of art. The underlying interest was the quest for beauty. As I have written elsewhere, that Warlock group comprised two English ages, the Elizabethan and the modern, as their music did; they were combinations of Thomas Nashe and Ernest Dowson, without the limitations of either. Bawdry, humour and liquor were essential ingredients of life. They lived far away from modern times and yet knew more about modern movements and music than their colleagues in Prince Consort Road.[77] The cold negatives of Puritanism had not reached their consciousness

77 The Royal College of Music.

since school-days (if then). They were positive, but they were also critical –
startlingly both. They created music that was listened to without either an
academic or a society *claque*. They just were brilliant, eccentric, passionately
alive (but aware of death), hedonist, utterly unselfish in the cause of music,
enthusiastically scornful, friendly, quarrelsome, drunk and sober by erratic
turns, but always with the fixed ideal of genius as their guide. 'What you do
not see, you miss' is an old maxim of good teachers. The Warlock Gang (as they
were dubbed) were intensely aware; their eyes were wide open, and their ears.
They knew and took pains to find out.

Philip Heseltine, who died untimely at the age of 36, produced a corpus of
English songs which I do not hesitate to rank with those of Wolf. They are as
much a part of the English heritage as the songs of Dowland and Campion,
the madrigals of Byrd and Wilbye. *The Curlew* is a minor masterpiece, *An Old
Song* and the *Serenade* say new things in an unexaggerated manner. Cecil
Gray was the prose-writer of the group, though he was also the most generally
knowledgeable musician amongst them. It ought to be unnecessary to suggest
that people should read Gray's prose before dismissing him as an upstart critic.
He was certainly as provocative as those complacent days demanded; he was
also truthful and prophetic. His analysis of our present day trends in music
ranged from 1924 to 1947, and should be read in date order, in conjunction
with Lambert's *Music Ho!* To Gray we owe the recognition first and later the
popularity of Sibelius in this country. Constant Lambert was a composer of
importance in his own right: *Summer's Last Will and Testament* alone estab-
lishes him, without *The Rio Grande*, the piano concerto, and the ballets. He lives
for us in each nightly performance of the Sadler's Wells Ballet, for he was the
musical genius of it from the beginning. E J Moeran was one of England's really
musical composers – no mere technician or note-spinner. His violin concerto
and string quartet (separated by many years) show the poetic continuity of his
musical thought.[78] Towering in intellect above them all was Bernard van Dieren,
the most versatile genius I have ever met,[79] who combined a doctor's training
with musical insight, business capacity with a subtle knowledge of languages,
celestial skill in counterpoint with techniques like revolver-shooting, book-
binding, and trick-cycling. His personality radiated influence, as Busoni's did.
I still believe that one day people will discover him as a composer though the
silent years pass since his works were printed in part. I forbear to do more than

78   Hubert wrote 'E.J. Moeran: a critical appreciation' for *The Musical Times*, 1 December 1930.
79   Hubert contributed an obituary on Bernard van Dieren for the *Daily Telegraph*, 2 May 1936.

mention the names of those two amazing conductors, Leslie Heward and Hyam Greenbaum.

The poets write of the lost continent. The Warlock Gang provide a lost age, an irrevocable nucleus of musical energy. The easiest thing in the world is to look over one's spectacles and say that they were wrong from the start. And if they were? Well, I could bear another spell of original wrongness – an ebullient Tudor-like outpouring of soul-felt love of living and passionate devotion to art and truth. Take them for all in all, we shall not look upon their like again – not in this 'planned economy.'[80]

John Ireland

34.   *28th June 1929   John Ireland to HJF*

Chelsea Arts Club, 143 Church Street, SW3

Dear Foss,

I listened to your lecture with great interest and appreciation – it represented an individual point of view and thank you all so much for all the trouble you have taken over it. I am very glad you still feel confidence in the Sonatina – it is perhaps too terse to be pleasant to most people, but on the other hand, whenever it is played it seems to make its effect, and I am sure what you said about it will go a long way to make people try to familiarise themselves with it.

Your illustrations, if I may say so, were very ably given, and the experiment with When I am dead[81] came off well, and scored the point you were making for.

Once more, ever so many thanks – I don't expect you to like all my work, and I value your good opinion, so nicely expressed, of the works in question.

Y[ou]rs ever

John Ireland

John Ireland came to dinner at Nightingale Corner [29 October 1930] in order to show Hubert some songs one of his pupils [Helen Perkin] had written. He came early so that they could run through the songs before we dined. John refused to play them himself, so Hubert sat down at the piano to read them at sight;

---

80   A brief extract from this article, read by Diana Sparkes (née Foss), was included in the CD *Hubert Foss and his friends – A recital of songs*, HJF001CD.

81   *When I am dead, my dearest*, a setting of Christina Rossetti for voice and piano, 1925, by John Ireland (1879–1962).

songs difficult to play and MS difficult to decipher. I could soon tell that Hubert was anything but favourably impressed. John was very excited about them and anxious for praise and admiration. Hubert hedged by saying 'Yes, yes, most interesting'. After playing two or three, all the lights in the house went out. I hastily brought candles but Hubert refused to play from the somewhat illegible MS in the wavering light. John was frantically disappointed and insisted on fetching a chair, climbing onto it and inspecting the fusebox, but the failure was not due to fuses, and we dined by candlelight. John left the MS with Hubert, who went through the songs in peace and quietude later. He made me laugh by saying the failure was heaven-sent as he just didn't know *what* to say about the songs of which he had a very poor opinion and at the same time didn't want to hurt John's feelings.

35.   *3ʳᵈ November 1932*   *John Ireland to HJF*

Studio, 14a Gunter Grove, Chelsea SW10

My dear Foss,

Many thanks for your letter.

Don't let there be any misunderstanding about my new songs. You said definitely you wanted to see them and even to have first refusal of them!

But in asking you to spend an evening with me I had no thought of approaching you as a publisher – but just as composer to composer. And I was (and always am) grateful for your opinions and criticisms, on my own or anyone else's work – for they are always acute and interesting.

As a matter of fact, long before I sent you them there were two publishers prepared to issue the songs – but as is my wont, (unbusiness-like, no doubt) I have preferred to keep them by me to see what they felt like after the first flush of composing them was over.

I am very anxious to see your violin sonata. Do show it to me soon – I was today looking at your Hardy Songs.[82] They are not, alas, for the public – but after all, it is something to have done them, isn't it. That is the only reward one can expect, with work of this calibre.

I tried to get hold of you last night, to get a free loan of a score of the Walton work [*Belshazzar's Feast*]. I had looked forward for a long time to actually

82   An extract from this letter (up to this point), read by Diana Sparkes (née Foss), was included in the CD *Hubert Foss and his friends – A recital of songs*, HJF001CD.

hearing this remarkable piece. How was the performance[83] to you, who know the work well?

I was sitting, too near, in the stalls, and at times the volume of sound was too great at such close quarters. I moved from the circle, because I saw a friend downstairs (not a musician!).

Walton is a truly remarkable person, and you are very right to put your faith in him so completely. His versatility is outstanding – to think that the composer of the Viola Concerto could so soon produce a work so completely different – not in personal style, but in outlook and execution. The invention, imagination and mastery of means are truly astonishing. What a passage 'Praise ye the God of Gold', etc. – at every point something crops up to show the vitality, and fertile and vivid imagination of this composer.

Well, we are all waiting for his Symphony, which I am sure will be as astonishing and epoch-making as this choral work.

(N.B. This letter is not for publication!) If you can give me Walton's address, I will write a line to him – in fact, I must.

Yours sincerely,

John Ireland

Constant Lambert

CONSTANT LAMBERT WAS OVERWHELMINGLY BEAUTIFUL as a young man. I used to see him at concerts and for some time I did not know who the angelic-looking boy was. One concert I particularly remember, as it was the first time I saw Philip Heseltine and E.J. Moeran there. It was at a Chamber Concert in June 1925.

Lambert, Heseltine and several other men sat in the row behind the one in which I was sitting. As they were both so striking in appearance, I own to having turned round on several occasions to look at them, which was easy as I was at the end of my row and they were in the middle of theirs. One time I was amazed to see a pipe being passed along from one to the other, each one having a puff or suck at it. It was not for some years that I met Constant. When I did, he was already being bracketed with Walton – Walton-Lambert, Lambert-Walton.

---

83   Queen's Hall, 2 November 1932, Dennis Noble, the Wireless Chorus, BBC Chorus and Symphony Orchestra, conductor Adrian Boult. John Ireland's *The Forgotten Rite* was also in the programme.

For many years they seemed, apparently, to pursue a parallel course, partly, I think, because they were both young and good-looking and because they were frequently seen about together, and were, indeed, great friends for many years – though their talents were very different.

There was never the same sort of personal and family friendship with Constant as there was with Willie, though Constant came to Nightingale Corner, Rickmansworth and to Corringham Road, London a number of times. Hubert saw a good deal of him in London, and, too, of Constant's wife, Florence, whom he took everywhere with him. Hubert was never as saturated with his music as he was with Willie's, though he had an unbounded admiration for Constant's genius and versatility.

36.   *29th March [1932]   Constant Lambert to DMF*[84]

15 Percy St., W1

Dear Mrs Foss,

My wife and I will be delighted to come on Saturday April 9th.

How Hubert manages to write a sonata on top of his other work I simply can't imagine.

Looking forward to seeing you both

Yours sincerely

Constant Lambert

An occasion we shall never forget was the party given by Arthur Benjamin at his home for the first chamber performance of Constant's *The Rio Grande*. The concert opened with Arthur and Julie Lasdun playing Arthur's *Music for Dancing*. Then followed *The Rio Grande*. The music was arranged for two pianos (played by Julie Lasdun and Arthur Benjamin), for percussion, played by Constant, for alto solo, sung by Albert Whitehead, and a small group of six singers. Hubert conducted.[85] The performance was exciting to a degree. Each and every performer gave of his or her best and I have never heard anything done with more urge and exuberance, and at the same time, with such beauty. Audience and musicians alike were carried away with enthusiasm, and to crown it all for me (and I laugh to think of it), after it was over, Hubert caught hold of

84   See plate 21.
85   At 66 Carlton Hill, London, 15 June 1930. See programme illustration, fig. 6, p. 71. According to Alan Frank, a flustered Walton turned the pages for Lambert.

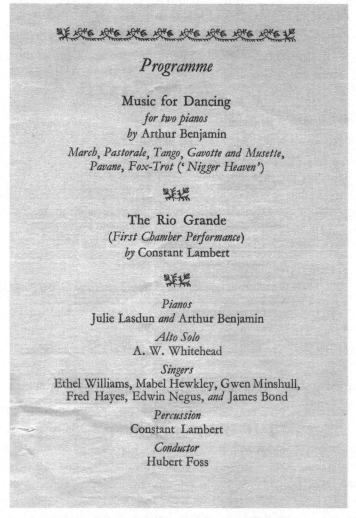

Fig. 6: Programme of Lambert's *The Rio Grande* in June 1930 at
Arthur Benjamin's house, with Hubert Foss conducting and Lambert
playing the percussion normally requiring up to five players

me and danced me round the marquee in the garden. The only time I ever knew
him to dance in or out of a ballroom. Hubert had no interest in or feeling for
dancing other than a mild liking for Folk Dancing, but I like to think he only
liked this because of its relationship to Folk Song. He was quite indifferent to

ballet and just felt it was an intrusion into the music. Ballroom dancing of any description was anathema to him. Though on a number of occasions we went to the Ballet, it was always on account of Constant, and Hubert was delighted with the success of the Camargo Society's performances and later, of the Sadler's Wells Ballet. He was a wholehearted admirer of Constant's work as a conductor.

37.   *1ˢᵗ March 1934   HJF to DMF*

I took my bags to King's Cross and went on to the Café Royal, where I quietly (and substantially) fed. But the peace did not last for long – I managed to avoid the more unpleasant habitués like Victor Gollancz and Richard Nevinson, but had a long talk with Constant and Florence (who was in black and powdered pearl colour) – he doesn't think he is going to write a book on Elgar, so one day I may do so.

38.   *1ˢᵗ July 1935   HJF to DMF* (Mundesley)
                                       Nightingale Corner, Rickmansworth

The C Lambert baby is called Christopher Sebastian L – both good names for their surname. He complains of it becoming vocal – well, <u>my</u> wee thing [Diana] sings 'Big bad wolf' very early in the morning and I love it!

39.   *1ˢᵗ February 1936   HJF to DMF* (Mundesley)
                                       Nightingale Corner, Rickmansworth

Constant's concert was heavily papered but had a distinguished audience. I made friends again with [John] Ireland,[86] and saw the world. I gather that white ties are taboo (your learned 'tabu' is only used by anthropologists!) but I knew no better, and was, thank God, covered by Lambert himself and Edward Marsh (CBE of Rupert Brooke fame). The performance was moderate; the work [*Summer's Last Will and Testament*] is much more difficult than CL thinks. CKS [Charles Kennedy Scott][87] confirmed to me how hard it is for the choir, which he trained. CL had a job to pull it off and worked himself to death. I think it very good, but not a public hit, but vide The Times of today – a splash for us.

---

86   John Ireland was shy and sensitive by nature and sometimes unapproachable. The reason for this lapse in friendship is not known.

87   Charles Kennedy Scott (1876–1965), renowned choral trainer and conductor of the Oriana Madrigal Society and the Philharmonic Choir.

The intellectual angle was so good – the classicised pictorialism (what a novelty of a cliché!) was beautifully done. Not liked by other wirelessites, according to my and my spies' accounts, but a great success in the hall. Not a popular work like Rio Grande or Belshazzar. We shall lose money. I cut the Mendelssohn, did my business jobs at the bar, and went to see Constant – rather tired and overwhelmed.

The Wimborne party was only 30 or so – good food, mostly standing up but some sitting. Excellent champagne in floods, and whiskey if wanted. Alice, Lady W[imborne], charming and enjoying the joke of Willie and Constant. C not really fêted but quite caught up by sitting old ladies! It would have amused you. Paddy H[adley] especially nice to me about you. So kind and interesting at once. Bill Primrose[88] came in full of beans and bursting with the [Walton's] Viola Concerto which he is playing (eccentrically well) with Beecham on Feb 27th (or so). Very brilliant.

We sang the work together in forgotten corners, where Paddy and I had previously hymned in concert about Lord Wimborne (who is unwell).

> 'It is believed that God knows best
> When He created Ivor Guest.'

Florence [Lambert], in whitish brocade (rather the colour of old tennis shoes, unwashed) with a period turn-up collar, etc. accepted the bounty and attacked me – 'not a half-bad composer, I think, anyhow!' I duly agreed, if coldly.

Paddy and I got away at 12 or so, but I gather Willie and the rest drank on till 3 or more at WW's flat. Primrose and I tried to talk business with him but found him a little loose, so I said I'd ring him about the Phil[harmonic] performance. Before I (next morning) could, he rang me – very precise and proper-like, but quite vague about what it was he had promised to decide!

I went with Paddy to the Oxford and Cambridge Musical Club where we yarned over a whiskey about things in general and war in particular. He is far more pessimistic about the peace of Europe than I am even. It greatly affects him. Then I went to R[edington] Road [the home of Dora's parents] and found your letter. In bed before 1 am. A good job done.

Constant's activities were so varied and ranged so widely that he never was occupied solely with composing, as Walton was. Indeed, Hubert hoped to write

88   William Primrose (1904–82), Scottish viola player who initially studied the violin with Eugène Ysaÿe. He gave the American premiere of Walton's Viola Concerto, which he was twice to record.

a study of Constant's life, not only of his musical life, but of his place in the post First War period among his contemporaries in the world of art and of literature.

We saw Constant twice within the last few weeks of his life – both fleeting moments; the earlier, as we were leaving a party given to celebrate the first performance of Alan Rawsthorne's Second Pianoforte Concerto, and then at the last performance he conducted of *The Rio Grande*. We felt on both these occasions that his time was short. Nonetheless, his death came as a shock.

Just before the funeral service at St Bartholomew's Church, Smithfield, Walton, who had been asked to give the 'oration', felt unable to do it and suggested that Hubert should take his place. I was not there myself, but several of those present told me how moving and inspired his words were. It was an ordeal indeed, and not only were his listeners touched, Hubert himself was almost overcome with emotion.

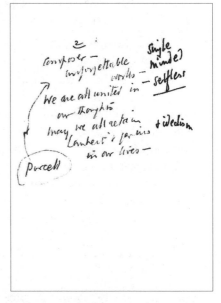

Fig. 7: These few notes, compiled at speed, are the disjointed phrases from which Hubert's spoken tribute was converted into a masterly address at Constant Lambert's funeral service, 25 August 1951

E.J. Moeran

40. *21ˢᵗ October 1930* **HJF (Moeran's father's house at Ling)** *to DMF*

I haven't time to tell you much as I have to go out and get petrol and also take Moeran out for his drive. He's doing splendidly and the nurse is excellent. You'd like him so much; he's quietened down a lot and is very nice indeed. His new work is very interesting – rather dry but beautifully written. It's a Sonata for Two Violins alone.

IN JUNE 1931 'JACK' MOERAN[89] came to stay with us. We asked him to luncheon. The appropriate hour arrived and passed but no Jack. About 3 o'clock he telephoned to say he had been held up but would arrive for tea. Tea time and no Jack, but Herbert Murrill arrived for tea – his first-time visit to us – and after tea he played through a number of his compositions to Hubert. About half past five Jack turned up a little worse for wear. He was at that time suffering from a tubercular knee (I think). His leg was in some form of iron splint, in spite of which he managed to be quite active. He metaphorically crashed into the drawing-room, all apologies and ebullience. Hubert introduced Herbert to him and told him he was listening to his compositions and asked Herbert to play an ear-tickling little piano piece which he had brought to him. Jack was enchanted. 'Play it again,' he said. Herbert played it again. 'Oh, I must hear it again,' said Jack, and again Herbert played it. When Herbert had played it three or four times he began to feel that we, his hosts, must think he was attracting too much attention, and, turning to Jack, said, 'Wouldn't you rather hear Mrs Foss sing your songs?' 'No, No, No,' said Jack, jumping up and down as best he could in a state of terrific enthusiasm, 'play it again.' Herbert went pink with embarrassment and Hubert and I hooted with laughter.

I went out down the garden with Christopher in order to make the situation less embarrassing for Herbert and listened to the rhythmic jingling of Herbert's piece which he played at least three more times for Jack. Afterwards Herbert wrote me an apologetic postcard.

Later on, in September, Hubert and I, with Christopher and his nannie, went to Somerton in Norfolk for a holiday. Jack had recommended to us a farmhouse of which he knew. It was situated at the end of a staithe and water

---

89   The English composer E(rnest) J(ohn) Moeran (1894–1950), known to his friends as 'Jack'.

almost surrounded it. It was not very comfortable and the food was execrable. However, we both loved the Broads country and we had a happy holiday there. We had the car with us and drove to many lovely places in Norfolk and Suffolk.

One day Jack came over from Ling and brought John Ireland with him. Earlier in the day we drove into the village and bought (at a very high price for that time) 12 chops. They were cooked by the lady at the farm and were so tough we could hardly swallow them. Jack and John were in melancholy mood (not, I think, entirely due to the disastrous luncheon, as they arrived in this condition, but to the effect each had on the other). Hubert was infected too with this miserable virus, and in desperation I left the three of them to their moanings and hopped into a boat and rowed up the staithe. Of course, I came back later and gave them tea and found them far more cheerful, having worked off on each other their divine melancholy.

A few days later we drove over to Ling with Christopher and Nannie to tea with Jack and his parents. His father was then Rector of Ling. We sat down to a dining-room tea at a long table with rounded ends, so it appears in retrospect: Jack, his mother and father, Hubert, Mark Raphael and myself. I think there must have been others as the long table, in my memory's eye, was full; I imagine they must have been parishioners and friends of Mr and Mrs Moeran, who would regard their musician son as someone rather strange and different, and of course his musical friends would come into the same category. Anyhow, there was a sense of strain and everyone was 'making' conversation. Even Hubert, seldom at a loss, was not at ease. Breaking through a barrier of silence, Mark Raphael, addressing Jack, rather tentatively, announced that he had been staying with (I think) the Robert Nichols[90] and that Mrs Nichols had had an operation. 'Oh, what sort of operation?' said Jack, much interested. A noticeable pause followed; then, 'Piles' very shortly from Mark. 'And where are they now?' immediately inquired Jack. I presume that Mark enlightened Jack as to the whereabouts of the Nicholses, but I was reduced like a 12 year old schoolgirl to almost uncontrollable laughter at the ridiculous implications. I felt red and jellyish and shaking and ashamed of myself as no-one showed signs of seeing the silly joke.

Later, as tea was ending, Jack's father handed round the cigarettes in a

90   Robert Nichols (1893–1944), poet and playwright, who adapted words by Whitman for
      Delius's *Idyll* (1932) and whose own words were set by Moeran in his *Nocturne*, written in
      1934 'To the memory of Delius'.

small tin which was largely and visibly labelled 'Suppositories'. Soon after this, Christopher and Nannie emerged from the housekeeper's room where they had had tea, and we left for Somerton. Hubert divulged that he had been bowled over by the cigarette incident, but the earlier incident had escaped him – having a more adult mind than mine was that afternoon. I was very relieved, though, that he had not noticed my disgraceful lapse into laughter.

In the late autumn of 1934, I was playing 'trains' with the children in our long low-ceilinged sitting-room at Nightingale Corner. It was about 5 o'clock in the afternoon, and we had had tea. The furniture was all awry; I was madly untidy. Christopher was six and Diana about fifteen months old – just staggering about. Nannie was out and we were having a wonderful game. Then the front door bell rang. Our young maid, Winnie, went to answer it. After an appreciable time, during which we sat hushed and wondering who our visitor could be, she came in. 'It's Mr Morland at the door,' she said. Thinking it was Dr Andrew Morland from Mundesley [Sanatorium], and also, feeling annoyed that Winnie should leave any caller on the doorstep, I rushed past her into the little square hall. There, standing in the porch, was Jack Moeran. I was naturally somewhat surprised to see him, instead of Andrew Morland, but I was doubly surprised by his appearance. He was wearing a huge Teddy bear overcoat in which he very nearly filled the doorway. He had the dazed look of someone coming into a strong light out of darkness and fog. Darkness there was, but no fog. His forehead was disfigured by scabs or patches of dried blood, of which he appeared completely oblivious. Through such of the doorway as was not occupied by Jack, I could see a woman dressed from head to foot in black of the most sombre description.

'Hubert said I could come in any time I was passing,' he said, and added, 'This is Nina Hamnett.'[91] (Where he was 'passing from' or 'passing to', or how, I cannot remember. I do not think I ever discovered.)

'Come in, come in,' I said, and led them into our chaotic but warm sitting-room, forgetting that the domestic scene was most unsuited either to Jack or his distinguished guest and unconventional artist companion. I introduced the children and then offered tea. This was firmly refused. I explained that Hubert was never back from London as early as this; it seemed impolite to enquire the cause of the gory marks on his face, as both Jack and Nina Hamnett seemed

91   Nina Hamnett (1890–1956), Welsh-born bisexual 'Bohemian' artist who studied in Paris
      and later frequented that area of London known as Fitzrovia.

unaware of anything wrong – not a word was said of any accident or mishap. What we started on, conversationally, I do not remember, but we arrived at the subject of French songs on which I was able to talk with some, if not a great, knowledge. At any rate, I knew the appropriate patter. At this point, Christopher went into the dining-room and came back with a box of dragées, chocolate, orange, yellow and red dragées; he offered them to our guests, who refused them. He then upset the box over the sofa and the floor. We picked them up as best we could. Miss Hamnett was sitting on the end of the sofa, her hand, with red lacquered nails, lying beside her. Diana lurched to the sofa and, to my horror, made a movement as if to pick up one of the scarlet-tipped fingers, her mouth opening in anticipation of a dragée. It was a scarifying moment. I hastily picked her up onto my lap and she stood there, her arms and sticky hands round my neck, while I tried to continue in an intelligent and sophisticated way the discussion on French song-writers. My sub-conscious thoughts were how much my guests must deplore the state of the erstwhile highbrow singer who had sunk to such untidy domesticity, but my mind was more immediately occupied by the fact that I hadn't a single drop of drink to offer them. In the early 1930s it was not nearly as usual to have the ubiquitous bottle of sherry always available as it is today. We had a reasonably good stock of drink in an admirable cellar under the house, but Hubert had the key! There wasn't a drop of anything in the dining-room. I suppose I felt that the less said, soonest mended. Anyhow, I remained silent on the question of alcoholic refreshment, and in about half-an-hour they left. This was one of the occasions on which I look back ashamed of my clumsy and inept handling.

A sequel to the anecdote occurred some years later in 1939. Hubert arranged a short recital of Roger Quilter's songs at Amen House which were sung by Sydney Northcote and myself.[92] Some little time before, Roger came to Corringham Road to go through the songs with me, and stayed to lunch with me, Diana (then aged five) and Nannie. He and I talked about songs and song-writers and for some reason I told him the Moeran-Hamnett story, ending by saying, 'I never knew what the blood marks were.' 'I 'spect they were lipstick,' said Diana in a bright, brisk voice. Roger turned in his chair and laughed with his face in his hands till the tears came down.

92   See letter from Quilter, p. 223. This all-Quilter programme on 22 June 1939 was Dora's 'first
      recital for some years after a period of severe illness'. She was accompanied by Hubert
      Foss, and Sydney Northcote by Quilter.

41.   *1ˢᵗ November 1933   E.J. Moeran to HJF*

Lingwood Lodge, Nr. Norwich

Dear Hubert,

I am very relieved to know you have got 'Lonely Waters'[93] back safely from USA. I had a spare copy which the B.B.C. have lost so I was a little anxious, as I hadn't even a sketch of the work. I am writing to Soho Square to get it here, as I want to revise the ending of it. I think the present alternative version to be used when a voice is not available is a bit slipshod.

I have heard from [André] Mangeot that Dec. 11th is the date fixed for my chamber music at the B.B.C., the programme to consist of the Pianoforte Trio, violin sonata, & string quartet. I would have liked something more recent as one item in the scheme, e.g. the string trio, but it is not to be. The Joyce song cycle would have been a good idea, but I gather the B.B.C., having engaged a pianist, Perkin, intend to make use of her! I also gather that some piano solos of mine were to have been included, but I am thankful ... [page torn] ... have been cut out. Excellent pianist as Helen Perkin [is, I] am not particularly proud of my achievements as a composer of piano music. If there are any notes to be written in the 'Radio Times', I shall be most grateful if you can be responsible. In the past, they have put in some tittle-tattle about Uppingham, which can well be avoided. Had I not wasted 4 precious years at an English public school, I would not have had to set to & become a student when I left the army at the age of 24. (You can bung that in if you like!)

When I first went to John Ireland I did not even know the compasses or clefs of the instruments (barring strings, having been a string player); at that time I could not follow a modern full-score at a concert, still less read it or attempt to write one, Uppingham being the public school for music, par excellence. Let me know if you are going to write any notes, & I will furnish you with any information you require about where & when the works were written.

Yours ever

Jack Moeran

---

93   *Lonely Waters*, a short orchestral piece based on a Norfolk folk song, possibly composed in the mid-twenties but not published until 1935 by Novello & Co., for whom Hubert Foss wrote a booklet, *Compositions of E.J. Moeran*, in 1948.

Edith Sitwell

O UR FIRST MEETING WITH EDITH SITWELL was in the nature of a happy ending to a most awkward and embarrassing incident.

In the early spring of 1932 we planned to give a small evening party at home [Nightingale Corner] to introduce to such of our friends as were especially interested in William Walton, his new songs [*Three Songs*] which he had written for Hubert and me, to words by Edith Sitwell, prior to their first public performance at the Wigmore Hall. We had given many parties at Nightingale Corner, and our friends came by car or train – a half hour from Baker Street, arriving round about 8.30ish – and after, or punctuating whatever entertainment we provided, was a very good supper.

As this party was to be small and informal, I wrote short letters of invitation to each friend, and, although I had not met her personally, I invited Miss Sitwell. As there had been some discussion between Edith and Willie on how 'Lucia' was to be pronounced in the song *Through gilded trellises*, it certainly had not occurred to me that Willie would set Edith's poems to music as solo songs, and have them published without her consent, and, perhaps foolishly, I took for granted her knowledge of THEIR existence, if not of mine or Hubert's more especially. To our horror, I received a most stinging reply from Edith's secretary, denying any knowledge of us and more or less accusing me of inviting Edith to the country without offering her dinner. Hubert immediately sent the letter to Willie from whom I subsequently received a large box of tulips and a penitent note. He wrote to Edith and explained what he had done and what we were trying to do. I then received a delightful letter from Miss Sitwell which was some consolation for the blow to my amour propre which her first communication had given me.

42.   *26ᵗʰ March 1932   Edith Sitwell to DMF*
                              22 Pembridge Mansions, Moscow Road, London W2

Dear Mrs Foss,

I have just received a letter from Willie Walton, which has explained to me that I was under a complete misapprehension when my secretary answered your kind invitation. I cannot tell you how sorry I am that this foolish misunderstanding has occurred.

The fact is, that until I received this letter this morning, I imagined that you were a relation of a family of the same name (not related to your husband's family) whom I knew in the past, and whom I have been obliged to stop seeing as they would prevent me from working – this impression was added to by the fact that I, more than once, received letters inviting me to parties from friends of theirs who were strangers to me.

I did not know that you lived in Hertfordshire, in fact, I thought you lived in London. So you see how this unhappy misunderstanding arose. I regret it very much indeed, and I can assure you that I should not have dreamt of sending that reply to your kind invitation if I had had any idea that it was you.

Believe me,

Yours sincerely

Edith Sitwell

As will be inferred, Edith did not come to the party, but came to spend a Sunday with us some time later on. As Hubert and I went on to the Rickmansworth platform to meet Edith and Willie, who brought her to luncheon, we laughed and said, 'Now we shall see if there are two of them.'

They emerged from a third class compartment and there began one of the most memorable days of our life. Edith was coruscatingly brilliant and witty all day. She gave us a side-splitting history – entirely apocryphal, I am certain, of other Fosses she had met, from one of whom she imagined my letter to be. In retrospect, I feel she was consciously anointing my wounded susceptibilities, but at the time Hubert and I just enjoyed ourselves to the limit – basking in the warmth of the entrancingly human personality that she showed to us. We sang and played the *Three Songs* to her and later in the day we drove her and Willie to Appletree Farm House where we introduced her to Sir Henry and Lady Wood, and where we again sang the *Three Songs*.

43.   *11ᵗʰ May 1932   DMF* (Rickmansworth) *to HJF* (Bristol)

I arrived at ES's at 4.45. My dear, she lives in a positive SLUM – I call her flat a tenement.[94] It is up five stories [*sic*] and stone steps. (Edith told me she lived at such a height and with no lift so that her father, who had a weak heart, could not visit her.) I got there – panting: a respectable sort of maid let me in and showed me into the sitting-room and Edith mountainously rose at me. She was dressed in some sort of furnishing material, unhooked at the back at intervals.

94   Edith Sitwell (1887–1964) shared a flat at 22 Pembridge Mansions, Moscow Road, in Bayswater, London with Helen Rootham, cousin of Cyril Rootham, until the latter's death in 1938.

She was extremely nice and I tried my best to be intelligent. The tea consisted of tea and farthing buns. The room is filthily furnished; you never saw such coverings to sofa and armchairs; it reminds me a little of Edwin Evans's[95] abode, although perhaps there was not so much LOOSE dirt about.

Edith showed me the poems she was working at and told me how she worked, (Edith showed me the large volumes in which she wrote and re-wrote her poems, altering words and phrases until they satisfied her, and the impressions the pages made on me was of an embroidery of precious stones – the exquisite words seemed to scintillate almost visibly.) She showed me a book of poems of Humbert Wolfe with 'illustrations' by, I think, Siegfried Sassoon – most awful bits of advertisements stuck in, and mid-Victorian illustrations cut out and inserted wherever appropriate. I laughed over this until I sobbed.

The walls of her room are plastered with paintings and drawings by a Russian [Tchelitchev][96] who, she told me, (with a suspicion of girlish coyness) was her greatest friend. Some of them I understood and appreciated, but some were most difficult. There was a huge one of a naked lady in a hammock and the proportions were most peculiar. You know if you lie in a rather loose hammock, your behind feels so heavy and huge – well, this picture was drawn like that. The parts that one feels are the heaviest, are drawn the largest. Then there was one of draperies draped up against portraits (heads) to look like weird bodies.

Well I evidently said the right things because she brought out portfolios of his drawings – ranging from sleeping cats to nude gentlemen. I gathered that some were for sale – at least she said that some were hers and then mentioned that one was sold to a Cambridge undergraduate who had not fetched it. The Russian (whose name I didn't get) lives in Paris and is coming over soon, and Edith and Osbert are going to give a party for him to which she is going to invite US!!! There's glory for you! There was a picture of tigers in the circus and we then discussed keeping wild animals – then a long story – too vague to relate – which finished with someone sending Edith the ring off a fighting-cock's leg – which she showed me. I was somewhat paralysed by this time. She begged me to come again, and I begged her to come to us. I clattered down the steps, found a taxi, and staggered into it.[97]

95   Edwin Evans (1874–1945), English critic and author, with a particular interest in Russian music and Debussy.

96   Pavel Tchelitchev (1898–1957), Russian-born surrealist painter greatly admired by Edith Sitwell.

97   See Victoria Glendinning's *Edith Sitwell: A Unicorn among Lions*, Weidenfeld & Nicolson, 1981, p. 170.

44. *14ᵗʰ May 1932   HJF* (Bristol) *to DMF* (Rickmansworth)

I am most amused at your account of Edith Sitwell. I've been to the place to deliver a note, you remember. Oh, those stairs. Apart from all eccentricities, you must remember she has no money, and spends it on party-dresses of a peculiar kind. And she capitalises her poverty as the Sitwells always capitalise every advantage or disadvantage. They are commercial first and nice second.

About the bottom-picture, I was struck with your excellent exposition of expressionism. The point of this theory is surely this: if, when in a hammock, your BTM feels large, it must be painted large to express your feelings. Also, a slight complication from a primitive sexual admiration occurs here. We all differ in our likes, you know; though I don't much care for large buttocks myself. I am told by aesthetes that West African natives do!

45. *[later]   DMF to HJF*

I DID enjoy my Edith Sitwell tea but I came away feeling she could be terribly malicious. She told me various tales of her encounters with people (over barking dogs etc.) and how rude they'd been to each other.

Donald Tovey [98]

THE FIRST TIME I SAW DONALD TOVEY was at Dorothy and Robert Mayer's beautiful house in Cumberland Terrace. It must have been in about 1926 or 1927 and the occasion was a musical party at which the players were that wonderful pair of artists Adolph and Fritz Busch. After they had played one sonata, there was some movement and to- and fro-ing among the guests. It was then that I saw Tovey's towering figure approach the piano, exuding a sort of amiable magnificence. He sat down and began to play – not Bach, not Beethoven, but a madly funny mock oratorio to the words of the nursery rhyme 'Hey, diddle, diddle, the cat and the fiddle'. He sang soprano; he sang tenor and bass and he sang choruses. I was entranced but of course, it was certainly not part of Dorothy's programme for the evening and before the 'oratorio' had come to an end, Dorothy beguiled him from the piano. In recent years I have heard similar 'mock' oratorios or operas given in public by well-known performers, and good as these have been, I doubt if they surpass or even equal the skill and musical invention of Tovey's 'comic turn'.

It must have been some time later [1927] that I can remember Hubert, white and exhausted, sitting in an armchair in my mother's drawing-room. He had just returned from Edinburgh where he had been staying for some days with the object of tackling Donald Tovey anent the proposed collection of his essays.

'Tovey has addressed me like a public meeting for three days,' he said.

I believe it was during this visit that Donald played the complete *Diabelli* variations of Beethoven to illustrate some minor point that was under discussion.

Hubert used to leave his hotel in time to reach Tovey at 10.00 am. and arrange for a car to fetch him early in the evening in good time for him to get back for dinner. Thus he had the excuse of the waiting car to extract him from the flood of talk, brilliant and erudite but completely without a sense of time, with which he was by that hour almost overwhelmed.

In November 1927, a few months after our marriage, Hubert and I went on

---

98   Donald Tovey (1875–1940), English composer and teacher, Professor of Music at Edinburgh University from 1914, and in 1916 founder of the Reid Symphony Orchestra, for whose concerts he wrote the programme notes later published by OUP as *Essays in Musical Analysis*. Knighted 1935.

a short tour starting at Newcastle where we gave a lecture-recital. Our second port of call was Edinburgh where we stayed for three days.

During that time Hubert saw a good deal of Tovey, although between whiles he managed to find time to take me to Edinburgh Castle and Holyrood. We went together to a rehearsal of the Reid Symphony Orchestra which, of course, was conducted by Tovey. It was fascinating to watch him and I was quite unaware of the passing of time. However, I noticed that a number of the orchestral players were, as discreetly as possible, retiring from the platform, and, on looking at my watch, I realised it was long past the hour when the rehearsal was due to end. Tovey appeared unconcerned or was oblivious to these defections, but after some considerable time he decided he had finished for the day and dismissed the remainder of the orchestra.

Hubert and I had been invited to luncheon with the Toveys at their house in Royal Terrace and walked there with them and several others. After our arrival, we went into the dining room. Lady Tovey, after indicating where we were to sit, herself sat at the head of the table. She was very small, and a huge leg of mutton which was placed in front of her, almost completely hid her.

As we moved into the room, Donald asked Hubert if he had read *Gentlemen Prefer Blondes*. Hubert replied that he had not, and Tovey rejoined, 'Oh, but you should; it is a most wonderful book, but' (going to a bookcase and extracting a bright yellow volume) 'here is an even better one: "NIZE BABEE".' He opened it and began to read from it before sitting down. We gradually seated ourselves and eventually he did too, and he read on and on. The book consisted of the usual nursery tales and fables, but written as if they were being told by a Yiddish Bowery woman to her children. I chiefly remember that each story had a very definite commercial slant.

Tovey read for what felt like hours. At first we were all highly amused, not only at the stories themselves, but at his pseudo-Bowery accent and his accompanying gestures. After a time I felt that my assimilation of what he was reading was practically nil and my appreciative smile had become stiff and set.

At this moment, Tovey's adopted son John, then a small schoolboy, who was at the table with us, rose from his chair and walked the length of the table to his father. In his hand was a piece of paper which he placed in front of him. Tovey stopped reading and inspected the message which was written on it in such large block letters that Hubert and I could not but see the legend too. It ran: DADDY YOU ARE AN FOOL.

Breathless, we waited for just wrath to descend on John's sandy head as in silence Tovey read and re-read the piece of impertinence. At last – 'You silly little boy,' he said, slowly and deliberately. 'Don't you know you never put "an" before a consonant?' John returned to his chair, deflated, and we breathed again.

46.   *21ˢᵗ October 1929   HJF* (Edinburgh) *to DMF* (Nightingale Corner)

> I rang up Tovey who wants to see me, so I am lunching there tomorrow. (Typical incident – I asked what time, so he said 'One o'clock. (Pause). Better say 1.15 to be on the safe side!') I've not seen him since our joint visit there, last November year.

47.   *22ⁿᵈ October 1929   HJF* (Edinburgh) *to DMF* (Nightingale Corner)

> Then I lunched with Tovey – as irrelevant as usual but marvellously interesting and really quite moderately practical at times. A very great man, who is just different enough from the world to be called a genius and not a lunatic. An inch more of difference or even a slightly more askew attitude and he would be put into safe custody! As it is, he is really most illuminating and, of course, incredibly knowledgeable and learned and thoughtful.

48.   *16ᵗʰ April 1930   HJF* (OUP, New York) *to DMF*

> At 4 or so I went and had tea with a publisher. He told me he had recently written a persuasive letter, with Richard Aldrich and Carl Engel behind him and using their names, to Tovey, proposing he should write a book on Brahms. After a suitable delay, they got back a letter, from Mrs Tovey, saying 'Professor Tovey can't be bothered' – and no more!

49.   *January 1931   HJF* (Caledonian Hotel, Edinburgh)[99] *to DMF*

> ... a formal meeting over the Anthem book and then a lecture by Tovey. I lunch with him Friday. He was as inconsequent as ever and, for once, poor in matter. He doesn't know the subject and he made rather a fool of himself.

---

99   Hubert was in Edinburgh for a Church Music Conference.

50. *7ᵗʰ January 1931   HJF (Edinburgh) to DMF (Rickmansworth)*

I am now waiting for Herbert [Wiseman] and David Latto to meet me and go with me to hear Whittaker[100] lecture. It will be rather funny because Tovey is doing the illustrations by conducting a Bach Cantata and he differs fundamentally from all [WG] Whittaker's principles of editing! I expect a crash before the end as only amateurs are taking part in the show.

51. *7ᵗʰ February 1932   HJF (Edinburgh) to DMF (Rickmansworth)*

I'm not feeling frightfully bright at the moment (4.00 pm.) having just left Tovey, who was in great form, I admit, but mentally as fatiguing as usual. We played the piano, the Emanuel Moor piano (two keyboards),[101] the harpsichord, and the clavichord, besides singing a good deal! We also only just escaped 'Nize Babee' once more; it is apparently still a rage and he still reads it out at every opportunity. But I was too wily this time and side-tracked him with other interests – at the moment chiefly the Haydn trios!

52. *14ᵗʰ January 1934   HJF (Edinburgh) to DMF*

Yesterday I had the Anthem book all the morning, wrote letters all the afternoon and had tea with the Toveys. I ordered my taxi to come back at 6.30, as I knew I should never get away if I didn't. I only kept him waiting a quarter of an hour – which shows great determination on my part. Tovey was in great form, but the result of the talk was that I've got to come up here again for the best part of a week – arriving March 1ˢᵗ. The object is to get those books finally going, and having tried every proxy known, I'm forced to do the job myself. So that's that.

53. *15ᵗʰ January 1934   HJF (Edinburgh) to DMF (Nightingale Corner)*

WGW [Whittaker] told me a lovely Tovey story. Bantock[102] was up examining at the University here and the small boy [Tovey's adopted son, John] was present at all the confabs. Eventually Tovey, much more attracted to the small boy than to Bantock, played trains with the lad, who had laid the rails across the top of

---

100 William Gillies Whittaker. See p. 236.
101 Emanuel Moor (1863–1931), Hungarian composer and inventor of a piano with two keyboards.
102 Sir Granville Bantock (1868–1946), English composer and educationalist, and from 1908 Professor of Music at Birmingham University.

the piano. They bowled an engine at each other! Eventually hilarity ensued and the small boy threw the engine at B's head. So B took him up and spanked his b-t-m and put him outside, locking the door! Almost the best Tovey yarn!

54. **2nd March 1934   HJF (Edinburgh)** *to* **DMF (Nightingale Corner)**

I can't write much as I am really very busy today, with Tovey's muck [*sic*] to get ready, and him to see at 3 this afternoon till evening arrives.

I went to hear Tovey's band last night. Fritz Busch is a good conductor without much technique of movement: he has plenty of control; but the band is awful – no tone at all – quite lost in the Usher Hall, and so dreadfully out of tune. The Mozart symphony was grotesque in its bad playing. Tovey played the Brahms quite pleasantly in a kind of explanatory way, but it wasn't concert piano playing at all. He got a huge ovation and about six or eight calls! I shall have to lie suitably this afternoon.

We had a grand talk about nothing yesterday – Elgar in particular – and I think I held my own well.

55. **5th March 1934   HJF to DMF**

I Toveyed again yesterday and lazed the rest. Things were a bit clogged but I think will straighten out today.

56. **6th March 1934   HJF to DMF**

I go out Toveying soon. I can't write about him but will tell you.

57. **7th March 1934   HJF to DMF**

I've still got to see Tovey once again, but that will not be arduous.

58. **21st–22nd March 1934   Donald Tovey to HJF**

39 Royal Terrace, Edinburgh 7

Q. Is this Sauchiehall Street on Tuesday?
A. Parrtly [*sic*].

Dear Foss

At last! As Carlyle or Johnson or one of those Gossers said: we may both of us be glad that we have the grace to thank God for anything.

Smatrrfact (a useful telegraphic word) I'm not at all glad or disposed to have done with you, being by nature inchellan and a burr. (Perhaps you don't know the word inchellan: it means one who if given a pinch, will take a Hell if you'll excuse such strong langwidge).

I hope you and your people can read my bad ritin and spelin; and I hope you won't want to bowdlerise this wind-up. It seems to me to mop up most of the mess fairly well, and I think the appearance of growing irritability will rather refresh the reader.

By the way, Sir Hugh Allen is a great success as External Examiner. How far I may be a fool to trust him with four-pence for a pot of beer on my death-bed I do not know, and am past caring. Anyhow, life is worth living only to the unsuspicious.

Yours sincerely

DFT

59.   *23rd March 1934   Donald Tovey to HJF*

39 Royal Terrace, Edinburgh 7

We don't go south till Tuesday.

Dear Foss,

Another slip for the Glossary. Just as I cut it off, Miss Tate's[103] 'cello concerto arrived. In fear and trembling lest it disappears among my geological strata, I read it at once and am sending it back. (I never lose anything, but the faults and reversals of the strata may occasion the delay of a geological epoch or two.)

The work is interesting, fairly practical, not unduly long and, as you say, shews humour and a capacity to keep going. But – I'm more and more certain that the conscientious avoidance of beauty, (–an avoidance which, Praise Be, is already beginning to 'date') owed its first vogue not to the pressure of imagination but to lack of imagination. The damnation of the pretty-pretty, and even of the chocolate-box, is a doctrine originated by people who would really have given their immortal souls for the chance of achieving something pretty.

I don't mean to class a composer of this degree of talent with the ordinary artistic vitriol-thrower. But she is the victim of her date. Walton has kicked like Jeshurun[104] and set himself free to be beautiful: and I hope she will too.

---

103 Phyllis Tate (1911–85), English composer, married to Alan Frank. A number of her works were published by OUP.

104 A poetic name for Israel, sometimes used to refer to the people of Israel.

This young lady also hasn't grasped the psychology of the solo instrument as such. She has a little of the woolly conscientious objection of the Paris Conservatoire students – (culminating in that, to me, boring Saint Chausson) which regarded all concerto style as sinful virtuosity. She gives the 'cello entrances which neither rouse attention as entries nor prove impressive as discoveries: e.g. towards the end of the finale where the 'cello enters with a slow descending chromatic scale as a not specially significant bass to the rest. Similarly, the solo 'cello as one of the voices in an otherwise orchestral fugue is not effective. Yes, yes, I know that 'effectiveness' is one of the seven deadly sins; but I don't believe pointlessness to be one of the cardinal virtues; and these criticisms of mine, though they are on general principles, are not a-priori. I think this composer's imagination is at present being dried up by the a-priorities of her Spiritual Uncles' Anti-Romantic Consciences. Why not see things as they are? It is natural, not artificial, to ignore inessentials when one can't help being thrilled. And it is natural to be thrilled.

Technically she is well equipped (though there are a few unnecessary difficulties). But she hasn't allowed herself to develop a vivid sense of colour as yet. There are various chinoiseries that are ready-made and safe; but I fail to see any chords or groupings that make you sit up and wonder why you never heard strings or wind like that before. And she ought to be able to produce such things.

Well, well, well –

Yours ever,

DFT

60. *October 1935   HJF to DMF* (Mundesley)

Back to the office and then on to an exhibition at the First Edition Club, and so, after some cheap oysters (but good) at De Hems, to the Bach Cantata Club. Tovey's recital. He was full of gout and old age, his hands crippled and himself miserable, but he played splendidly.

61. *21ˢᵗ January 1936   HJF to DMF* (Mundesley)

Nightingale Corner, Rickmansworth

Taking Tovey to bed with me tonight.[105]

---

105 Possibly the proofs of Tovey's *Essays in Musical Analysis*; vols III and IV were published in 1936.

62. *22ⁿᵈ January 1936   HJF to DMF* **(Mundesley)**
                                         Nightingale Corner, Rickmansworth

I will take these letters (yours from Rose and me and my office letters which I had to bring home) to the post, cut my nails, and sleep (chastely) with Tovey.

63. *23ʳᵈ February 1937   HJF* **(Edinburgh)** *to DMF* **(Corringham Road)**

I had tea with Tovey – he read to me at length and I had to cut him short. I go there all day tomorrow.

64. *24ᵗʰ February 1937   HJF* **(Edinburgh)** *to DMF* **(Corringham Road)**

I Toveyed all the morning, and this afternoon went to call on a rich patroness of his, a Mrs Maitland, who has some very lovely pictures – including two well-known Gauguin paintings.

65. *16ᵗʰ September 1937   Donald Tovey to HJF*
                                         Hendenham Lodge, Bungay, Suffolk
Dear Foss

I'm delighted with the production of the 'cello concerto[106] and am very glad you like the MS. As to your part, I can only endorse what Peggie Sampson said, after revising the proof of MS. of the 'cello part, in a letter which I have either mislaid or already sent to you, to the effect that nobody produces music more beautifully than the OUP.

I am enclosing some strips of paper, in accordance with Schweitzer's method of dispatching friends' complimentary copies.

You can cut the postal address off (where I know it) and use it for the parcel, and affix – (a much less salivaly word than 'stick') – the personal allocution to

---

106   Tovey's Cello Concerto was first performed in Edinburgh by Casals on 22 November 1934. Unlike Tate's concerto (which Tovey had described as 'not unduly long'), his lasted over an hour, compelling Constant Lambert, on reviewing a Queen's Hall performance on 17 November 1937 with Boult conducting [issued on CD Symposium 1115], to comment that 'the first movement ... seemed to last as long as my first term at school'. It was published that year by OUP in full score, 'reproduced in facsimile of a beautifully clear manuscript by the composer, and bears the inscription, "written in honour of Casals by his friend Donald Francis Tovey"' (Mary Grierson, *Donald Francis Tovey – A biography based on letters*, OUP, 1952, p. 298).

the copies. If, as is possible, I am exceeding my allowance, I will not question anything you may reckon thereto on my next bill.

Casals I take for granted, also Boult and the BBC. (By the way, I must send you betimes the corrected orchestral parts – there's rather a lot to be done to the strings, and I fear some (one certainly) of the violinists have been insulting; I had to remove something with India rubber.) It is curious how violent the prejudice of today is against anything classical in a contemporary style: a composer is damned if he doesn't use 50% of language that would have been totally unintelligible in 1850: and as for our critics, to them all musical phrases current before 1900 are equivalent. It's about time musicians began to see that there is no more inherent need for this prejudice in music than there is in literature. I wouldn't mind if there were a ha'pworth [sic] of popularity in all this intolerable disciplinarian diet of modern sackcloth and ashes.

On the gummed side of each slip I have pencilled instructions as to which is to be score and which only pfte and 'cello, or only score.

I return proof of the last pages of Vol. V of the Essays; I can find only one mistake, a misplaced (decrescendo) on page 253. I hope the volume will appear in time for term: my students are howling for it.

In haste

DFT

PS I'll send further slips as I think of names, but meantime could you proceed with some which don't at present need inscriptions?

First (complete set) [to] Dr Sophie Weisse,[107] Hotel Rappen, Freudenstadt, Germany

Then Cassado[108] (address unknown to me). He wants it soon as he intends to play it shortly in Denmark.

66.   *17th September 1937   Donald Tovey to HJF* [postcard]

Many thanks to your all-seeing and omniscient Reader! Harz-forest it shall be – 'ence the word 'Arzreise, as Barry Pain's Conductor said of the word orse-air.

I thought I had already corrected the mistake – probably in another issue of the analysis (we have done the Brahms Rhapsodie more than once). Your Reader may be interested to know how the mistake arose. I was fortifying myself with a B & S, and, there being too much soda in it, the Sch got schwepped into the

---

107 Sophie Weisse (1851–1945), Tovey's piano teacher.
108 Gaspar Cassado (1897–1966), Spanish cellist and student of Casals.

Harzwald, thus producing the Schwarzwald. I hope you are producing Vol. 5 immediately, if not sooner: my students can't pass their imminent examinations without it: or with it.

Yours
DFT

67. *21st October 1938   Donald Tovey to HJF*

39 Royal Terrace, Edinburgh 7

Dear Foss

Yes, yes, yessissimo: that Deneke Lecture always was the key to the whole caboodle. If we can incorporate it we can clear up the whole mess, and I shall begin to feel less gloomy. But at present I don't see how to make the stuff readable and it fills me with gloom. I don't even know where to begin.

If you could come up here – preferably for a week-end (but <u>not</u> round the 30th of this month) – I have no doubt we can see daylight through what is to me an impenetrable fog at present.

About Vol. 6, there are some lacunae that I could fill up beautifully if I could have one appendix-page devoted to music-type illustrations, which would avoid disturbance to the text.

I shall never be able to trust myself as proof-reader: here comes a letter from a borrower (by your permission) who has been puzzled by the following astounding statement about the 3rd movement of the Cheekwhisky Pathetic Bosphony:

Vol. II, p. 88 'At all events it would, if translated into literature, be the triumph of the real hero not the story.'

For which, of course, read 'Would not be the triumph of the real hero of the story.'

Sorry, sorry, sorry.

Gosh!

Yours gosshously
DFT

PS. What a perfect jewel the Holst Life is.[109]

Tovey was a great admirer of Dorothy Sayers's books. He was very anxious to meet her as he had nebulous thoughts of writing an opera using one of her books as the libretto – I believe it was *The Nine Tailors*, but I am not sure. Hubert

---

109   Imogen Holst, *Gustav Holst – A Biography*, OUP, 1938.

had met Miss Sayers on one or two occasions so he arranged a luncheon party at the Étoile in Charlotte Street for the two to meet. This must have been in 1936 or 1937. For some reason I was unable to go. What I do remember is Hubert returning home about half past three and on my asking how the portentous occasion had gone off, he said in mock despair, 'Well, Tovey batted first and never gave a chance for an hour and a quarter.' Apparently, after that, Dorothy Sayers 'went in' but could make very little headway. Past 3 o'clock, when the restaurant staff was getting restive, Hubert, with Lady Tovey's aid, guided them outside and into a taxi, Donald still talking, and then slipped unobserved into his car and escaped.

We never heard of any results – musically – of this meeting.[110]

68.   *29ᵗʰ October 1934   Thomas Banks Strong to Humphrey Milford* [postcard]

Extracts from Jamieson's Scottish Dictionary:-
TO TOVE ... to talk familiarly, prolixly and cheerfully ... to carry on a free conversation with great glee, without regard to the lapse of time.
TOVIE (adj.) babbling, talking in a silly and incoherent manner.
These may interest you as an etymologist.
TBS

---

110   Tovey had what he referred to as 'my mild flirtation by post' with Dorothy Sayers. Unfortunately his letters to her were lost during the war (Mary Grierson, pp. 324–25). After Tovey's death in 1940, Hubert Foss contributed an article, 'I knew Donald Tovey', to *The Listener*, 4 September 1941, p. 343, based on a broadcast with the same title on 24 August 1941.

Ralph Vaughan Williams

Dora Foss never wrote about Vaughan Williams (1872–1958), unlike the other musicians in this section. However, it is quite likely that she intended doing so, and Vaughan Williams is therefore represented here by correspondence almost exclusively between him and Hubert Foss[111] and also some letters of Hubert's and Dora's in which they write about RVW.

69.   *30ᵗʰ October 1928   HJF to DMF*

> We've got the Te Deum which VW has written for the Archbishop's enthronement![112] A scoop!

70.   *27ᵗʰ July 1933   Ralph Vaughan Williams to HJF*

> Dear Foss,
>
> Thank you very much for your letter. I am perfectly well – only there is this wretched ankle and I mayn't put my foot to the ground for another week at least. So sorry to hear of your gout.
>
> Yours
> RVW

71.   *2ⁿᵈ November 1933   HJF* **(Shrewsbury, writing of Bristol)** *to DMF* **(Nightingale Corner)**

> Jane [Dawkins][113] and I met Vaughan [*sic*] and ate sandwiches, and VW said he hoped he wouldn't go to sleep. Actually I did instead! And Jane said I should, and that VW laughed loud! But that is just cattishness I think. The show was awful![114] Just like death. In Act IV VW turned to me at one of the jollier moments and said 'Another funeral coming in'. He, poor man, had rashly let himself in for staying with the producer-conductor. I pitied him and he bewailed his weakness. His ankle is still groggy, poor old chap.

---

111 Further correspondence between Vaughan Williams and Foss is included in Hugh Cobbe (editor), *Letters of Ralph Vaughan Williams 1895–1958*, OUP, 2008.

112 *Te Deum in G*, first performed at the enthronement of Dr Cosmo Gordon Lang as Archbishop of Canterbury, 4 December 1928.

113 Jane Dawkins was a music teacher at Clifton High School, Bristol and a close personal friend of Hubert and Dora Foss.

114 Vaughan Williams's *Sir John in Love*, 30 October, Bristol Opera School, conducted and produced by Robert Percival.

72.   *12th April 1935   Ralph Vaughan Williams to HJF*

Dear Foss,

Thank you very much. I owe everything to Boult who was really creative over it[115] and to his orchestra who were superb.

Yours

RVW

73.   *6th June 1935   Ralph Vaughan Williams to HJF*

Dear Foss

One word of thanks for your letter.[116] The good wishes of friends is the best part of all this business.

Yours

RVW

74.   *24th November 1935   DMF* **(Mundesley)** *to HJF* **(Nightingale Corner)**

I quite enjoyed going into the Days. Jack [Moeran] was as usual. I gather that Arnold [Bax] says that VW's 4th Symphony is the greatest work of the century and will outlast Willie's, (although he allows that Willie's is a fine work).

Why isn't VW's symphony being recorded etc.?[117] There is a definite rage for him it seems among other composers, brought on, I suspect, by Willie's success. It is only natural, I suppose and to be expected.

75.   *7th December 1935   HJF to DMF* **(Mundesley)**

Nightingale Corner, Rickmansworth

I had a hasty lunch, and started on at two with the audition for the Cambridge people of VW's Magic (Poisoned) Kiss[118] – Rootham, Gwendolen Raverat,

---

115   He is referring to the Symphony in F minor (No. 4), first performed on 10 April 1935. 'Ralph ... said that Adrian had *created* the second movement – he himself had not known how it should go, but Adrian had.' Ursula Vaughan Williams, *R.V.W. A Biography of Ralph Vaughan Williams*, OUP, 1964, p. 205.

116   Hubert Foss had been congratulating Vaughan Williams on being awarded the Order of Merit.

117   The Fourth Symphony was recorded by HMV, with Vaughan Williams conducting the BBC Symphony Orchestra, on 11 October 1937.

118   *The Poisoned Kiss*, first performed at the Arts Theatre, Cambridge, 12 May 1936, conducted by Cyril Rootham. The spoken dialogue was written by Evelyn Sharp [see following footnote].

Mrs Prior (producer), VW, Evelyn Sharp[119] and BBC man present, with Sydney Northcote and Mrs Field [Gladys Currie] singing much of the stuff at sight, and I the rest (aided by Rootham).

76.   *24th October 1937   Ralph Vaughan Williams to HJF*
The White Gates, Westcott Road, Dorking

Dear Foss,

Thank you very much.

I thought I must accept – though honours from Germany[120] are not what they were.

Yours

R. Vaughan Williams

77.   *6th November [1941]   Ralph Vaughan Williams to HJF*
The White Gates

Dear Foss

This is sad news indeed[121] – how shall we get on without you? I did not realize how much I counted on you – 'Ask Foss' advice' – 'Ask Foss to see to it' or 'I'll ask Foss to play it over to me at Amen House'[122] – But perhaps it is not all over as regards all that – and any way it is a selfish and material way of looking at things – and I ought to think only of how grateful we all are for all you have done for music (and incidentally musicians; so many people who think they are doing a lot for music seem to forget that music is made by musicians). But you must have a glow of satisfaction when you think of Walton & [Robin] Milford & Van Dieren – & if in the two latter cases (in the first (Milford) I think wrongly and the second (Van D) rightly) the horse has refused to drink – it is in spite of you not having merely led him to the water but positively shoved his nose in it.

---

119 Evelyn Sharp (1869–1955), author, journalist and supporter of women's suffrage. At the age of sixty-three she married the author and fellow suffragist Henry Nevinson.

120 'He had ... received an offer of the first award of the Shakespeare Prize, given by an anonymous Hamburg merchant ...', Ursula Vaughan Williams, p. 216. After much thought he accepted the prize and travelled to Germany to receive it, although it 'was rather in the nature of fairy gold, for he could not take it out of the country' (p. 221).

121 Hubert Foss's resignation as head of the Music Department at OUP. See plates 28–29.

122 The London offices in Warwick Square, EC4, of the Oxford University Press (the '*a*' pronounced as in 'p*a*y').

As regards myself I know that I owe any success I have had more to you (except H P A[llen] who insisted on shoving the S[ea] Symph[ony] down people's throats after it was a compete flop at Leeds) than to anyone.

Well the next lot of people who get the advantage of your energy & insight will be lucky and though your official relations with music & musicians may cease I know that you will continue to keep a fatherly eye on even those of us who are really old enough to be your father.

I always admired the way in which you took an interest in even the humblest of music makings – choral competitions, school music etc. – realizing the profound truth that without that foundation the Elgars & Waltons cant exist.

Well good luck to you in any new ventures & congratulations to those who get you for a cooperator.

Yrs

R. Vaughan Williams[123]

78.   *31ˢᵗ August [no year]   Ralph Vaughan Williams to HJF*
The White Gates, Dorking

Dear Hubert,

I always want to do what you ask. But in this case [it] isn't politic – one of the duties of your society will be to push (among other people's) my compositions – can I therefore become president of such a society?[124] What do you think?

Yours

RVW

79.   *23ʳᵈ September 1942   Ralph Vaughan Williams to HJF*
The White Gates, Dorking

Dear Hubert,

I have lost a letter from you asking me I think to write out something to broadcast to the Dominions.[125] Here is a bit of hot air which I hope will do –

---

123 An extract from this letter, read by Diana Sparkes (née Foss), was included in the CD *Hubert Foss and his friends – A recital of songs*, HJF001CD.

124 Probably the Society (formerly Committee) for the Promotion of New Music, of which Vaughan Williams became president when it was formed in January 1943.

125 Seventieth birthday tribute by Hubert Foss to RVW, broadcast on 12 October 1942 on the Home and African Services, most of which he included in the Prologue to his book on Vaughan Williams published eight years later.

Music is the one thing which defies bombs and blitzes.

Music is the one thing which binds together those who live at opposite ends of the globe.

Music is the one thing which makes friends of those who have never met, and perhaps will never meet except through the power of the greatest of the arts.

Yours

RVW

---

80.   *14ᵗʰ October 1942   Ralph Vaughan Williams to HJF*

The White Gates, Dorking

My dear Hubert,

Thank you both so much for remembering my birthday – which I spent quietly and fairly normally – except for eating too much cake.

Yours

RVW

---

81.   *20ᵗʰ October [1942]   Ralph Vaughan Williams to HJF*

The White Gates, Dorking

Dear Hubert,

Thank you both for your friendship & your good wishes. Thank you also very much for all you have done for me anent the BBC.[126]

I listened to everything – though sometimes I wish I had had the courage not to. I think I get more & more incompetent as a composer. My later things seem to come off *much* worse than my earlier – so it is certainly time I retired.

Your extravagant praise alarmed me – and might cause the enemy to blaspheme – but thank you all the same, because I know you meant it.

Yours with much gratitude

R. Vaughan Williams

---

126 Because of Julian Herbage's illness, Hubert had been asked by the BBC to organise the season of RVW's major works to celebrate his seventieth birthday on 12 October 1942. He also gave a broadcast talk (see previous footnote).

82.   *13ᵗʰ November 1942*   **Ralph Vaughan Williams to HJF**
The White Gates, Dorking

Dear Hubert,

The Pfte version of Greensleeves[127] has just been sent me – it looks very good – I say looks since not having four hands I can't play it through (even if I had I couldn't).

Yours
RVW

83.   *[November or December 1943]*   **Ralph Vaughan Williams to HJF**
The White Gates, Dorking

Dear Hubert,

I shd very much like to meet you soon, and to talk over this hymn idea is as good an excuse as any other. I shall be in London on Saturday for the concert and could meet you afterwards – but I suppose Saturday is no use to you.

After that the only 'necessary' journeys I am making to London are on Sunday December 12th and Tuesday December 14th – but I suppose this is rather far off and also Sunday is no use for you.

In both cases I have appointments at 4.30.

Yours
RVW

84.   *[1948?]*   **Ralph Vaughan Williams to HJF**
The White Gates, Dorking

Dear Hubert,

Many thanks for interesting programme – I am again in the film way[128] (9 months does not seem to apply in this case – I'm more like a cat) – & I am rationing my visits to London – I am sending you my 'musical influences'[129] in a few days.

Yours
RVW

---

127   *Fantasia on 'Greensleeves'*, arranged for pianoforte duet by Hubert Foss, OUP, 1942.
128   The film was probably *Scott of the Antarctic*, first shown 29 November 1948.
129   'Musical Autobiography by Ralph Vaughan Williams', which Hubert Foss included as chapter 3 in *Ralph Vaughan Williams: A Study*.

85. *26ᵗʰ July 1950 Ralph Vaughan Williams to HJF* [typed]

The White Gates, Dorking

Dear Hubert,

First, forgive a typewritten letter because I want you to be able to read this. I am quite overpowered by the affection and thought in your book.[130] I feel hopelessly unable to live up to it. Indeed, I owe you rather a grudge because I had hoped for the rest of my life, to be able to live comfortably following my lower instincts, without ideals. Now everybody will be able to refer to your book to find out what I ought to be like! But, alas, I am not and I shall have to try and live up to my (or rather your) ideals.

I will not try to thank you any more. I am sure you will understand.

Just one small point. It looks rather like 'looking a gift horse in the mouth', but I have found a slight misprint on Page 33 – the word printed 'snuggery', should of course be 'smuggery'.

Well once again, my affection and admiration

Yrs

RVW

86. *18ᵗʰ October 1950 Ralph Vaughan Williams to DMF and HJF* [all typed except last sentence]

The White Gates, Dorking

Dear Dora and Hubert Foss,

Thank you very much for your kind greetings. I think it is wonderful that you should remember my birthday. I am so sorry I couldn't come to your party.

Yours

R. Vaughan Williams

87. *24ᵗʰ June 1951 Ralph Vaughan Williams to HJF* [postcard]

Before you write more about P[ilgrim's] P[rogress],[131] you shd see my revisions especially of Act 3 which will be ready soon.

Will gladly support a scheme for honouring CSK [*sic*][132] – it would help if you would tell me what to say to A[drian] B[oult]. More later.

R. Vaughan Williams

130 Hubert Foss, *Ralph Vaughan Williams: A Study*.
131 *The Pilgrim's Progress*, first performed at the Royal Opera House, Covent Garden on 26 April 1951.
132 Clearly CKS (Charles Kennedy Scott) intended – see letter 88.

88.   *27ᵗʰ June 1951   Ralph Vaughan Williams to HJF* [typed]

The White Gates, Dorking

Dear Hubert

I am so sorry I have been so long answering your letter. However, I will try and do so in detail.

I was interested in your article, though I do not altogether agree with your criticisms of the production.[133]

I have come to the conclusion that certain places want altering and occasionally enlarging. This is especially the case in 'Vanity Fair'. As soon as the sketch is ready I am going to get someone to play it through, probably Leonard Hancock,[134] and if you could come and listen I should be very grateful.

I should very much like to see the review of your book,[135] but it has not arrived yet.

About Kreisler playing in the orchestra at the Worcester Festival, that is my story,[136] not Cranmer's. Anyway, it is merely a funny story and would be quite out of place in a book which professedly deals not with personalities except insofar as they directly influence my music.

I do not think I want to hear Jenning's [*sic*] film. I had a lot of trouble over my talk but I don't think I want to hear it again.[137]

I will try and write something about the LSO[138] when I can think of anything.

---

133   Hubert Foss, 'Vaughan Williams and Bunyan', *The Listener*, 26 April 1951, p. 684.

134   Conductor of the first performance of *The Pilgrim's Progress*.

135   *Ralph Vaughan Williams: A Study* by Hubert Foss.

136   While conducting his *Five Mystical Songs* at the 1911 Worcester Festival, Vaughan Williams was amazed to see Kreisler at the back desk of violins. He was to play the Elgar Violin Concerto after the *Mystical Songs* and was 'playing himself' in.

137   A ten-minute Central Office of Information documentary, *Dim Little Island* (1949), produced and directed by Humphrey Jennings (1907–50) and concerning four men's views of Britain: artist Osbert Lancaster, industrialist John Ormston, naturalist James Fisher and composer Ralph Vaughan Williams, each providing his own commentary, with music by Vaughan Williams. Jennings had died in 1950 from a fall in the Greek island of Poros while scouting locations for another documentary. In February 1956 Vaughan Williams wrote to *The Musical Times* that he had 'never heard of this film' and had not 'spoken part of the commentary'. It is possible that he recorded his contribution separately, never saw the film and had forgotten his involvement in it.

138   At the time of his death, Hubert Foss was writing a history of the London Symphony Orchestra which was completed by Noël Goodwin (*London Symphony: Portrait of an Orchestra*, The Naldrett Press, 1954). Vaughan Williams provided a Preface.

As regards a lecture at Epsom, I really do not think I can face sitting still the whole evening while someone else talks about me, so I am afraid I must ask you to let me off.

I have already answered you about Kennedy Scott. I shall be glad to add my quota to the requests for an honour to be given him. Perhaps you could indicate to me more or less the line I ought to take?

I fear this is rather a wet blankety letter.

Yrs

RVW

89.   *14ᵗʰ November [1951]   Ralph Vaughan Williams to HJF*

The White Gates, Dorking

Dear Hubert,

I remember a great many years ago (early '90s) that the 'Strand' Magazine started the fashion of personal interviews & sent round a questionnaire to several eminent composers – Hubert Parry's reaction was 'I'm damned if I'll tell those fellows whether my bottom is painted blue'.

I feel the same with the BBC snoopers trying to get a factitious interest in my music by telling people what I eat for breakfast and what sort of lavatory paper I use.

– If my music cannot stand on its own bottom, I have no desire for it to stand on mine.

Of course, I sh[oul]d love to have you write about my music – but you have already done that.[139]

I'm sorry but there it is!

Yrs

RVW

---

139   Foss had been asked by the BBC to persuade RVW to agree to a short television documentary about himself, for which Foss would write the commentary. RVW had so far refused (Cobbe, pp. 490–91).

90.   *17ᵗʰ March 1952   Ralph Vaughan Williams to HJF*

The White Gates, Dorking

Dear Hubert,

I am ashamed not to have answered your delightful letter before. I have been having a slight dose of 'flu myself – and on the top of that St John <u>and</u> St Matthew Passions.[140]

I was so sorry to hear of your illness and much relieved by a card from Martin that you were improving.

Ursula and I went to see a television show the other day – in the studio – very interesting – but how a whole masque is to get into a frame about 12 inches square passes my comprehension.

I was much worried that I could not go to St Martin's next Sunday – but now that you cannot be there I do not mind so much. That was an interesting letter from the Dean – but I feel rather ashamed of being dubbed as 'religious'; it makes me feel a fearful humbug.

When next I am in London, I shall find out if you are able and willing to let me come and see you.

Yours

RVW

91.   *14ᵗʰ October 1952   Ralph Vaughan Williams to HJF* **[all typed except additional note]**

The White Gates, Dorking

My dear Hubert,

A personal thought from you is a better present than all the marble clocks and Purdoneums[141] in the world. I cannot hang up anything so laudatory for my friends to see, so I shall keep it in a drawer, where I keep my other valuables.

Yours

RVW

My love (if I may make so bold) to Mrs Hubert.

---

140 Works that Vaughan Williams conducted at Dorking. A 1958 performance of the *St Matthew Passion*, RVW conducting (broadcast in 1960), was issued on CD GEMS 0079.

141 A purdonium [*sic*], *Collins English Dictionary*, is a type of coal scuttle named after its inventor, a Mr Purdon.

To Ralph Vaughan Williams[142]
In homage on his eightieth birthday
12th October 1952

Music stands in the skies, stirring this strong
Truth-seeking poet (broad frame and valiant heart)
To English thoughts, uttered with sensitive art
Now in the lark's, now in the angels' song.

Shakespeare and Blake, Herbert and Bunyan throng
This stage, where ale-wife Elinor takes her part
Next Pilgrim, Galanthus, cockney, Hugh from his cart
And scholar from his Vulgate. Here is young

England's music. His quest has spanned the years
And made sweet sounds of them. Here greatness lies.
He will out-sing our wonders and our fears.
England's beauty he found, in hymn, symphonies,
A child's song or a man's. His outlines fold
In mist of history. England, he is not old.

Hubert Foss

Further correspondence from Vaughan Williams, after Hubert Foss's death, is
included in the Tribute section: letters 265, p. 242 and 272, p. 252.

142   In this birthday tribute, Foss makes reference to a number of Vaughan Williams's works,
      including *The Lark Ascending*, *Five Tudor Portraits*, *The Pilgrim's Progress*, *The Poisoned*
      Kiss, *Hugh the Drover* and *An Oxford Elegy*. With 'cockney' he is possibly thinking of 'the
      cockneys [who] are hit off to a "t" in the livelier parts' of *A London Symphony*, as Foss writes
      in *Ralph Vaughan Williams: A Study*, p. 131.

William Walton

O N 27ᵀᴴ APRIL 1926, I first saw William Walton when *Façade* was given its second performance at the Chenil Galleries in Chelsea.[143] I had read the reviews of the first performance and my mother and I decided, that whenever it was repeated, we would go. The morning the performance was announced, I set off for Chelsea and bought five, I think, of the best seats. My mother, my two sisters, Sylvia and Angela, and my brother Geoffrey went. I shall never forget the excitement of that evening, the extraordinary sense of this being a portentous occasion.

The work itself was a complete novelty to me and to very many there – the scintillating music, spiky and brittle, combined with the enchanting poems, with their wit and coloured words seemed to me completely fascinating and I was entirely captivated. William came on to receive the wild applause. Pale, willowy and shy – apparently, but rather appealing and charming withal, he made his bows. It appeared to me to be the beginning of his public career.

At last the clapping and shouting stopped and we turned from the platform and wound our way through the crowd down the Hall, seeing many famous faces there, including those of Arnold Bennett and Augustus John.

When we next saw Hubert, we were still overflowing with enthusiasm and my mother said to him, after we had tried to describe the charm, originality and brilliance of *Façade* – 'Here is the new composer' and I can see Hubert's kindly but incredulous smile. 'I can't form any opinion till I've heard it', he said.

It cannot have been very long after this that Willie came to see Hubert at Amen House, Warwick Square, EC4, the OUP Headquarters in London from where he ran the Music Department, the 'shop' at that time being in Wimpole Street, in the charge of Norman Peterkin. Some early memory made me think that John Goss brought Willie there, but Hubert himself was not sure of this and was, indeed, rather vague about the actual circumstances of their first meeting.

However, after our marriage in 1927 and during the winter of 1927–28, we met Willie frequently at concerts; he and Hubert were on very friendly terms and *Façade* was definitely the OUP's. Hubert was enchanted by Willie's airy

---

143   Second *public* performance. The first private performance was given at 2 Carlyle Square, London on 24 January 1922. The first public performance was at the Aeolian Hall, London on 12 June 1923.

nonchalance, amused by the shafts of lightning and acid which would suddenly illuminate his conversation, and, above all, enormously excited by the musical possibilities he divined in him.

In September 1928, Hubert wrote to me from Siena:[144]

92. *10ᵗʰ September 1928   HJF* (Siena) *to DMF* (Belsize Park Gardens)

Yesterday evening I copied music and then Lambert and Walton and I dined most pleasantly and cheaply (it's very cheap here – excellent wine at 1½d per glass!) and we went to bed earlyish.

93. *12ᵗʰ September 1928   HJF* (Siena) *to DMF* (Belsize Park Gardens)

Pat Hughes[145] and the Brosa Quartet[146] turned up at our restaurant ... We all had a jolly time and then the three, Lambert, Walton and I, went to the party. All the way up the stairs at the Palazzo Pubblico were standing gentlemen in mediaeval dress with halberds, and pages at the top in black and white stripes, looking like bull's-eyes! The party was excessively dull. Long Italian speeches, and then the Venetian Quartet (who are so nice) played some old music – but alas the 'cello had two strings out of tune! When it came to a real hooter of a lady-singer, Walton and I left, having shaken hands with the world in general. We went for a walk round Siena and, my goodness, it was hot. But it was so lovely by that pitch-black starlight. Up one little street we stopped on hearing music. We were at the top of the steps to a lower level, and at the bottom was a tiny open space lit by one lamp. Four people were playing tangos on mandolins and whistling the tunes with a flexitone to help, and one or two couples were dancing. It was such a beautiful sight, so simple and romantic and peasant-like, and such a change from the idiotic reception. We went quite a distance round, and then found others about in the town, and as usual, on the first Festival night, we sat up yarning till about two!

---

144 The International Society for Contemporary Music Festival in Siena, Italy, September 1928, which included the first European performance of *Façade*. In fact, two performances were given, with William Walton conducting and Constant Lambert reciting. Foss reviewed the festival for *The Musical Times*, 1 October 1928.

145 Patrick Cairns ('Spike') Hughes (1908–87), composer and jazz musician, son of the composer Herbert Hughes.

146 Founded in 1925 by the Spanish violinist, Antonio Brosa (1894–1979).

94.   *14th September 1928   HJF (Siena) to DMF (Belsize Park Gardens)*

I helped rehearse Façade in the morning (Sitwells[147] in great evidence) and then lunched rather urgently with Dent[148] over getting the Festival to come to Oxford. Then more Façade and then letters. I was taken out to dinner and then more Façade! In about two minutes I must go and help again with the lights (the Sitwell lot seem to know nothing about such things!). I shall be pretty tied today, lunching with them over the question of rights, America, etc.

95.   *15th September 1928   HJF (Siena) to DMF (Belsize Park Gardens)*

Façade was done twice yesterday – a huge success! I really think we shall do well with it, and performances are looming up in all sorts of places.

96.   *5th January 1929   HJF (London) to DMF (Mundesley)*

There was a most exciting parcel for me today from Amalfi,[149] a Xmas present from Willie Walton. It's so nice and jolly and novel that I'm not going to tell you a thing about it, but bring it down (at great expense and inconvenience) to show you, and you shall participate therein.

This present consisted of a large net, as I remember it, filled with little packets of raisins swaddled in vine leaves – charming and delicious.

In the late summer of 1929 we moved to Rickmansworth where we rented a pleasant house which we re-named 'Nightingale Corner'. It was built about 1899, and very well constructed. The exterior had little architecturally to commend it, rather mock Tudor, but all the rooms had heaps of windows and every room had charm. The garden was old-fashioned with an Edwardian tennis court – hedges and trees on two sides. We used it for the simpler and less strenuous game of deck tennis and had many happy times playing there.

Willie's first 'staying' visit was in the early summer of 1929, again in

---

147   The siblings Edith, Osbert and Sacheverell Sitwell, who 'adopted' William Walton who lived with them in Chelsea. The first and most famous outcome of this patronage was the entertainment *Façade*, a setting of poems by Edith Sitwell.

148   E.J. Dent. See pp. 196–7.

149   The Italian coastal town where the Sitwell brothers, with Walton, would often stay at the spectacularly situated hotel Cappuccini Convento (a converted monastery) for working winter holidays.

October 1929, and then again in 1930. He was then living in Osbert Sitwell's house in Carlyle Square, Chelsea. He was rather shy and diffident, and at that time desperately hard up. He had borrowed Osbert Sitwell's pyjamas, a most striking orange and black pair, to come to us with, but his hairbrushes and other dressing table accoutrements appeared to date from his choirboy's days. However, he always appeared to be immaculate and extremely elegant in what he informed me, sometime later, were Moss Bros misfits.

On this first occasion Willie overcame his natural antipathy for being energetic and after some persuasion on Hubert's part, played deck tennis.

We loved Willie's visits. We spent hours listening to his playing of whatever the current composition was – *Belshazzar's Feast*, the Symphony, etc. and Hubert discussed, advised and encouraged him and grew to know the works intimately. He was a sort of nurse to Willie's musical offspring and loved them almost as if they were his own.

But Willie's visits did not only mean music. We sat long over meals while Willie regaled us with current gossip and comments on friends and foes alike. How we laughed!

He was most appreciative of good food, and as Hubert and I were too, we always took the greatest pains to give him the best within our means – and how (comparatively) easy that was then! He loved simple things to eat too, like the home-made pickled shallots that he could not stop eating! He helped to lay out apples in the stable loft one time he was with us.

One Sunday Hubert wanted to work in his room, quite undisturbed, so I took Willie for a walk which he found completely exhausting. We took the bus up the Chorleywood Road, then walked to Chenies[150] and back mostly across fields – a very few miles, but Willie was allergic to physical exercise in any form and he was most tried by this unaccustomed pedestrianism, although he quite forgave me for taking him out.

He was very anxious to further a very superficial acquaintance with Arnold Bax, so we invited them both to dine with us quietly without any other guests. For me, it was an entrancing experience of just listening. I doubt if I spoke at all, other than uttering the necessary 'hostess' remarks at dinner. Hubert initially pushed the conversational wheels with a few interpolations, but by the time we returned to the drawing-room, the two composers were more or less oblivious

---

150   A village in Buckinghamshire.

of us and we just sat back and enjoyed ourselves. Most of the discussion and general talk was about other composers, both past and contemporary – and the contemporary ones were wholeheartedly and jovially pulled to pieces. One incident I remember: for some reason or other they turned on the wireless to a programme of Russian music and 'guessed' the composers – nearly always incorrectly – which caused them much amusement. Arnold left by the last train and Willie stayed on with us for the weekend.

It was while Willie was staying with us that he first met Sir Henry Wood. We took him up to the Woods' at Appletree Farm House one Sunday and it was on that occasion that Hindemith[151] was there too. We walked round the gardens together and a grey squirrel crossed our path. Hindemith made some remarks on the habits of squirrels and was at a loss for English words and spoke in German. I felt rather pleased with myself when I knew that 'Magen' meant stomach.

I look back with pride and emotion on those days when Hubert and Willie sat for hours at the piano, sometimes Willie playing with his 'composer's' technique – sometimes Hubert – and we heard the great works growing.

97.   *[postmarked 18ᵗʰ June 1930]   William Walton to HJF* [postcard]

Thank you so much – I shall be delighted to come on the 28th & I hope, carry off us [*sic*] the championship.
yours
Willie Walton[152]

98.   *20ᵗʰ August 1931   Arnold Bax to HJF*

155 Fellows Rd, NW3

My dear Foss,

Thanks very much. I should be very pleased to come to Rickmansworth one evening. (I imagine there are plenty of late trains back to Swiss Cottage.) I like

---

151   Paul Hindemith (1895–1963), German composer, conductor and violist. He was soloist in the first performance of Walton's Viola Concerto when initially rejected by Lionel Tertis; Henry Wood Prom, 3 October 1929, Walton conducting.

152   Further correspondence between Walton and Hubert and Diana Sparkes (née Foss) is included in Malcolm Hayes (editor), *The Selected Letters of William Walton*, Faber & Faber, 2002.

the idea of the party you suggest, for you are always stimulating, and I am ever glad to meet Willie Walton.

With best wishes,

Yours

Arnold Bax

In 1931–32 Willie wrote the *Three Songs*[153] which he dedicated to Hubert and me. We had some hilarious times working them up and I felt very flattered and pleased to think he wrote them for me to sing. They are extremely difficult as the tessitura is, on the whole, very high – but enormous fun to do.

On April 9th we had a little party to introduce them to musical friends and out of the invitation to that arose the contretemps which I have related under the heading, 'Edith Sitwell'.[154] As a party, it did not go off terribly well. It was a brilliantly sunny evening and I don't think anyone felt like a concert. Our living room was flooded with the setting sun and somehow it seemed an effort to sing – not physically, but mentally. On that occasion I also sang three songs for voice and clarinet written for me by Gordon Jacob, with Alan Frank[155] playing the clarinet. Louis Godowsky played a violin sonata of Hubert's – a work full of lovely and moving moments.

99.   *21ˢᵗ December [1931]   William Walton to DMF*

Faringdon House, Berks.[156]

Dear Dora

Thank you so much for your letter. It is kind of you to ask me for a week-end.

Would it be possible for me to come instead of the dates you mention, for the week-end of the New Year? If that is too inconvenient I will come on Jan. 15th.

It is sweet of you to ask the Baronin[157] as well, but alas! alas! she returned to Switzerland about ten days ago.

153   Settings of Edith Sitwell: *Daphne*, *Through Gilded Trellises* and *Old Sir Faulk* (OUP, 1932), first performed by Dora Stevens and Hubert Foss at the Wigmore Hall, 10 October 1932. They recorded the songs for Decca on 20 March 1940. See Discography, p. 269. These are the only commercial recordings of Dora singing.

154   Pages 80–1.

155   Alan Frank (1910–94) joined OUP in 1927 and was head of the music department 1954–75. In 1935 he married the composer Phyllis Tate.

156   The home of Lord Berners.

157   Baroness Imma von Doernberg, dedicatee of the First Symphony.

Here is one of the songs [*Through Gilded Trellises*]. Don't hesitate (because it is dedicated to you) to severely criticise it, if it doesn't meet with your approval. It is not so difficult as it first looks, especially the piano part which sounds difficult but is in reality as easy as Sidney Smith,[158] & I may say not unlike.

However I hope you will like it. I will send the others as they are finished.

I've now to write a Xmas carol by tomorrow morning for the 'Daily Dispatch'.[159] It is bad to be tempted by filthy lucre!

With all good wishes for Christmas & the New Year to you, Hubert & Christopher.

    Yours

    Willie Walton

100. *[January 1932]*   **William Walton to DMF**

Faringdon House, Berks.

Dear Dora

Here is another song [*Old Sir Faulk*], alas! not the 'Lydian' one which is proving a little obstreperous.

I am not sure that you will approve of this one, but it is I think fairly good of its type, & at any rate ought [to] evoke a touch of inconsequent lunacy in any programme.

Looking forward to the 16th,

    Yours,

    Willie.

101. *12th January [1932]*   **William Walton to DMF**

Faringdon House, Berks.

Dear Dora

Thank you for your letter. I am glad my 'effort' has not gone down badly. I had considerable misgivings about it.

Hubert will soon be joining the B.B.C. dance band!

I don't mind a bit about the room, as long as Paddy [Hadley] won't object to my seeing his wooden leg in the flesh, so to speak.

I will let you know what time I arrive.

158 Possibly referring to Rev. Sidney Smith (1771–1845), Anglican cleric and writer known for his witticisms.

159 *May We Joy Now in This Fest*.

I just had a wire from Harriet [Cohen] saying that as a token of – [*sic*] she is playing the Sinfonia[160] in Montreal & paying for it herself. Which, all things considered, is extremely nice of her. Also I've had a very aimiable [*sic*] letter from Harty.

Yours

Willie.

PS. The new song is not fit to be seen, & there's not much of it as yet.

The Beginning of the Symphony

102. *[c. February 1932]   William Walton to DMF*

The Daye House, Quidhampton, Salisbury[161]

Dear Dora,

I am so very sorry to hear that you have not been well, & I hope that by now, you are recovered.

Here is the last song [*Daphne*]. I am sorry to have been such a time with it, but I could not get it satisfactory – this is the 3rd version – all I can say about it is that it is better than the other two.

I am here for some weeks, trying to start on a symphony. What a fool I am, treading where so many angels have come a 'cropper'. However I shall be able to be in a better position to judge, by April 1st.

I asked Edith about the pronunciation she prefers 'chee' – 'chi', anglicised if incorrect.[162] Are you going to have the Recital on March 20th?

Yours

Willie Walton

103. *[February or March 1932]   William Walton to DMF*

The Daye House, Quidhampton, Salisbury

Dear Dora

Thank you for your letter. I am so pleased to hear that you are better and that your voice is making a 'come-back'.

---

160 Walton's *Sinfonia Concertante* for orchestra with piano 'continuo' (OUP, 1928).

161 The home of Edith Olivier (1872–1948), writer and socialite, friend of Stephen Tennant, Cecil Beaton and Rex Whistler, and first cousin of Laurence Olivier's father.

162 The word was 'Lucia' in *Through Gilded Trellises*.

I feel that you both know best about giving a party for the songs. I personally feel that they are hardly worth taking so much trouble about. As regards the date April 9th would suit me best, if it is all the same to you.

About the concert, June 15th seems a good date, but whether I shall be back from Switzerland I can hardly say at the moment. It all depends on how expensive it is, and how long my money lasts. It probably won't last anywhere near June 15th.

The symphony is unspeakable, it has been christened the 'Ichabod'[163] or the 'Unwritten', only time will decide which, if either are appropriate.

Yours
Willie

104. *[March 1932]   William Walton to DMF*

The Daye House, Quidhampton, Salisbury

Dear Dora,

I have been waiting to hear from Edith S. before I wrote you.

I heard from her last night, & I expect you will have also received a letter from her.[164]

Her explanation seems adequate and genuine & I hope that you will accept it as such.

I felt sure that there was some misunderstanding & that she was labouring under some misapprehension & non-realisation as to who the invitation was from.

So I now trust that this unfortunate contretemps is amicably settled.

About the order of the songs, I had conceived it as being –

1. Daphne
2. Through gilded trellises
3. Old Sir Faulk.

but perhaps Hubert is right & 1 & 2 should be reversed.

Though I think my order better as I think 'Old Sir Faulk' won't come as such a shock after (2) as after (1).

163 Biblical reference to the grandson of Eli, born after the Ark of the Covenant had been seized by the Philistines (I Samuel 4:19–22). Loosely translated it means 'without glory', symbolising the difficulty that Walton was having with the symphony.
164 Letter 42, pp. 80–1.

I don't think the matter of speed really enters into the question as (3) is quite sedate & altogether the styles of the songs are so different that contrast will be there in whatever order they appear.

I will arrive for lunch on the 9th & look forward to seeing you both.

yrs

Willie

Note enclosed with box of tulips received about this time:

The Daye House, Quidhampton, Salisbury

Please accept these as propition [*sic*] for my sins.

Willie

the 'sin' being that he had <u>not</u> told Edith S that he was using her poems for the songs he was writing and thus, inadvertently, placed me in the very awkward position of which I relate under my E[dith] S[itwell] memoir.[165]

Hubert, of course, went to every first performance of Willie's works, and very often to the rehearsals. I, too, went to the first performances (with the exception of that of Belshazzar's Feast, which was at Leeds) and for many years we went to every performance we could attend. Willie's music was part of us – we were elated or depressed, thrilled or moved as new works were conceived and born, and repetition never seemed to blunt the fine edge of his musical mind, to numb the poignancy of his slow movements or to quench the fire of his more electric and thunderous moments.[166]

Through Willie, we met the Sitwells and in the chapter on Edith Sitwell, I have told of my meetings with her.

In 1932 on our way to Oundle, Hubert and I lunched at Weston Hall, the home of Sacheverell Sitwell and his wife Georgia. Willie was then staying with them and was writing his symphony.

Sacheverell – tall – Georgia dark and beautiful, in spite of a really shocking cold.

There were eight or nine at lunch – including Roger Fry and Arthur Waley and Reresby, the (then) only son of the house. Lunch was very late; Sacheverell

---

165 Pages 80–1.

166 Brief extracts from these memories of Walton, read by Diana Sparkes (née Foss), were included in the CD *Hubert Foss and his friends – A recital of songs*, HJF001CD.

kept on retiring to back stage to see if it was ever coming. There was a butler and a young boy waiting. We started the meal with baked beans which appeared (and tasted) as if they had been an hour in the oven. This course was followed by slices of meat (species unidentifiable) covered with white sauce. The butler, when this was finished, solemnly dealt plates to all, and equally solemnly, removed them and replaced them with small pudding plates. A very small apple pie and a minute jug of cream was then rather gingerly partitioned.

Willie told us he worked in a stable near the house where a piano had been installed. Reresby at this point interrupted to say somewhat brutally that Willie had been made to work there so that he did not disturb the household.

Hubert and I then accompanied William to the stable. The piano was a senile, disintegrating upright which Willie kept together and attempted to keep in tune with the aid of a spanner. I have never seen a more decrepit instrument. On this pathetic wreck Willie was composing his great symphony.

105.   *17th May [1932]   William Walton to HJF*

Casa Angolo, Ascona, Ticino, Switzerland

My dear Hubert,

This is all very well. You know that my life is already an open book & I can't think of anything more which can with strict propriety be divulged to the public. However as you ask – here goes.

Perhaps it is wiser (& more profitable) to cast a doubt about the parentage, – only born March 29th 1902.

It is said that he could sing before he could talk (doubtless untrue).

Anyhow he remembers making a scene (tears etc) because not allowed to sing a solo in local church choir when about the age of 6.

Won probationership to Ch[rist]. Ch[urch]. Cath[edral]. Choir at 10 (after being very sick on first long train journey).

First signs of composition 'Variations for Violin & Pf. on a Choral[e] by J.S.B.['] didn't progress (like his latest composition) more than a dozen bars. Not very interesting & wisely decided to stop. However broke loose again about 13 & wrote two 4 part songs 'Tell me where is fancy bred' & 'Where the bee sucks'[.] After that fairly went in for it & produced about 30 very bad works of various species songs, motets, Magnificats etc.

First composition to show any kind of talent Pf Quartet (ultimately published not very much revised by the Carnegie Trust – very black mark in 1924) though written in 1918.

At this date became undergraduate at Ch. Ch. & failed consistently in all 'schools' & was ultimately ignominiously 'sent down' (though he passed his Mus. Bac. exams like [a] lamb, except the compositions!!)

The most fruitful things about that period was gaining the friendship of the present Bish. of Ox[ford]. & S. Sitwell & ultimately with the rest of that talented family.

Apparently idled away his time from the time he was sent down, (1920) though went to Italy for 1st time, till suddenly appeared as an unpopular 'bolt from the blue' at the I.F.C.M.[167] with a String Quartet at Salzburg 1923.

Though not too popular a work in England, nevertheless it excited the interest of the great Alban Berg, who took the shy & nervous young composer to see the even greater Arnold Schonberg, who gave the little brute his blessing (luckily he has not, to the composer[']s knowledge heard any of his later compositions).

After this, the composer not knowing which way to turn produced some rather bad works in various styles (he is self-taught) now mercifully in the fire. And it was not till 1926, again at the I.F.C.M. this time at Zürich that he produced that exciting work P.P. [*Portsmouth Point*] on which so much of his fame wrongly rests.

This was all 'great fun' (as Dame Adrian [Boult] would say) for the composer, as all the English musical world considered him dead & a 'flash in the pan'. After that with the production of 'Façade' at the I.F.C.M. at Siena in 1928 & the[n] again the Viola Concerto at Liège in 1930, the young composer seemed well on the lower rungs of the ladder of fame.

The rest you know, & I hope really very much that sometime I shall produce a good work – till then with this pious wish,

auf wiedersehen,
Willie

The Baroness [Doernberg] sends her love to you both.

In 1932 Walton's Viola Concerto was played in Worcester Cathedral during the Three Choirs' Festival. Hubert, Willie and I stayed for this week in Malvern at the Foley Arms, driving in to Worcester for rehearsals and whatever performances we wanted to attend.

Willie was excessively nervous before the performance of the Concerto and Hubert took him on to the terrace outside the Cathedral and above the river and

---

167   Actually ISCM, International Society for Contemporary Music.

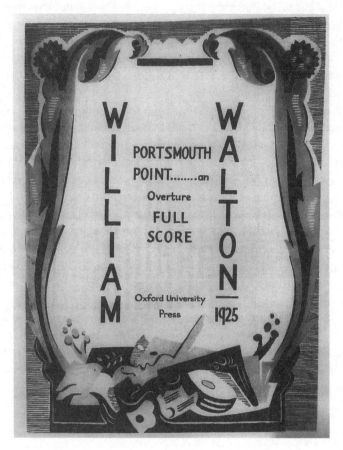

Fig. 8: Cover design by Gino Severini for Walton's
Portsmouth Point, his first work to be published by OUP © OUP

gave him a good swig of brandy from our flask which gave him the immediately
necessary courage!

The performance was a great success and the work sounded heavenly in the
cathedral. Lionel Tertis's playing was ravishing. We laughed afterwards when
Willie said that if the authorities had known what the Concerto was all about
(or to that effect), it would not have been considered suitable for the Cathedral!

It was during this Festival that Willie first met Elgar. It was at an evening
concert and Willie commented that Elgar would not have any form of musical
conversation with him, but would only discuss horses and racing.

While we were in Malvern, Hubert and Willie went out for a drink and came back in great glee having watched Bernard Shaw reading from beginning to end a poster giving details of a Noel Coward Festival!

During that week, we drove into the lovely Wye Valley country and photographs were taken at Symonds Yat.[168] At the end of the week we left Willie at Bath with Siegfried Sassoon.

106. *[September 1932]   William Walton to DMF*
    [postmarked Salisbury, after the Worcester Three Choirs Festival]

I enjoyed so much being with you both, in fact I don't know what I should have done without your presence at that dismal festival which we so successfully avoided.

We [WW and Siegfried Sassoon] arrived here somewhat late owing to a valve exploding, otherwise life is peaceful & pleasant.

Willie

107. *[October 1932]   William Walton to DMF*

In the train

My dear Dora,

You must forgive me, but I've had a rush of telegrams from the baroness asking me to join her at once. It is so difficult to know how bad she is, but I feel she must be otherwise I'm sure she wouldn't have wired for me.

I've had such a rushed two days getting ready for my unexpected return.

I am truly sorry that I sha'nt be present on the 10th but I'm sure my absence will make no difference to the quality of the performance, & I'm sure all will go well. You have all my best wishes for a huge success.

I've done all I can in the way of propaganda & I've written to Osbert to carry on the good work.

It seems very bad my rushing off like this, but I'm so distracted that I feel I've no option.

With kindest regards. I'm writing to Hubert.

yrs.

Willie

168 A popular beauty spot in the Forest of Dean, Herefordshire, overlooking the Wye Valley.
    See plates 8–9.

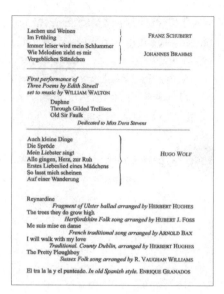

Fig. 9: Programme for the first performance of Walton's *Three Songs*, October 1932

108. *[October 1932]*   ***William Walton to DMF*** [telegram]

> MISS DORA STEVENS WIGMORE HALL LONDON[169]
> ALL LOVE AND BEST WISHES FOR WONDERFUL SUCCESS
> MISERABLE AT ABSENCE WILLIE

109. *[mid-October 1932]*   ***William Walton to DMF***

Ascona

Dear Dora,

Thank you so much for your letters, and I'm delighted to hear that all went well, though it is a distinct pity that it should have collided with the Courtauld Concert. The cuttings Hubert sent me seem quite amusing, but are chiefly pre-concert so I hope there will be some more.

I am really very sad at missing the recital, not only for my own songs, and I am sure that it was a magnificent performance. But without doubt, I hope I shall be able to hear them again.

---

169 The first performance of the *Three* (Sitwell) *Songs*, by Dora Stevens and Hubert Foss, at the Wigmore Hall, 10 October 1932.

I must say that when I was sent the programme for the Music Club, I nearly wired you to sing something more dreary. I can feel the shivers now.

What a good thing that the B.B.C. has thought fit to allow Hubert to broadcast on 'B. F.' [*Belshazzar's Feast*].[170] I shall try & listen.

Will you tell him that I will try a[nd] produce a low masterpiece for him, I don't know quite when, but miracles sometime happen.

Imma sends her love. She is getting better slowly & I hope next week that she will be able to go to stay a[t] Pallenza [*sic*] further down the lake in Italy with some rich friends[171] to recuperate.

Meanwhile the symphony shows definite signs of being on the move, a little spasmodic perhaps, but I've managed to get down about 40 bars which for me is really saying something. What hopes for it being completed for April I should hardly like to say.

I should like a pen-picture-post-card of Harriet's goings-on if you've time, now that you will be full of domestic worries. I wish the other Edward Clark[172] would go & do likewise.

It seems a pity that Christopher should so truculently follow in his father's foot-steps & refuse to take the floor. I secretly sympathise with him completely, embarrassing as it may be for you.

So with much gratitude to you both for all the trouble you have taken over those songs, I must now stop.

With love to you both

Yours ever

Willie

170 Broadcast of 2 November 1932, introducing the Queen's Hall concert that included *Belshazzar's Feast* with Adrian Boult conducting the BBC Symphony Orchestra. This was probably Hubert Foss's first broadcast, the first of 547 known broadcasts. See Eleanor Geller's M. Mus. dissertation *A Musician Talks – Hubert Foss's broadcasts (1933–1953)*, University of Southampton, 2010, 321579482.

171 The wealthy Scot, Neil McEacharn, who in 1931 had bought an estate close to Pallanza, on Lake Maggiore, which he transformed into English-styled gardens and renamed *Villa Taranto*. He was later to marry Imma von Doernberg. Today the botanical gardens, which he gave to the Italian state, are open to the public.

172 Edward Clark (1888–1962), conductor and administrator, and later husband of the English composer Elisabeth Lutyens. The Fosses had a manservant also called Edward Clark who had given notice, with his wife, their cook, about this time.

110. *[November 1932]   William Walton to DMF and HJF*

Casa Angolo, Ascona, Tessin/Schweiz.

My dear Dora & Hubert,

Being in dire arrears with correspondence, you will forgive me, I hope, addressing you both. I adored your marvellous description of Harriet's concert & I have destroyed the letter but couldn't find heart to do the same with the drawing which I'm keeping.

I'm sorry the B.B.C. have this uncompromising attitude to your singing my songs. It's fantastic. Do you think it wise if I write a snappy little note to Clark or do you think it too undignified.

I listened to 'B.F.' [*Belshazzar's Feast*] on the Radio from Berlin. It didn't come through too well – in fact I was horrified, but am considerably cheered up at receiving Hubert's letter. From the point of view of 'tempi' I didn't think it too good the slow parts being too slow & the fast being too fast. But I'm glad it wasn't the 'flop' I thought it was going to be. What have the notices been like, rude I suppose.

I heard from various people in Germany, it came through excellently & there is a good notice of it in the Berlin 'B.Z. am Mittag'.

Will you send two copies of the latest edition to bore Hans Reinhart as he still wants to have a go at the german version? Perhaps you might send the songs as well he may try his hand a[t] translating them.

Alles gut

yours

Willie

P.S. I heard Hubert well, & how clear & resonant was his voice. Really what a 'broadcasting' voice should be.

Four letters from Sir Hamilton Harty have been included from this point as they relate to the progress of the symphony.

111. *5th December 1932   Hamilton Harty to HJF*

My dear Hubert

(Aren't we friends? My name is 'Hay').

'Belshazzar' came off quite well at Nottingham – and made its usual sensation. The Chorus – inspired partly by terror – sang much above themselves – and of course, my boys are clever and efficient and dealt faithfully with the Orch. part.

By the way, I am a little troubled and wish you would help me. You know Walton very well, of course – I fear he may have been annoyed by a letter I wrote to him recently in which I rather questioned whether his work needed all the complexity he has given it in order to produce his desired effect.

Anyway, he has not replied to it. The work is certainly one of genius and it may be no other way was possible to him. If you could get it into his head sometime that I am a terrific admirer of his and that – to be frank – I am by no means quite convinced, on reflection, that my point of view is definitely right – it would be good of you, and probably give him a better idea of what I really meant, which was all friendly and all tentative.

Let's keep the L.S.O. pot boiling like mad! I am told you are being a terrific sport about it.

Bless you – and spit on your hands.

> Yours ever,
> Hamilton Harty

112. *[December 1932]   William Walton to HJF and DMF*
Casa Giachetti, Ascona, Tessin, Schweiz

My dear Hubert & Dora,

I know that it sounds unbelievable, but nevertheless it is quite true, that I had just taken up my pen to write to you when the telephone rang & Imma brought in your telegram announcing the glad tidings about Amsterdam. Doubtless you are both as happy about it as we are – it indeed sets, what I believe is understood as, the 'seal' upon it – 'highbrow, lowbrow, rich & poor, one with another' that is undoubtedly the text, at least I hope so. We would get the Queen [of Holland] there, but she hates noise so we shall have to put up with Princess Juliana (a violin virtuoso) instead, that is if Imma can persuade her to come which I understand won't be very difficult. But really, high spirits & joking apart, I think it is good news & I hope that you will ultimately sell your 10th thousand copy. When, by the way, is the Festival? All such questions as to who is singing, conducting etc will be settled later, I presume.

Now I ought to try and excuse myself for not having written you before & thanked you for your two news letters – if I had any adequate excuse I would glibly offer it, but the honest truth is that I hav'ent [sic], except to confess to sheer laziness & a certain shyness to owning up to the sad fact that this .... [sic] symphony is not getting on in the way I feel it should do. You may remember in 'Belshazzar' that I got landed on the word 'gold' – I was there from May to December [1930] perched, unable to move either to right or left or up & down, & I'm now in a similar distressing position, but that it is not such a nice chord (in fact it is only an octave on A) – when I'm likely to move, is I regret to say unknown.

I've written to Harty cancelling the April date & explaining everything, & how delighted I was with his taking so much interest etc. in 'B.F.' & I must say he's behaved beautifully about it & seems to understand perfectly, & we stand on extremely good terms. It is proposed that the Viola Concerto shall be put in instead of the symphony – whether this will actually be I am, till now, uncertain.

I'm delighted that the Manchester[173] & Nottingham performances of 'B.' were so good – I'm sure that Harty is really the man for it.

We spent 10 lovely days in Rome (there is a 70% reduction on everything) & I had hopes that the change would perhaps freshen me up, but alas as I've already said, nothing has happened until now. But in any case whether it might be finished in time for the April date, I consider it wiser to sit on it for some months longer & produce it next season.

I should like to hear your considered opinion on Bax's 4th [symphony] & the new Bliss work. Instinct tells me that with the Bax, we have heard it all before at perhaps even greater length. Harriet told me it was all so gay & just like Beethoven, but perhaps better than that master, but my instinct (or is it predjudice [sic]) tells me otherwise.

It seems that I've no other news. Life is very quiet, & under other circumstances would be positively dull & nothing of any interest happens except continual reminders from jolly old Hans, who is becoming a colossal bore, to say the least.

I enclose the german [sic] cuttings which may be useful for your next bulletin – one, the 'B.Z. Mittag' is very amenable about the B.B.C. & tolerably so about me, the other more so about me.

Imma sends her love & so do I.

> Yours ever
> Willie

113.   *9ᵗʰ June 1933   HJF (Amsterdam)[174] to DMF (Nightingale Corner)*

I rang Willie up: we are meeting at 12 for lunch ... I must do a bit of printing now before Willie comes.

---

173   Hallé Chorus and Orchestra, Sir Hamilton Harty, 17 November 1932.

174   The venue for the 1933 meeting of the Contemporary Music Society, at which Constant Lambert conducted *Belshazzar's Feast*.

114. *10th June 1933   HJF (Amsterdam) to DMF (Nightingale Corner)*

Willie and Constant [Lambert] came to lunch and were most amusing yesterday. We pottered round and had an amusing lunch at an old-fashioned restaurant I know here, and then went on to the Bureau of the 'Feest' and from there to the Rijksmuseum to see the permanent exhibition of Van Goghs – a wonderful sight showing his development from ill-drawn picture postcard stuff – so badly done and dull in subject – through his first French pictures and later to his mind gradually giving way.

Also there is an exhibition of old instruments which is thrilling and Willie behaved abominably of course: beating all the drums in ecstasy and turning a plaque of Richard Strauss to the wall!

Then to the reception – C. and W. going to Rotterdam for an extra chorus rehearsal (of Belshazzar's Feast) – which is held (literally) in a post office! C. says it's like a conductor's nightmare. He was most witty all day ... Willie comes to lunch alone – I want to talk about my book [*Music in My Time*] to him and to see his symphony. Later I must write an article.

Willie's go is tonight. Imma couldn't get away so he's leaving Monday, I think. Everyone very nice here.

All my love, darling,
Hubert

4.30 pm.
The food here is excellent but dear!

Willie is looking thin. He approves such notions as I have for my book, which will not, I gather, conflict with the one Constant is just finishing [*Music Ho!*]. He talked today about whether it was bad for him to be so much away from England, and I told him you thought it was. So he's coming back for six months soon.

I'll write about the symphony tomorrow.

115. *11th June 1933   HJF (Amsterdam) to DMF (Nightingale Corner)*

Darling,

First of all Willie had a huge success last night [*Belshazzar's Feast*]. An ovation and half-a-dozen calls, and so did Constant. I don't think I've ever seen such a success at these Festivals. Casella and Labroca entranced, all the band (many of whom I spoke with) thrilled and so far not one adverse criticism from all whom I asked. A very good performance considering all things. I could hear the words of the choir (sometimes too clearly, as in 'Yee, we wopt'!). Constant did it with enormous drive and rather too fast if anything, but most thrillingly.

The one trouble was lack of contrast in dynamics owing to lack of rehearsal. It was all very exciting.

Harriet came over and made a most horrid fool of herself with Willie who was abominably rude to her. I deeply detest that woman. So does he and so does Constant.

The orchestra was really splendid – so solid and resonant and the hall – a big one – just the right size.

Willie's symphony is most exciting – really on the big scale and in the purest symphonic manner: just like Beethoven and Sibelius and yet very personal. Rather tragic, and the second movement Scherzo really sinister. I think I have persuaded him to use for the slow movement that ravishing idea he played to us ages ago when he was starting the work. It will I really think be a great work and of importance in re-establishing a symphonic ideal other than Brahms's.

His scoring made the other composers sound so muddy!

He was talking about Christopher[175] a lot yesterday and urging me to have him taught the violin soon so as to train his ear early. I agree. What do you think?

116.   *12ᵗʰ June 1933   HJF* (Amsterdam) *to DMF* (Nightingale Corner)

Yesterday I worked all the morning, lunched with Constant and Florence and then we all went out to a garden party at a swell banker's house – rather less grim than it was to be expected. I saw many friends and drank a lot of champagne cup! Last night a rather dull a capella concert and a final talk with Willie. He left this morning and Harriet, thank God, tonight.

On September 20th 1933, my daughter Diana was born. Under doctor's orders I went into the nursing home at 27 Welbeck Street some time before she was due to be born. I had a minute room and on one occasion, a few days before the baby's arrival, I had three visitors at once – Lady Wood, very tall and big, my father [Mr Alfred Stevens], also tall, and Willie, tallest of all, with a huge armful of gladiolas; he had just returned from a year in Switzerland. After Diana was born, he came to see me with Hubert, having been staying with him at Nightingale Corner. He told me he had been going through the last movement of the symphony with Hubert. He was very depressed with its progress, and this mood was rendered even darker by Christopher, then aged five, who, after

---

175   Hubert and Dora's son.

listening for a few minutes to Willie's playing of the new movement, pleaded 'And <u>now</u> play some <u>good</u> music, Uncle Willie.' 'And I expect he's right,' wept Willie!

117.   *13ᵗʰ January 1934   DMF* (en route to and at Nightingale Corner) *to HJF* (Edinburgh)

The concert[176] was very successful and Daddy [Mr Alfred Stevens] thoroughly enjoyed himself. I spoke to Willie, Paddy [Hadley], Arthur Benjamin, John Ireland, Jack Moeran, Phyllis Tate and her mamma, Eric Blom, Florence Lambert and Lady Snowden.

Willie was very nice, but is not looking well – worry and malnutrition, I should think. I saw him before Belshazzar and not afterwards. He had a terrific reception and many recalls and much shouting. Boult did it really pretty well. It seems to be <u>too</u> strong for him to vitiate it. Roy Henderson – much improved – the choir better than it promised by its ghastly performance of The Hymn of Jesus.

Daddy was very agreeable to Willie and patted him on the back!!!

Paddy was a little distrait and distant – he looked very well. I heard him kow-towing to Sir John Reith[177] (who sat alone in the front row giving a poor imitation of Mussolini). Paddy's work was delightful and had a really good reception. I don't think it is a <u>great</u> work, but it is a string of very lovely things.

Ireland was his old pussy self. I liked the concerto, especially the 1933 dressed version of 'We'll to the woods no more'[178] – the beginning I found a little percussive and dry at a first hearing. Helen Perkin played well – and stood no nonsense from Adrian – or so it sounded.

176   Queen's Hall, 12 January 1934. The last of six BBC concerts of British music, with Holst's *Hymn of Jesus*, the first performances of Delius's *Fantastic Dance* and John Ireland's *Legend*, Hadley's *The Trees so High*, Moeran's Rhapsody No. 2 and Walton's *Belshazzar's Feast*. Roy Henderson, Helen Perkin, BBC Chorus and Symphony Orchestra, conductor Adrian Boult.

177   John Reith (1889–1971), founder of the BBC; the first general manager in 1922 of the British Broadcasting Company; and when it became a public corporation its director general 1927–38. Knighted in 1927.

178   John Ireland's Piano Concerto, premiered in 1930 by and originally dedicated to Helen Perkin, a pupil of Ireland's, includes a motif from the composer's Housman song-cycle *We'll to the woods no more*. But it seems that Dora may have confused the Concerto with Ireland's new *Legend* for piano and orchestra that was receiving its first performance at this BBC concert. The Concerto was not on the programme.

You had warned me that The Hymn did not wear well. I found it impressive at a first hearing, but not enormously.

Moeran was there with his mother and brother. I like the 'Rhapsody' but I think it was a mistake to put it after 'The Trees' – even though there was an interval between them. They are both too Folk Song-y to be near each other. He was very nice and pleasant indeed.

Arthur came and talked for some time. He is very jealous of Willie – otherwise he was extremely nice and I was very glad to see him again. He seems very pleased with the success of his violin concerto.[179]

Mrs Tate and Phyllis were charming. I gathered that the 'cello concerto was fairly successful. Peers Coetmore[180] played it much better than in London.

Among others there were V.W., E.E. [Edwin Evans], Constant, Arnold, [Frank] Bridge (just behind us), Sir Hugh [Allen] – nearly next to us, [Cyril] Rootham, Margaret and Thelma Reiss Smith. The female portion of the audience was distinctly drab. Willie was joined at half-time by a young blob of a girl. He didn't seem particularly interested in her – he only wanted a couple of warts on his face to look like an Anglicised and angled Buddha – he wore the same kind of smile!!!

[Same letter] In the afternoon.

Soon after I got home, Willie rang up all unexpected like – to be petted and patted, I suppose. He is delighted with last night's performance and with his reception. He says he doesn't think Boult could do it better and it certainly was the best performance he had heard. He is very pleased with Roy Henderson now. I must say that I was very struck with his new reading. One did feel, last night, that everyone knew his or her bit, and there was none of that sense of extreme difficulty that one felt before.

Willie sent his love to you and wants to see you when he is not ashamed to look you in the face. He is rather frightened of you at the moment, it appears!

We chatted slightly for a bit and I told him I was going to make you take a long weekend off and he at once invited both of us to Towcester. I don't fancy it terribly – the foraging arrangements seem so inadequate. What do you think about it? Anyhow, it was very sweet of him and we must talk it over. I'm not

---

179   Arthur Benjamin's Violin Concerto, dedicated to Walton, was first performed on 29 January 1933, with Antonio Brosa the soloist and the composer conducting the BBC Symphony Orchestra.

180   Peers Coetmore, English cellist who married E.J. Moeran in July 1945. She gave the first performance of Tate's Cello Concerto on 10 January 1934 at Bournemouth, Sir Dan Godfrey conducting the Municipal Orchestra.

sure if it would be a holiday for <u>you</u> to have Willie's woes as a leitmotiv. I told him he had looked like Buddha and he said he had <u>felt</u> like that. He is very thrilled with the News Chronicle notice. Who is the critic? It reads as if written by a complete ignoramus to me.

118.   *15ᵗʰ January 1934   HJF* (**Edinburgh**) *to DMF* (**Nightingale Corner**)

... I greatly revelled in your account of the concert. I know what Willie needs – a great bouncing houri like you to bully him as you do me! (Fury registered at once!) So glad your father liked the show. He could come oftener if he would. Ireland – yes, his pussy self, but the work is a grand bit of stuff as far as I can judge from the score. John told me H.P. [Allen] had improved greatly in strength. Did H P A[llen] talk to you? If not, he oughted to [*sic*]. I liked your description – very libellous and cynical.

As for the holiday, I'm in favour of Towcester – lovely country, an easy drive and company, and not far from Spurling[181] if we want to go over. But I agree about rations – what is the system? Is W. in town for a bit? A night out at home would rid him of his fears, I'm sure.

Towcester for discussion please: I can't decide now.

119.   *6ᵗʰ March 1934   HJF to DMF*

Willie hasn't phoned me but Norman [Peterkin] has, about him – whether to allow the second performance of the Symphony to the Courtauld Sargent Concert. N is dealing with it.

120.   *21ˢᵗ July [1934]   **William Walton to DMF***

Weston, Towcester, Northants.

Dear Dora,

Thank you so much for your letter & the delicious cream.

In spite of having progressed a little with this last movement I feel at the end of my tether & am longing to get off to Denmark for a few days. Actually the food situation will be better on my return as the cook will be back from London.

As a matter of fact I'm not at all sure that I shan't have to begin this movement all over again & only a chance remark of the gardener[']s wife as she brought in the famous ham saved me for [*sic*] destroying it already. 'How pretty your music is getting – it sounds just like a great big band'. Considering that it is more than

---

181   Clement Spurling, head of music at Oundle School.

likely she knows what she likes than I know what I like & perhaps it may be a
piece for the mob at any rate I thought I'd keep it to see what Hubert thinks on
Monday. But on the whole I feel pretty gloomy.

I hope you have enjoyed your holiday in spite of the adjacency of the Bliss's
[*sic*]. I love your description of his studio & of course he is just like a mousta-
chioed cod-fish so he will be in the right environment. I hope it won't make his
music even more watery.

Yours
Willie.

(I had merely described Arthur's studio as being made chiefly of glass and built
on piles in the middle of a wood and said that one felt like a fish in a tank. It
was a lovely place and we had had a very happy day with them!)

121.   *13ᵗʰ September 1934   Hamilton Harty to HJF*

Dear Hubert,

'Ecco! Il Duomo!' as the little Fiesole tailor said to me after the 12th fitting
of the suit he was trying to make for me. (I had, at last, in despair, professed
myself satisfied, and he was as sardonic as he dared). Poor little man – it was
a frightful suit.

I shall not be sardonic, but very thankful when I can say these words to
Willie W. – but the poor boy is right to wait until he is quite satisfied. I do so
hope (and think) it is going to be all right this time.[182]

But what a difficult accouchement! No matter – pass the chloroform – Nurse
– these are the authentic pains!

Yours ever,
Hay.

I'm going to Ireland – back in about a week. Let's drink claret somewhere!

After the first performance of Walton's Symphony [without the last movement]
on December 3rd, 1934, Lady Wimborne gave him a sumptuous supper party at
Wimborne House. It was a never-to-be-forgotten experience. We passed through
a series of ante-rooms till we came to a large salon where we were received by
Lady Wimborne. Huge pyramids and columns of white lilacs and lilies rose from
the floor; champagne cocktails and I got entangled with mine and my handbag

182 The symphony.

trying to shake hands with Lord Wimborne in the middle of this spacious room with no flat space near on which to park my drink. We then moved into the supper room where we sat at a number of round tables. I counted thirty-five guests and seventeen footmen. The tables were massed with yellow roses in silver tankards; we drank soup out of silver plates and ate the most exquisite food.

After supper, we moved into the vast music room, with its fantastically lovely crystal chandeliers lit by hundreds of candles. It was a scene of great splendour and beauty – yet as a <u>party</u>, it was ineffably dull.

Siegfried Sassoon joined Hubert and me and we sat together on a brocaded seat and contemplated the magnificent room and the distinguished company. 'This is Rome before the Fall,' Siegfried Sassoon said.

The second party given by Lady Wimborne to which we were invited was on November 6th, 1935 after the first complete performance of the symphony. This was a much larger affair with a buffet supper, and minor Royalty present. It was regally done and was meant, I suppose, to be a triumphant sequel to the concert, yet it didn't seem to have anything to do with the music. It was just a terrific social occasion. Willie had had a whole page about himself in the *Evening Standard* that day and I remember Mrs Constant Lambert unhappily bemoaning the fact that Constant had no rich patroness to procure him such attentions from the Press. We were able to tell her that it was through Hubert's agency that the newspaper article had appeared and not through aristocratic influence – which somewhat consoled her.

122. *4ᵗʰ December 1934   Hamilton Harty to HJF* [after the first performance of the incomplete symphony]

Dear Hubert,

A thousand thanks for your little note of encouragement to the Queen's Hall.

I was satisfied that what powers I possess were all given to the Symphony the other night. Whether these are powerful or mediocre is not a thing I have any means of judging. One just hopes.

Someday I should like to talk to you about the young man. Enormously gifted – something further has to happen to his soul.

Did you ever notice that nothing great in art has lived that does not contain a certain goodness of soul and a large compassionate kindness? Perhaps he has not noticed it either!

Yours ever,

Hay.

123.   *5ᵗʰ December 1934   Hamilton Harty to HJF*

My dear Hubert,

Many thanks and appreciation of what lay beneath the lines of your letter
– which touched me.

I'd like a good talk with you about WW. All is not well there, I feel. Ring me
and we'll fix something.

(Dear generous Hubert, who is often so bothered by his own worries and yet
so warmly interested in the destinies of his friends!)

Yours ever,

Hay.

124.   *12ᵗʰ December 1934   HJF to DMF*

W's letter is rather a shock.[183] I wrote tactfully to Hay [Harty] about it.

125.   *3ʳᵈ April 1935   Malcolm Sargent to HJF*

12 Wetherby Place, London SW7

My dear Hubert,

How very kind of you to write me such a charming letter. I am naturally
delighted that my performances[184] have pleased you and Willy.

For my part, it was a great privilege to have the opportunity of conducting
anything of his. I have the greatest admiration of his genius and faith in his
powers, and if at any time I can do anything to get his works known, I shall
always look upon it both as a joy and an honour.

I congratulate you for being so far-sighted as to recognise his genius and
help with the publication. I know that this side of your business can never
really be a profitable one.

Yours ever,

Malcolm Sargent

183   Walton's letter, date and recipient (possibly Dora) uncertain, has not been located but it
      quite likely concerned the decision to perform the symphony without its last movement, to
      which Walton reluctantly agreed. Harty had been willing to wait for its completion but the
      London Symphony Orchestra committee pressed for its incomplete performance. Walton
      was now faced with the daunting challenge of writing a finale that lived up to the success
      of the first three movements. As he wrote to Paddy Hadley, it was a 'pit that I've dug for
      myself'. Foss's letter to Harty has also not been located.
184   Sargent conducted two performances of the symphony (still in three movements) at the
      Courtauld-Sargent Concerts on 1 and 2 April 1935.

Fig. 10: The fugue for the last movement of Walton's symphony

126. *9th July 1935   William Walton to HJF*[185]

Weston, Towcester, Northants.

My dear Hubert,

Thank you for your letters & the copy of E[scape] M[e] N[ever].[186] The cover is grand – if only the inside was as good!

The parts are in the possession of B & D[187] & I don't [know] whether they will part [with them].

I've been here some ten days or so & have produced this for the 3rd subject, but am shivering on the brink about it I need hardly say.

[fig. 10]

I may be in London on the 18th for a day or two & then on to Renishaw[188] for the week-end to discuss this ballet question with these Russian people who are coming also.[189] I think it is almost as good as settled that I do it.

Love to Dora and yourself,

yrs

Willie

What about going [with] the enclosed?

Has the score of the first two movements arrived safely? There are still one or two things in the 3rd I've not yet made up my mind about, but will let you have it soon for engraving.

---

185 See plates 24–25.

186 A film directed by Paul Czinner, with music by Walton (his first film). Walton's next three film scores were for films directed by Czinner.

187 British and Dominions Imperial Studios, the production company of *Escape Me Never*. It ceased production in February 1936 when the studios were destroyed by fire.

188 Renishaw Hall, the Derbyshire seat of the Sitwell family.

189 *The Princess Caraboo*, to a scenario based on an idea by Osbert Sitwell, intended for Colonel de Basil's Russian ballet, with music by Walton. It never materialised.

127.   *9ᵗʰ August 1935   HJF to DMF*

Tomorrow I go to tea with Willie – see postcard enclosed – oh, I forgot to complete the Willie story – he is within 1½ minutes of the coda, which is written, so I'm going to hear the great work tomorrow.

128.   *11ᵗʰ August 1935   HJF (Oxford) to DMF (Mundesley)*

After lunch and a suitable interval I drove over to Willie to tea.

Everyone at Weston was perfectly delightful. Sachie most tender about you, and Georgie also. Edith came to tea, as the beginning of her stay and was charming about you. She is going to send you a copy of her new book on Queen Victoria as in her words 'The only thing she can think of to cheer you up!'·

Sachie was dressed in a (dirty) bright yellow open-necked shirt, an old coat and red trousers! Willie in grey flannels and a blue tennis vest, and Edith in a black hat like a mortar board without the stiffening, and a fawn (veal) dress, with enormous jade bracelets and a vast jade ornament on her chest.

Georgia goes to the nursing home on Sept. 7th or so. Reresby[190] was very spoilt and conceited, I thought. He was annoying and Sachie tried to do the heavy father with great failure, Reresby just refusing to go upstairs and defying him.

They couldn't have been kinder than they were to me or to you in message, and the garden looked lovely. They have miniature roses – perfect specimens in every particular but four inches high!

Willie looks and seems very well. You'll be glad to hear that the last movement is nearly complete, only 1½ or 2 minutes to do yet. Apart from the fugue subject, he's actually thought of another idea altogether and is working them all together. I'm delighted with it and think he really will complete in a week or ten days. The next thing is a ballet to a libretto about Bath by Osbert [Sitwell]: I read it and thought it very good. It's for the Basil Ballets. His royalties this year are £96+ – really more than that but there are some deductions for arrangers' fees. Quite good. Far better than Lambert's.

It was a pleasant day and I enjoyed the whole thoroughly.

Oh, Anthony Eden told Osbert Sitwell that there is imminent risk of a war between England and Italy over the Sudan and Abyssinia and that war is expected to be declared early in September. Cheerful!

190   First son of Sacheverell and Georgia Sitwell, born 15 April 1927.

129. *30ᵗʰ August 1935   HJF to DMF* **(Mundesley)**
                                        Nightingale Corner, Rickmansworth

Life is one long round of telephone calls – since I began this second section I've had three! VW, one of them, and also I've just heard that Willie rang up to say he'd actually finished his Symphony! So I've put a call through to him. Isn't that good news?

I've just had Willie on the phone – he seemed pleased about the Symphony and sends his love. I shall see him before I get to you – he gets to Town on Monday.

130. *2ⁿᵈ September 1935   HJF to DMF* **(Mundesley)**
                                        Nightingale Corner, Rickmansworth

Willie comes to tea [at Amen House][191] tomorrow with Symphony.

131. *3ʳᵈ September 1935   HJF to DMF* **[telegram]**

... Hay approves Willie's last movement.

132. *11ᵗʰ November 1935   Henry J. Wood to HJF*[192]
                                        Cumberland Lodge, Ealing Common, W5

Dear Mr Foss,

Unless the price is prohibitive, I should so like to purchase a full score of Walton's Symphony.

I heard it for the first time, last Wednesday night[193] – what a work, <u>truly marvellous</u>, it was like the world coming to an end, its dramatic power was superb, what orchestration, what vitality & rhythmic invention – no orchestral work has ever carried me away so much.

Sincerely yours

Henry J. Wood

191   Simon Wright, '"Willie Comes to Tea with Symphony": Hubert Foss as Walton's Publisher', *Brio* Vol. 37 No. 2, 2000, pp. 2–14.

192   See plate 26.

193   The first performance of the complete work, Queen's Hall, 6 November 1935, Harty conducting the BBC Symphony Orchestra. The first performance of the incomplete work, also conducted by Harty, had been with the London Symphony Orchestra.

133.   *18ᵗʰ November 1935   Percy Scholes[194] to HJF*

Dear Foss

WALTON

I quite understand your being wrapped up for the moment in the sequentials of that great success, and if I don't for the present get full replies on all points shall not grumble.

We here heard the performance very well and were greatly impressed.

I take this opportunity of alluding to an incident of very little importance. A little time ago, in the bar at Queen's Hall, I told Walton and you something that had greatly struck me when I heard the Viola Concerto performed abroad – Guido Adler's[195] coming to me almost 'with tears in his eyes' and saying, in effect, 'Here's the real thing at last!'.

I assumed that Walton and you would know all about Adler, but you didn't and so my recounting the experience seemed to you pointless – if not patronising.

If you will turn up Adler in Grove (or, better still, in Einstein's edition of Riemann's Musiklexicon) you will see the point, such as it is. Here was an old man (then over 75) and perhaps the deepest-read musicologist in the world, whom one might (from his age and from the nature of a good deal of his life's work) suppose to be unlikely to be impressed by the present day work of a younger man and was yet moved by that fine thing to a sort of Nunc Dimittis.

I consider this little passing occurrence to be, in its way, a compliment that a young Mozart or his publisher need not disdain. (Not that you two did disdain it, so far as I know, but you were clearly completely puzzled.)

No need to reply to this letter, the fundamental purpose of which is to congratulate you on being Walton's publisher.

Yours sincerely,

P A S[choles]

194   Percy Scholes. See p. 226.
195   Guido Adler (1855–1941), Austrian critic and musicologist.

134. *[c. 22ⁿᵈ November 1935]   HJF to DMF* **(Mundesley)**

Nightingale Corner, Rickmansworth

Willie still causing trouble – not himself but his symphony. Dates are devilish awkward. We'll scrape through somehow.

135. *[c. 23ʳᵈ November 1935]   HJF to DMF* **(Mundesley) [telegram]**

Nightingale Corner, Rickmansworth

WILLIE'S SYMPHONY RECORDING FIXED DEC. 10TH.[196]

136. *23ʳᵈ November 1935   HJF to DMF* **[telegram]**

WILLIE HAD GREAT SUCCESS AND FINE PERFORMANCE LAST NIGHT[197]

137. *24ᵗʰ November 1935   HJF to DMF*

I finally fixed up with Yeomans (Decca) about Walton's symphony recording – Dec 10th, as I wired you.

I lunched late at the George (Oxford) and arrived in Brum at 5. I rang Willie who wanted to see me. By the time I'd seen him and unpacked, it was time to feed and change and go to the concert which was at the awful hour of 7.45. It really was a magnificent performance [Leslie Heward] – the band is not really full of good players but they went all out for this and pulled it off. The tears were rolling down my cheeks during the Epilogue, and so they were down many others! In some ways it was better than Hay's but not in breadth of experience. The thing that pleased me was the way it gripped the public: Willie had an ovation and the notices (enclosed) are fine.

We go on from the Brum concert. Willie (who luckily refused to dress – I was so glad) took his bows splendidly and was noble all through. Leslie H. threw a small party.

196 The symphony was recorded in Decca's Thames Street studio, near Cannon Street Station, London, on 9 and 10 December 1935. Hubert Foss was the producer and amongst those attending the recording sessions were Constant Lambert, Alan Rawsthorne and Spike Hughes. Foss recalled the occasion in an article in the February 1953 issue of *Gramophone*.

197 In Birmingham, with Leslie Heward conducting the City of Birmingham Orchestra.

138. *26ᵗʰ November 1935   William Walton to DMF* [typed]

56a South Eaton Place, SW1

Dear Dora

Thank you for your letter and the photographs.

I was in Birmingham a few days ago, where I saw Hubert, and we all enjoyed the magnificent performance of the symphony there.

I hope your cure is being less grim.

Isn't it good about the records?

Yours ever,

Willie.

139. *9ᵗʰ December 1935   HJF to DMF* (Mundesley)

Nightingale Corner, Rickmansworth

Recording sessions with Willie's symphony fairly good – I think rather rushed and fussed, and I had to have a few words (which Willie meant but would not say!) with Harty. He became like a lamb after losing his temper. We got five sides down which means seven tomorrow.

140. *12ᵗʰ December 1935   HJF to DMF* (Mundesley)

Nightingale Corner, Rickmansworth

When I met Willie on Tuesday, late for recording session, I asked him how he was. He said – 'I think somebody must have stolen my Eno's!' [Fruit Salts]

141. *['Monday evening'] December 1935   HJF to DMF* (Mundesley)

Nightingale Corner, Rickmansworth

Willie does not type but hires an occasional secretary. We played the last movement on his records – fair. He's being a bit awkward but very nice and sweet-natured about it all.

142. *31ˢᵗ December 1935   HJF to DMF*

Willie's case of wine has turned up – a dozen port – Taylor 1924. An excellent vintage. Now what to do? One of three things:

1. Tell him I'm off port and will he change it?
2. Go to the wine seller and ask him to change it unbeknownst?
3. Put it down (we have no port and it will keep) for occasional use.
    I favour 3.

143.   *1st January 1936   HJF* (London) *to DMF* (Mundesley)

Willie very sweet on the phone this morning. The Cochran ballet[198] is, he says, a 'wow', but the rest of the show has not got a funny line in it, so I fear it may not run in London. But the Ballet will sell alone.

He says he has it from Sam Courtauld that Beecham has gone off to USA with all the Phil. Orchestra's funds, and Sam refuses to pay up, so the LPO is likely to be abandoned! Why trust Beecham anyhow?

Osbert and Willie have sent me a case of wine, I hear. It arrives tomorrow, having been non-delivered at Ricky [Rickmansworth]. Very sweet of them.

144.   *13th January 1936   HJF to DMF* (Mundesley)

I hear that the performance of the WW records by the BBC is to be prefaced by my note verbatim, under my name![199] Lunching with Willie tomorrow. He's been wired to do the overture for the Cochran Show.

145.   *21st January 1936   HJF to DMF* (Mundesley)
                                          Nightingale Corner, Rickmansworth

Poor Willie has suffered through the Sovereign's death – he was to have conducted the ballet (Siesta 1st go-off, Façade and Escape Me Never Ballet[200] as an entr'acte) tonight at Sadler's Wells. Also Cochran has postponed his first night.

---

198 *The First Shoot*, a short ballet in Cochran's revue *Follow the Sun*. The scenario was by Osbert Sitwell, the choreography by Frederick Ashton, and the designer was Cecil Beaton. It opened in Manchester on 23 December 1935, transferring to London on 4 February 1936 after a postponement owing to the death of King George V.

199 Before the symphony had been recorded, Walter Yeomans of Decca had approached the BBC about the possibility of having the records broadcast. The BBC's initial response had been uncertain because of the 'vexed question of broadcasting complete and lengthy works', especially as 'few recorded works are fifty minutes or so in length'.

200 A ballet sequence in the film of the same name, directed by Paul Czinner and starring his wife Elisabeth Bergner. Walton's first film score, it was first shown on 1 April 1935 in London.

146. *[date uncertain]   William Walton* (Ravello)[201] *to DMF* [postcard]

My dear Dora,

The 'geist' of old R. N. [unidentified] has had a fatal effect, ask Hubert re 'In Honour'.[202] It is quite lovely here, but rather hot over 90° in the shade. I feel there was a serious omission in the Coronation honours,[203] surely Harriet should have been created a 'Dame'. I hope that you are getting on well & are better.

Love

W. W.

147. *16ᵗʰ December 1937   William Walton to DMF* [typed]

The Clinic, 20 Devonshire Place, W1[204]

My dear Dora,

Thank you and Hubert ever so much for your telegram and the lovely flowers and present, which have cheered me up no end.

It was a bit grim for the first day or two, but I am much better now. I hope to be out by Christmas after all, as I am getting on much better than they expected, so perhaps you will give me a ring and let me know if you could come and see me some time, as I should be delighted to pass one of the weary hours in your pleasant company.

I do hope Hubert's voice is better – I know what a burden it makes life to lose one's voice.

Yours ever

William

148. *8ᵗʰ January 1938   Thomas Strong to HJF* [on *Athenæum* writing-paper]

49 Coleherne Court, SW5

Dear Foss,

I will put down what I can remember about W. T. Walton but, of course, my memory is not wholly trustworthy, and my intimate acquaintance with W. is long past.

---

201 From the Villa Cimbrone, Ravello, Italy, where Walton wrote much of the Violin Concerto.
202 Probably referring to Walton's choral work *In Honour of the City of London*, first performed at the Leeds Festival (as *Belshazzar's Feast* had been) on 6 October 1937.
203 King George VI was crowned on 12 May 1937.
204 Walton underwent a double-hernia operation.

He was a boy in the choir at our Cathedral: as far as I remember his home was in Lancashire. In those days the six senior boys used to come to my house every Sunday morning after Cathedral, ie about 11.30 am. It began by being a sort of little Bible Class: but they gradually developed the habit of staying till 1 pm and messing about with my books, etc. I think, but am not quite sure, that he used to strum on my piano. It was rather fun for them, because I often had distinguished people staying with me whose autographs the boys used to secure. I remember Lord Rosebery being seized upon in this way. All this was just before the War. I have never quite lost sight of W. but, of course, I do not often see him.

One Sunday, when he was in the Choir, he brought with him a large bundle of music-paper covered with his compositions; he was then about 15. He asked if he might leave them for me to look at and dumped them on the table in my hall. It so happened that the Examinations for music degrees were going on just then and Parry was staying with me. He picked up W's MSS and was interested. I remember his saying 'There's a lot in this chap, you must keep your eye on him'. Soon after this he left Ch. Ch. He had made up his mind to make music his profession and I gave him, I think, introductions at the R[oyal] C[ollege of] M[usic]. But he did not get on with the people there, and I do not know exactly what he did do. I have heard from him from time to time and he has stayed with me more than once at Cuddesdon.[205] But I know very little in details about what he does. I went to hear Belshazzar in London on its first performance there, and he sat next to me. He does not, I think, like conducting; he certainly did not conduct on that night. I had heard of his illness; there was a mention of it, I think, in The Times.

I am quite out of the musical world now and I really do not know what W's position in it may be. I always liked him, and am very glad when I come across him.

Yours very sincerely

Thomas B. Strong, Bp.

He has been, I think, a good deal in Germany.

205   A theological college near Oxford.

149. *[26ᵗʰ January 1938]   William Walton to HJF*

Ashby St Ledgers, Rugby[206]

My dear Hubert

[Walter] Legge[207] writes me that Mengelberg wants scores of the Symphony & Viola Concerto. He leaves on Friday, but you could send them round to Q[ueen's]. H[all]. tomorrow (Thursday) where he's conducting the Phil.

(Also Furtwängler wants the big score of the Symphony as there is an idea that he will do it at his concert of English music in June.[208] C/o Prof J Plesch 40 Hereford House Park Lane will get him.)

'Morning sickness'[209] is beginning, but otherwise not much progress.

Love to Dora & yourself

William

150. *11ᵗʰ May 1938   William Walton to HJF*

Ravello, Prov. di Salerno

My dear Hubert,

This is a letter, which I am writing for the sake of clearing my mind.

In the last fortnight I've had weighty decisions to make & I do hope you will think that I have acted rightly.

What has happened is as follows. About a fortnight ago, Bliss authorised by the British Council, wrote me, for the moment in strict confidence, asking me to write a violin concerto for the concerts at the New York World's Fair adding that three others were being asked, himself for a Pfte Concerto, V.W. for a choral work, & Bax for a orch[estral]. work.[210] Terms being £250 for 1st perf only & no other rights being asked for except maybe the dedication. Also £100 extra for a trip to New York.

---

206 The address of Alice, Viscountess Wimborne, with whom Walton had a very close relationship after parting from Baroness Doernberg. Alice died from cancer in 1948.

207 Walter Legge (1906–79), English impresario and important recording manager, later director of music for ENSA and, in 1945, founder of the Philharmonia Orchestra.

208 In the event it seems that neither Mengelberg nor Furtwängler was to conduct the symphony.

209 Referring to the Violin Concerto.

210 Bliss's Piano Concerto, Vaughan Williams's Five Variants of *Dives and Lazarus* (not a choral work) and Bax's Seventh Symphony. These were all premiered in June 1939 at Carnegie Hall, with Sir Adrian Boult conducting the New York Philharmonic-Society Orchestra. Walton's Violin Concerto, which had been intended for the same concert, was not performed until December, at Cleveland (Ohio), with Artur Rodzinski conducting.

I replied in the affirmative, stipulating that Heifeitz [*sic*] should play 1st perf. The B.C.'s terms not clashing with Heifeitz, I felt I could try & kill 2 birds with one stone, for he can do whatever he likes about [it] after the 1st perf. (I've not heard that the B.C. will accept H, or demand a British violinist).

This I felt settled the American question which has been worrying us previously & knocks out any 'In honors' etc.

Everything in the garden seemed lovely & I settled down to it, determined to undertake nothing else till it was finished. And knowing what I'm like it is not any too much time.

Next occurs a telegram 'Please undertake music "Pygmalion" film terms £550 guineas.' I answer 'no'. This started last Thursday & has been going on ever since, Pascal the producer not taking 'no' for an answer.[211]

It takes too long to describe the temptations being in front of me, the telephone calls (I might be Garbo) but I've persisted in saying no.

The most difficult one to refuse is the offer of the next two pictures at the same if not a higher price. Which means refusing £1,650 within the next 12 months. But to accept would mean refusing the American offer, for I should have to return now, & there is about 30 mins music in this film & it is going to take a month to get through, & at least one other film would be ready by Xmas & that would mean another month – quite apart from the distraction & settling down again to the V.C.

But as I say I've turned it down. Whether it is a wise decision I am in some doubt. Consider the B.C.'s american proposition again, financially what with what I shall get from Heifeitz, I'm not much out of pocket if it concerned this one film only.

But there are other doubts as well. Heifeitz may not like the work, he may have other dates & be unable to play. This I've not yet had time to find out, & at any rate H. is hardly likely to commit himself until he has seen at least part of the work & at the moment there doesn't seem much to show him.

Of course I suppose in the case of H. refusing, I can always find someone else, but it would be bad, I think for the work.

What, however, seems to me the greatest drawback is the nature of the work itself. It seems to be developing in an extremely intimate way, not much show & bravura, & I begin to have doubts (fatal for the work of course) of this still

---

211 The Hungarian producer Gabriel Pascal had approached Walton for a score for a film of G.B. Shaw's *Pygmalion*, but Walton was too busy with the Violin Concerto to accept. He did, however, later agree to provide a score for a film of Shaw's *Major Barbara* which appeared in 1941. Pascal held the film rights to Shaw's plays.

small voice getting over at all in a vast hall holding 10,000 people. Whether my original plan to have the 1st perf. with Courtaulds in the 1939–40 at Q.H. is not the best after all. At least there would be some in the audience who would know what I was talking about. In fact, under the american conditions, however good the work may turn out to be, I can't see it being a justifiable success at that particular perf. & that means the end of it, & of most of my works in America for some time to come.

Anyhow I think I can leave the idea of refusing the american perf. for a little while, at any rate till the end of July.

But as it is, it all boils down to this, whether I'm to become a film composer or a real composer.

I need hardly say that noone likes refusing the prospect of £1,650, but on the other hand, with the OUP subsidy, my old royalties, and P.R.S. dues etc and what I've got of my own, I am fairly alright for the moment. In fact I think I can safely wipe out films, which have served their purpose in ennabling [sic] me to get my house etc.

Nevertheless I should like your approval & views especially on the american question. Even if I come to refuse that I believe I'm right about the film decision. Sorry to bother you with such a long letter.

Love to you both
William.

151.   *[end of May or June 1938]   William Walton to HJF*

My dear Hubert,

I am so sorry to have been so long writing to you, but I have been undergoing the usual travail & have dropped at last the 1st movement. Not too bad.

Having been bitten by a tarantula a rare & dangerous & unpleasant experience I have celebrated the occasion by the 2nd movement being a kind of tarantella 'Presto cappriciosamente alla napolitana'.[212] Quite gaga I may say, & of doubtful propriety after the 1st movement – however you will be able to judge.

I return about July 5th having let my house till thereabouts.

I am most distressed to hear about Dora & do so hope that she has made a good recovery. You must have been having a bit of a time of it what with that & the ISCM etc.[213]

---

212 The second movement of the Violin Concerto, actually marked 'Presto capriccioso alla napolitana', is an example of Walton trying to match Heifetz's virtuosic style of playing.

213 International Society for Contemporary Music.

I will let you know as soon as I'm back & we will meet.

With best love to you both & looking forward to seeing [you] again.

Yours ever,

William

152.   *2nd August [1938]*   **William Walton to DMF**

Ashby St Ledgers, Rugby

My dear Dora,

I am most touched by your kind thought of sending some flowers to my mother and for offering to go & see her. It really is too kind of you & I am most grateful as I am sure she is.

She seemed to be on the improve already when I left her and in good spirits. With love to you both & ever so many thanks again.

Yours ever

William

P.S. Would you ask Hubert to send Massine[214] at Drury Lane min. scores of Symphony and Façade I.

153.   *14th December 1938*   **DMF to HJF (Canada)**

60 Corringham Road, NW11

Alan [Frank] had a long telephone talk with William who hopes to finish the Violin Concerto by the end of Jan. He is doing some film work which is holding it up. I expect you'll hear all details from Alan. I gather the work won't be played (if it is) in NY till June – late – and Heifetz is still being prima donna-ish!!

154.   *18th January 1939*   **DMF to HJF (USA)**

60 Corringham Road, NW11

Pause – telephone – William rings up to say he is 'stuck' but plans to get the goods posted to you about Feb 1st. He says his difficulty is making the last movement elaborate enough for Heifetz to play it. He says he will never write a commissioned work again. He is at Rugby and did not come up for the première

---

214 Léonide Massine (1896–1979), Russian-born dancer. Massine had choreographed ballets to Tchaikovsky's Symphony No. 5, Brahms's No. 4, Beethoven's No. 7 and Berlioz's *Symphonie fantastique*.

of the Bergner film 'Stolen Life'[215] – he asked me to go and see it and let him know what I thought of the music – so I'll try and get there next week with Helen Sandeman. He says he will come and play the concerto to me as soon as it is done and will ring me up. I'm longing to hear it.

155. *2ⁿᵈ February 1939   DMF to HJF* **(USA)**

60 Corringham Road, NW11

Helen and I met Ella [Hackworth][216] at the Plaza and we all saw *Stolen Life* the new Bergner-Walton film. It is a good entertainment in its way. I've never seen Bergner as good before – the photography is fine – mountain and sea scenes are superb. The hero very passable, but the story very unconvincing and several parts completely unbelievable, but with a little common sense introduced, the story could have been made almost credible. However, although Helen was so moved by the story as to be unable to hear the music, I was harder-boiled and managed to take in a lot. It is first class cinema music – and by that I mean that it is streets ahead in quality of any I've heard, but still fills the bill. It is very very Waltonesque and as I said in my 'report' to him, 'I thoroughly enjoyed meeting some old friends, so to speak!!' Bits of the Symphony etc. The storm movement is fine – I wonder if it all could be resolved into a suite?

156. *4ᵗʰ February 1939   DMF to HJF* **(USA)**

60 Corringham Road, NW11

William for the best part of an hour on the telephone. I want to try and remember what he said as a lot is significant. He feels Heifetz won't do the Concerto – he's a bit 'off' Szigeti who 'whines' – Kreisler is W's latest idea – a sort of repetition of the Elgar Concerto triumph in his later years. William isn't at all pleased with the last movement – says it wants two months' more work – Brosa[217] not very enthusiastic – William repeats that he will never work to commission again. I asked what he was planning next. He said he was going to learn composition and start on Chamber music, beginning by a duet, a trio,

---

215 The last of four films directed by Paul Czinner and starring Elisabeth Bergner, for which Walton supplied the music. The others were *Escape Me Never* (1935), *As You Like It* (1936) and *Dreaming Lips* (1937).
216 Ella Hackworth, pianist and friend of the Fosses; Diana's godmother.
217 Antonio Brosa, who had played on the soundtrack of the film *Dreaming Lips*, gave Walton some advice on the Violin Concerto. Brosa was to give the first performance of Britten's Violin Concerto in America in March 1940.

a quartet and so on, but <u>not</u> unaccompanied violin! He is telling Heifetz that <u>if</u> he does it, he (William) will go over any time after Ap 1st and hold his hand while he learns it etc.

He'd been to the Bergner film last night and said you could hardly hear most of the music. (I must say <u>I</u> didn't hear 27 minutes of music). He says he has had two more offers of film music as a result of it. He says he'll be terribly busy now orchestrating the concerto – he says if Kreisler should do it, he'd have to alter it a bit – some parts, I gather, really only playable by Heifetz. I tried to cheer him up about the concerto and said in farewell, 'Anyhow, I'm sure it's better than anyone else could write' (or something like that) and he said breezily 'Oh, I've <u>no</u> doubt about that' which was so typically William. He said a great deal you know – Heifetz's fee etc., and he talked politics for hours. He is very anti-Jew au fond. Thinks that they <u>do</u> want war and that <u>they</u> create the 'jitters' that the ultra-left intelligentsia get. He says that they have got a German 1924 out-look – completely démodé. He says he can't afford to be rude to the Jews as they are so powerful musically (or to that effect). He says he thinks it's a menace all the German Jewish musicians that are coming in the country and taking work from Christians etc., etc.[218]

He hopes to come up for a couple of days the weekend after this next one, so he says he will try and play me the work then.

I've tried to remember what he said – it's very unconnected – what I've written.

Oh, he says it's the first piece of <u>bad</u> music he's written. I <u>do</u> hope he's mistaken, but I do feel he is so detached that he can really judge his own work.

157.   *3rd March 1939   DMF to HJF* (Glasgow)

60 Corringham Road, NW11

William telephoned at length all about Heifetz having cabled 'accept enthu-siastically'. He wants to see you at once! I've told him to write to you at Glasgow. He's terribly excited.

218 Anti-Jewish sentiment is evident nowhere else in Walton's correspondence. Speaking at
      length to a close friend may have brought to the surface feelings that were uppermost in his
      mind relating perhaps to incidents of which he was aware while living on the continent.

158. *[15ᵗʰ May 1939]   William Walton to HJF* [postcard with a picture of the *Normandie*]

SS *Normandie*

Arrive tomorrow after a very good passage in this miracle of a ship.
    Love to you both,
    W[219]

159. *[postmarked 6ᵗʰ June 1939]   William Walton to HJF* [postcard with picture of Empire State Building]

Shall be back possibly before you get this. All news when I see you both.
    W

160. *17ᵗʰ December 1954   William Walton to DMF* [typed]

Lowndes Cottage, Lowndes Place, London SW1

Dear Dora,
    It was kind of you to write such a nice letter about 'Troilus and Cressida'.[220]
I am touched to hear that you were there and that you saw the work on your
own and on Hubert's behalf.
    With love to you all from us both,
    Yours ever
    William

161. *25ᵗʰ February 1978   William Walton to Diana Sparkes*

***La Mortella*, Forio d'Ischia, Italy**[221]

Dear Diana,
    Thank you [very] much for your letter telling me about the death of your
mother. I am pleased to hear that the end was peaceful, for when I knew her
she was always, or nearly always suffering from T.B which in those days afflicted
her, and I am happy to hear that she lived to such a great age as 84 and that she
was still capable of being her old self.

---

219   Walton sailed to America, accompanied by Alice Wimborne, to see Heifetz so that the solo
        part of the Violin Concerto could be shaped to the violinist's liking.
220   The first performance of Walton's opera *Troilus and Cressida* was given at Covent Garden
        on 3 December 1954, conducted by Sir Malcolm Sargent.
221   William and Susana Walton's permanent home, on Ischia. They had made the island their
        home in 1949.

Living here practically always, I did not see so much of her as I should have liked as our stays in England were always very short & were so overcrowded with affairs. I am fairly well, but disliking old age greatly & not in fact suffering it gladly. Who does I'd like to know.

I am pleased to see my name on the service sheet, as you know, both your father & mother were so kind & helpful to me in my early days.

With best wishes from us both,

Yours very sincerely,

William

Walton died on 8 March 1983. Further correspondence from Walton, after Hubert Foss's death, is included in the Tribute section: letter 267, p. 243.

Charles Williams

HUBERT KNEW CHARLES WILLIAMS for many years, as Charles had already been on the staff of the Oxford University Press for some time when Hubert went there. My own first meetings with him were in connection with the production of the first of the Masques which he wrote for the Amen House staff. This Masque, *The Masque of the Manuscript*, was first performed on 28th April 1927.[222] Hubert wrote the music for it, simple and tuneful for the greater part. A song, *The Carol of Amen House*, difficult, both musically and vocally, was interpolated, and I was asked to sing this. I do not know if Hubert asked Charles to write this carol or if it was part of the original scheme of the Masque. If he <u>did</u> write it especially for me, it was a great and understanding kindness to both of us, as it brought me into the world of Amen House. I did not appear before the audience, but sang from behind a screen. Charles and everyone else treated me with the greatest friendliness, and I was never made to feel an intruder. I am just called 'the singer' in the tiny programme.

Hubert had no mean part in the Masque. As Master of the Music, he not only composed it, but played it and even sang some of it. None of the performers was a musician, so the vocal line had to be essentially extremely accessible, using nursery rhyme tunes (e.g. *Baa baa black sheep*), and basic original melodies. By accompanying them with ingenious and varied harmonies, there was no sense of monotony. (It is interesting to note that during the rehearsals and performances of a revival of the Masques in 1955,[223] the very musical participants adored the music, as did the audience.)

Charles Williams wrote the following poem for me, incorporating the names of some English songs which were among my repertoire:

> Into <u>my own country</u> (a)
>> when <u>the galliass</u> (b) brings me home
> to <u>Yarmouth Fair</u> (c) or Sussex
>> from <u>Rioupéroux</u> (d) to Rome

---

222 Both Masques were privately printed in 1997.

223 At St Anne's House, Soho. In 1998 the Masques were once again performed, at the OUP in Oxford, to great acclaim, to celebrate the seventy-fifth anniversary of the OUP Music Department.

I shall hear <u>the jolly carter</u> (e)
    beside <u>the windmill</u> (f) go
and a <u>sleep</u> (g) song and a <u>laughing song</u> (h)
    under the <u>green willow</u> (i)

<u>When I am dead, my dearest</u> (j)
    and no <u>gavottes</u> (k) prolong
<u>O cam' ye by</u> (l) or cam' ye not
    I shall have my own <u>dream song</u> (m)

C W 15 June 1926

a) Peter Warlock	b) Norman Peterkin
c) Peter Warlock	d) Hubert J. Foss
e) E.J. Moeran	f) R. Vaughan Williams
g) Peter Warlock	h) Gordon Jacob
i) Gordon Slater	j) John Ireland
k) Herbert Howells	l) [Benjamin Burrows ?]
m) Roger Quilter	

Hubert loved Charles dearly and had an enormous admiration for him and his poetry, though he owned he could not follow Charles's mind into the mysteries wherein he was completely at home. The affection was mutual.

162. *26ᵗʰ January 1927*   ***Charles Williams to HJF***
Amen House, Warwick Square, London EC4

My dear Foss,

Yes – but 'what was the hat of Foss doing on the head of the black man from Borneo?' That is what I wanted to know, and Phillida – the others don't read Edgar Wallace, being highbrows. Foss, of course, wasn't a nice man, though a cinema-scenario-editor, and his name was Lawley Foss,[224] though that was no doubt a blind; there can't be two Fosses of any standing.

Your relations – certainly, but I don't feel that they are likely to be so fascinating.

However I found out, I won't stop to tell you yours because it's all very long and complicated, and Mr Lawley Foss was decapitated by the descendants of

---

224 A character in Edgar Wallace's thriller *The Avenger (The Hairy Arm)*, first UK publication 1926. Lawley Foss meets his death by decapitation, and the story also features an orangutan.

the hereditary executioners of France in an underground cave, but as he had a sinister connection with Sir Gregory's ourang-outang [*sic*] and stuck bits of white paper on the windows of an 'extra', before he was more or less petrified by dropping water, and that was before the black man went or was going back to Borneo, whence he had come with a large sword, but not the sword that decapitated Foss – not that Foss suffered by a sword at all, no – that was all Mr Wallace's guile – and the policeman married the 'extra'. All most satisfactory. I do like my Edgar Wallace.

But let us return to our sheep. 'My dear Foss! O my dear Foss!' (as my admired H.C. Bailey[225] says) – I really do admire you, I really do admire you, I really do admire you, I really do admire you, I ... but I cease. If that doesn't convince you, nothing will. How much more clever you are than I! How much more adaptable! How much more talented! How much ... etc. So far as I have studied your notes, I find – with a delight almost superhuman – that they reinforce my own vague ideas.

Honestly. I think you are a noble and beautiful character. A little wooden-necked, perhaps, a trifle insistent. But I do not tread on your tail at present.

The date won't be fixed till your return – so it shall give you plenty of time to deal with your immediately more important matters before you turn to us. God bless you.

I await your verbal statements about America with interest, if you can make them. I have written a tragedy for Balham and a Shakespeare frame-work for the City of London Literary Institute. My own Shakespeare – a nice pleasing verse-writing creature. For the 23rd of April. You must come and see five minutes of it.

Always yours,

Charles Williams

---

225   H.C. Bailey (1878–1961), English writer of crime stories.

Charles enjoyed composing poems about his friends. Here are two he wrote for
Hubert who played the parts of The Master of Music and Thyrsis in *The Masques*.

TO THYRSIS – ON HIS BOOK ON PRINTING

Thyrsis, when in the night I lie awake,
considering, somewhere about half-past two,
          how very many things my friends can do,
          and what intelligential marvels make;
doubtful if in the end my small heart ache
          wholly with wonder or with envy too,
          I come at last to meditate on you,
and then, content, myself to sleep betake.

For envy, Thyrsis, needs similitude
          to work on; no similitude is here;
what, 'twixt a room with candlelight endued,
          and the large sky, illumined far and near,
where you in your activities are seen,
Phosphor and Hesper and all the stars between?

                                        C W 19 March 1927

Across the fosse, my Foss, that parts this world
          from that of colour and disposed light
in movement by no rough displeasure swirled
          to eddies of confusion and affright;
across the ditch where fantasy enisled
          presents some lovely and melodious thing,
where snow and wolves pretend to haunt the wild
          (itself pretended), whence the sleigh bells bring
new joy, new love, new laughter, and new song,
          too swift to tire, too aery-sweet to cloy,
and a fair wrath is posed but to prolong
          new song, new laughter, new love, and new joy:
across this fosse who lets the drawbridge down?
          who but yourself, my Foss, and charms the town?

They had a relationship in which Hubert loved and accepted all Charles's gentle and not-so-gentle mockery as demonstrations of affection, as indeed they were. He wrote the following verse in appreciation of his friend:

CHARLES WILLIAMS

But does he really only *talk*,
to hardening ears that do not listen?
Those gestures, that impatient walk,
the tilting of the chair, are they
not mannerisms, while the ray
of changing-coloured thoughts that glisten,
sparkle resplendent, iridesce,
through all the London Business,
uplift condensed accounts, and blow
the sombre sales-sheets to and fro,
lightens our book-strewn path of care,
pouring the health of sun and air
on Amen House, distilling rare
and beautiful gleams in Warwick Square,
and on us humble groundlings there?
And if he talks thus, is it wrong?
My children, we must change our song.
If his is talk, then ours is chat,
finicking scraps of this and that,
of weather, rations, the new hat
Miss X was wearing, mouse and cat,
spider and fly, nurseling and brat,
the relative joys of house and flat –
anything, so the words come pat.

The wisdom of sure judgement, sane
and laughing toil for daily fee,
a mind of books that manages
(earthly) to keep the ideal plane,
words to construct his images
flooding reports, reviews, his pearled

verse, and his letters equally –
stintless, he offers us his world.

Talk on, my friend, so that you may give
my thoughts your radiance, and I live.

                                                    Hubert Foss

Charles was unique. If I say he radiated goodness – it sounds priggish – and he never gave any impression of priggishness, but there was an aura around him that seemed to embrace everyone. In appearance he was tall and gracefully angular.

Apart from writing the music to the *Masque of the Manuscript*, Hubert wrote the music for the second Masque, the *Masque of Perusal*. Again, unsophisticated music, but extraordinarily effective. This Masque was performed in 1929 when I was recovering from TB. Hubert's letters to me at Mundesley Sanatorium in the early part of 1929 are full of references to the rehearsals.

Hubert's other literary connections with Charles were in the production of the beautiful edition of *Heroes and Kings* which Hubert designed, and which was published by the Sylvan Press. It was bound in scarlet coarsely-woven silk and stamped with a golden design of a crown surmounting an archway from which, apparently, is suspended a sword, and illustrated with wood-engravings by Norman Janes.[226] Later Hubert wrote a set of Shakespearean songs to be sung in Charles's *A Myth of Shakespeare*.

163. *30ᵗʰ July 1929   Henry Hadow to HJF*

                                    The Grange, Ecclesall, Sheffield

Dear Foss,

Very many thanks for this most interesting book.

I delight in the 'Myth of Shakespear[e]' – indeed I don't mind confessing that I hear some of his music in the verse. I hope that it will have a wide success. It ought, among other offices, to be of great use to schools and colleges at their annual festivities.

I shall be proud to see the Shakespear[e] songs when they are ready.

Yours ever

W.H. Hadow

226 Norman Janes (1892–1980) was a well-known watercolour artist and a close friend of Dora and Hubert Foss.

Charles was unmusical,[227] that is to say, he had no knowledge of its technical processes. It did not really interest him. He probably could not recognise a tune if he heard it a second time, but he was not impervious to it. In 1930, he and his wife Michal came to see us at Nightingale Corner, and we played and sang (probably among other things) Hubert's settings of Blake: *Infant Joy*, *As I walked forth* and *Nurse's Song*. These two poems he sent us later, and on reading them even now, I feel wonder and gratitude to Heaven that we – and Blake – should have been able to evoke such intensity of experience in Charles's mind.

TWO POEMS   3 JUNE 1930
FOR DORA AND HUBERT FOSS

I

Blake and you and the song and light
    of the sky amid dark trees;
I saw Blake go by in the night,
    as a friend his friend sees.

His forehead was as the topmost sky,
    full, strong and clear therewith
as the voice that sang while he went by,
    his eyes upon his myth.

Outside the window I saw him pass
    in the music I there looked on.
Half he glanced in through the glass
    as he went by, and was gone.

But the whole room was full of Blake
    and you and a voice and the light
which did not yet the heaven forsake,
    being in the song and the height.

II

How lovely music is!
All the fair animals of the forest came

---

227   He called himself 'The One-Eared Man' in an article he wrote for *The Dominant*, 1 December
    1927, p. 11.

running before a flame.
There was a fire in a forest; this
nor saw I nor felt –
but herd by herd, company by company,
beautiful things broke audibly:
the fair birds flew,
the fair beasts poured forth leaping in me,
toward the temporal hut wherein my heart had dwelt.
Hastily it withdrew,
fearing the overthrow of walls and roof,
hastily aloof.
All in a wonder, a grace of sound,
wild and ordered, fierce and controlled,
broke the quick-rushing movement around.
I was rapt to behold
the lives, the forest lives, the lives of my life,
forgetting their strife,
surge towards the hut that was once a heart; but O
as it shook to its overthrow,
all stayed, all vanished, all ceased.
Bird and beast,
diverse multitudinous lives that came
hurrying, hurrying, hurrying from the flame
in the forest beyond my heart,
all that my thought spied
in the great incantation, the magical art,
vanished; the music died.

Charles Williams

When the OUP moved in 1939 to Southfield House in Oxford [see p. 41], Hubert and his depleted staff shared a converted bathroom with Charles and his staff for about eight months until Hubert went back to London. I remember a thrilling 'reading' of *The Doctor's Dilemma* in Bartlemas, the house we had rented. I also remember an evening at Lady Margaret Hall when Charles recited Shakespeare and I sang English songs – to a small audience. I had not heard him recite – publicly, at any rate, before, and he made me completely lost to the outside world for the time. An experience never to be forgotten.

164. *9th December 1941   Charles Williams to HJF* [typed]
OUP, Southfield House, Hill Top Road, Oxford

My dear Hubert,

I have owed you a letter for so long that I am ashamed to think of it. But my son has been swept into the Air Force and we have been rather rushing about and that has confused everything. Now your second letter makes me still more ashamed and I hasten to thank you. I am very glad you liked the poem. It was written for an old lady here, a friend of mine, but it does not, I think, for all that, express more than I really think. If I had been given the opportunity when I was much younger I should have loved music, but I shall never have time to settle to it now.

Your other letter affected me very strongly. I am very sorry that all these difficulties have cropped up – very sorry indeed, with a purely personal regret. Few things have been more agreeable to me in this odd place than your companionship, and tiresome though we must both have been to each other on many occasions it is, I think, true that that tiresomeness never became serious. Which is much more than I should care to say about those of my colleagues whose existence I can be said to be conscious of. We shall, I hope, see each other soon in London, or here if you are down. At any rate it would be against all my own instincts to let you go so easily.

Yours always,

C. W.

Hubert was deeply grieved when Charles died, and in later years I heard him say many times, 'If only Charles were here, I would ask him ...'

Henry J. Wood

IN JULY 1927 HUBERT WAS INVITED by Sir Henry Wood to have lunch with him and his wife and family at their home at Chorleywood in Hertfordshire. The Oxford University Press was shortly to publish Sir Henry's *The Gentle Art of Singing* in three volumes and he was anxious to discuss at leisure various details regarding publication and publicity with Hubert.[228]

The day suggested was the Sunday before our wedding. Without telling him this, Hubert said the day had been promised to me, whereupon the invitation was at once and with the greatest kindness extended to me.

On that Sunday, July 17th, Hubert and I met at Baker Street Station at midday and before one o'clock we were climbing up the hilly side of the Chorleywood Common on a gloriously hot and sunny day. We found our way to Appletree Farm House, which we approached through a garden blazing with flowers.

(In retrospect, the Appletree garden seemed always, save in the depths of winter, to be glowing with the largest, most brilliant and quite perfect flowers. In spring with sheets of daffodils and bluebells; roses and madly tall and exotic lilies in the summer, followed by the most gorgeous dahlias and I particularly remember scores of golden roses literally shining in the misty early October morning, seemingly tied together with tinsel cobwebs.)

We were welcomed with great warmth by Sir Henry and Lady Wood[229] – Sir Henry small, rather plump, with merry twinkling blue eyes was obviously delighted to see Hubert. Lady Wood, tall and dignified and a little awe-inspiring at first sight, introduced their daughters, Tania and Avril, then about fourteen and twelve years old. We were then introduced to Dame Ethel Smyth, the one other guest, who loudly and with cheerful heartiness demanded cocktails.

After drinks in the small drawing-room we had lunch in the hall and I have no recollection whatsoever of the conversation during that time. With Sir Henry, Dame Ethel and Hubert there, there must have been a great deal. However, after lunch Sir Henry insisted on playing tennis and we played several sets. Sir Henry was a strong and wildly inaccurate smash hitter, revelling in his strength and blithely unconscious, apparently, of any need for keeping the

---

228 Much later Hubert wrote a Prefatory Note for Henry Wood's *About Conducting*, Sylvan Press 1945.

229 Godmother to Diana Sparkes (née Foss).

ball in court. Hubert was a somewhat similar type of player, though far less strong, far less enthusiastic. Tania and Avril were moderately good schoolgirl players and I was, though a more orthodox performer than Hubert, anything but brilliant. As an exhibition of lawn tennis it must have been abysmal – but it was terrific fun. We took it in turns to sit out and I remember as if it was yesterday Sir Henry and Hubert dashing about and the girls laughing and the sun shining – and I was watching them – all of us, for the moment, completely carefree and happy.

Hubert and I returned to my parents' house that evening feeling we had not only met a great man and musician, but had been accepted by him and his wife and family as friends.

On the following Wednesday [20 July 1927] Hubert and I were married. After a few days at Hawkhurst in Kent, we went to Luxembourg. First to the capital itself, then to Vianden, a beautifully situated little town with a river winding between wooded hills, and there I received my first letter which began 'Dear Mrs Foss'! It was from Lady Wood. We had not told her our wedding day was so near, but on seeing the announcement in the papers she at once wrote with great warmth and kindness to me. Sir Henry, later, sent Hubert a travelling clock[230] which accompanied him all over the Continent, many times to America, and it lived in his study at home. [It is now owned by Mrs Norah Foss.]

In October 1927, Vol. I of Sir Henry Wood's monumental collection of singing exercises and instructions, *The Gentle Art of Singing* was published by the Oxford University Press and he writes to Hubert on October 3rd:

165. *3rd October 1927*   **Henry Wood to HJF**
                                       Appletree Farm House, Chorleywood, Herts.
Dear Mr Foss,

   I am more than satisfied and delighted with Volume I of the *Gentle Art of Singing*; it is charmingly produced and I am eternally grateful to you for the pains and trouble you took for so many months past, in bringing this about. I only hope you and your firm will be rewarded financially.

   Only got back last night from Belfast, leaving tonight for Glasgow, so looking [forward] to your little dinner party on Thursday night.

   Sincerely yours,

   Henry J. Wood

230   See plate 14.

The Thursday night to which Sir Henry referred was an ordeal – in antici-pation for me, as a very inexperienced housewife. I was lucky enough to have a maid, and a retired parlour-maid of my mother's came to wait on us, so all went well on the domestic side.

Our other guests were Dorothy Helmrich,[231] the very charming Australian mezzo-soprano, and Arthur Benjamin, then known far better as a pianist than as a composer, Australian too.

The party was a success and though I [look] back on it without remembering any salient detail, I can still feel the warmth and kindliness extended to Hubert and me by all our guests. My main recollection is a ridiculous one – we had a fruit cocktail consisting of Muscat grapes in liqueur – maraschino, I think it must have been – and I can see myself now endlessly peeling them and feeling I should never get them done in time.

A few days later, Lady Wood herself arrived with armsful and armsful of the most superb chrysanthemums and dahlias from her garden. It was a sweet and generous gesture to a newly-married woman and was only the first of innumerable kindnesses that we received from her in later years.

Muriel Wood was not an easy person to know. She appeared austere and aloof at first sight, but Hubert and I were allowed, for some reason, behind the barriers of her reserve, and we loved her for her thoughtfulness for us and for her loyal friendship, and we revelled in her slightly acid wit and her sprightly and discerning comments on the many and varied people who crossed her path. We admired her too for her unswerving devotion to her husband and all his activities.

166. *16th February 1929   HJF to DMF* (Mundesley)

I am sending you a letter from Lady Wood which I am duly answering, probably tomorrow. That is to say if not tonight, then certainly tomorrow. Very sweet of her. I shall probably send you a copy of my letter. I leave you to judge whether a pretty little note from you would do good. HJW so loves me that I'd like to cement the friendship as much as possible. I think it most nice of her. She's

---

231 Hubert Foss accompanied Dorothy/Dorothea Helmrich in recordings of Schumann's *Du bist wie eine Blume* and Brahms's *Auf dem Schiffe* in the 'Columbia History of Music by Ear and Eye' devised by Percy Scholes. See Discography, p. 269.

quite a dear if a little over-inflated and he's just lovely. I do hope he gets made a member of my dining club.[232] Harty, you remember, is bringing him as a guest, which is a necessary preliminary of membership.

167. *7th April 1929   HJF to DMF* (Mundesley)

Yesterday was very nice. I lunched with Claude [Lippman][233] and caught the 2.40 to Chorleywood. HJW was taking a piano rehearsal of *The Apostles* with Horace Stevens and stuck at it (playing himself all the time!) till about 5.00. Then we had tea and then HJW devoted himself to me.

Of course everyone was frightfully nice about you, and they sent messages, and will look for houses for us and do anything that is wanted. I told Lady Wood all about things at Mundesley, and Sir Henry too. Lady Wood ended up by inviting [us] there for the day as soon as you were fit to go and said she'd insist on your resting the proper amount of time.

Our talk was really very satisfactory – he gave me lots of information which was most useful and good and I greatly enjoyed the sun and air. It is a lovely place. I should really very much like to live there. I really cannot retail all the stuff he gave me – five pages of notes in my book.

I had developed TB after my son Christopher's birth in May 1928, and had to spend the following winter and spring at the Sanatorium at Mundesley in Norfolk. I returned to Hampstead where we stayed for two months in a hotel and later for a month with my parents in Redington Road. On medical advice we looked for a house on gravel soil and had some difficulty in finding a suitable one. The house agent eventually persuaded us to look at a house at Rickmansworth. It seemed far too large for our needs, judging from the house agent's leaflet, although the rent was reasonable. With rather pessimistic forebodings and a good deal of protestation, we accompanied him to the house which was then called Bowlands. We fell completely in love with it. It was built by a doctor for himself and his family in the late nineties – solidly and sensibly. It hadn't much to be said for it architecturally but all the rooms had heaps of windows and were light and of a comfortable size and the garden was a delight.

232 The Dominant Dining Club, which lasted for a while. See pp. 198–200.
233 Hubert's best friend at Bradfield College. They remained life-long friends.

We moved there at the end of August 1929, renaming the house 'Nightingale Corner' (it was indeed at the corner of Nightingale Road). We were welcomed by Lady Wood's letter which greeted us on our arrival as neighbours.

168. *26ᵗʰ August 1929   Lady Wood to DMF* (Nightingale Corner)
Appletree Farm House, Chorleywood

My dear Mrs Foss,

A note seems a silly sort of way to welcome you to the neighbourhood, but I can't think of any other as your garden is sure to be full of flowers, so just let me say that we hope you will be as happy in Nightingale Corner as we have been at Appletree Farm and that we shall see you more often than one often does one's neighbours. (<u>What</u> a sentence to send to someone connected with the OUP!)

With <u>very</u> best wishes

Yours v sincerely,

Muriel Wood

We were less than two miles from Appletree Farm House and the friendship begun two years previously grew and ripened quickly. From 1929–1935 we visited the Woods on innumerable occasions and they came to us many, many times.

Every Sunday in the summer, if Sir Henry was at home, during the afternoon and for tea there was an invasion of the well-known in the musical world. I suppose all the famous musicians of the day went there at some time. The huge barn in the grounds was the centre of the afternoon gatherings. It had been floored and made into a vast room, completely suited to the sort of al fresco entertaining which was so delightful in the summer – and in retrospect all the days there seem to have been fine. The barn had part of one side removed, or, to put it another way, it had a very wide entrance and just inside this was a huge round table spread with the most delectable cakes. This was presided over by Lady Wood with Tania and Avril as attendant under-hostesses, as it were.

We were privileged to lunch at Appletree many times and we were given carte blanche to go to tea there whenever we liked. We took Constant and Florence Lambert and Patrick Hadley there, and we took Willie Walton there for his first visit, soon after *Belshazzar's Feast*'s first performance. On this last occasion we encountered Harriet Cohen, who with ardour told Willie that he <u>must</u> have Jewish blood in his veins as no one who <u>hadn't</u> could have written the chorus in BF 'By the waters of Babylon'. Anything less Jewish than Willie appears would be hard to find.

(Incidentally, I heard her tell Vaughan Williams that he must have Jewish blood, after the first performance of his Fifth Symphony, again referring to the Waters of Babylon. I'm afraid I interpolated here, 'It's not the Waters of Babylon, it's the Book of Common Prayer and the peace that passeth all understanding'.)

Another time, we took Willie and Edith Sitwell to Appletree where I sang to Sir Henry the three songs which Willie had written for Hubert and me to words by Edith Sitwell.

Many times we dined there in a purely 'family' way, generally without other guests. On one occasion Sir Henry was discussing other conductors and spoke of Malcolm Sargent. He told us that he had been warning him against combining a too active social life with his work as a conductor – he said that he, himself, could not work if he had too many late nights, and then he told us how very often he was asked to parties by Duchesses and ladies of rank and wealth and how he refused to go to them. 'And they always want something, my dear,' he said, 'there's always a protégé or a friend whom they want me to take up.'

In fact Sir Henry and Lady Wood lived as quiet a life as was possible for a man in his position. Having heard his opinion on late nights I have since wondered how he stood the many functions to which, in later years, he was persuaded to go.

One day we went up to luncheon and on reaching the house discovered Sir Henry on the roof of a half-built South African verandah which he was building himself. He was a first-rate carpenter and was making this external attractive addition to the house with complete competence and skill. Lady Wood made us laugh by saying 'Look at my old man'.

On occasions we drove Sir Henry and Lady Wood, with one or both of the girls, back home after the Saturday Prom. One time we brought back Frederic Lamond,[234] then far more Teutonic than Scottish, and when, as we approached Rickmansworth, he referred to 'Richmanshof' I was unable to decide whether this was a form of wit or a natural translation into German of any English name.

Sir Henry was anxious that Walton's *Three Songs* which he wrote for Hubert and me should be sung at the Promenade Concerts. He had heard me sing them in the Concert Hall and in his own home, and considered, apparently, that not

234   Frederic Lamond (1868–1948), Scottish pianist and composer who studied with Liszt.

only were the *Songs* worth putting in the Prom programme, but that I was a suitable singer. Walton had offered to score them if I sang them.[235]

In November 1932, when Christopher was four and a half, we considered he was old enough to enjoy some fireworks, so we bought a 15/– box of assorted rockets, Catherine wheels and so on. Sir Henry and Lady Wood were to dine with us on Guy Fawkes' Day, so Hubert hastened to let off our fireworks early so that all noise would be over before they arrived. He put in stakes for the rockets, a tall pole for the Catherine wheels and Christopher's firework show was over in time for us to dress for dinner. Not, alas, without an unpleasant incident, as one of the fireworks misfired and slightly burnt Hubert's arm which became distinctly painful. However, he felt relieved that the parental 'good deed' was over and, with me, was anticipating a stimulating yet peaceful evening with the Woods. Half-past-seven and they arrived. To our horror Sir Henry was nursing a box of fireworks, the counterpart of the one which we had so recently let off. 'I can't do without fireworks on Guy Fawkes' Day,' he said, beaming, 'and I know you'll let me have them, won't you?' His childlike enthusiasm was, of course, irresistible. All the same, I knew that Hubert was blanching at the thought of letting off another boxful but he played his part nobly and I don't think Sir Henry guessed that Hubert was not as thrilled as he was. After dinner and coffee were over, Sir Henry and Hubert went into the garden, Sir Henry in the thickest of thick overcoats and a huge scarf; Lady Wood and I went into my bedroom, the better to watch from the windows which looked down the garden. This time all the fireworks performed according to plan and Sir Henry enjoyed himself as much as Christopher had done earlier. But my mind's ear can yet hear the amazement in Lady Wood's voice as the Catherine wheel turned on the previously-erected – for our fireworks – pole. 'Oh, Mr Foss is wonderful; he thinks of absolutely everything.'

I think it must have been during the following summer that Christopher and I were up at Appletree and he shattered me by remarking loudly to Lady Wood, 'I fink it ought to be Sir Henry HALL, too'!

We invited Sir Henry and Lady Wood to meet Sir Henry and Lady Hadow on April 18th 1931, at our house, so they came to dinner with us. The conversation at dinner was mainly carried on by the men, both ladies in their entirely different ways being shy and rather on the defensive. However, as the men thoroughly

---

235   The *Three Songs* were performed at the Proms on 22 August 1938, sung by May Blyth and with Sir Henry Wood conducting.

enjoyed each other's verbal prowess, the ladies listened and were as silent as they liked. When we left the dining room and were females alone in the drawing room, it was a different matter. Try as I would, I could introduce no subject in which both my women guests were interested. Lady Wood, no musician herself, but able to hold her own in musical society, could find no point of contact with Lady Hadow whose outlook on music seemed confined to her own family's interests. As she was a Troutbeck, her knowledge of music seemed bounded by the ecclesiastical horizon of a world of which Lady Wood appeared completely ignorant. In vain I struggled to weave some sort of connecting thread. It was quite useless. Lady Wood, usually so positive and forthcoming, stiffened to a ramrod. Lady Hadow, usually so pleasant and gentle, melted into a dim nothingness. After a silence that seemed endless, I became quite desperate and began recounting Christopher's sayings and doings, because that seemed a mild and neutral subject. This maternal chatter tidied over the remaining minutes before the men left the dining-room and joined us.

During the years 1929–1934 we saw Tania and Avril Wood from time to time and grew extremely attached to them. At all the Sunday parties they hovered on the circumference of the circle round Sir Henry. Lady Wood was a completely adequate hostess and her time and energies were fully occupied, not only with her guests, but in keeping a guardian angel's eye on her husband. He was never allowed even to have the chance of sitting in a draught, and scarves and coats were always at hand in case a breeze arose, or the temperature fell. Tania and Avril, though fulfilling the duties of daughters of the house, appeared in an indefinable way to be outside the entourage – of it, but not in it. All the celebrities wanted to talk to other celebrities and I think little notice was taken of *them*. I cannot remember ever seeing young friends of theirs at Appletree – neither young men nor girls. It was Henry's musical circle and no-one else. (On one occasion, Hubert and I were asked to dinner in order to form a sort of bridge between Sir Henry and some neighbours of the Woods – a distinguished but non-musical couple whom Lady Wood was anxious to entertain.) We sometimes invited Tania, when grown-up, to dinner or to deck tennis without her parents and very real affection grew between us. In latter years it was Avril of whom we saw most.[236]

236   Avril Wood gave the address at Dora Foss's service of thanksgiving in 1978. See pp. 266–7.

I suppose it is inevitable that men of the stature of Sir Henry, whose whole life was devoted to music, should involve those near to him in an undue amount of self-abnegation and self-sacrifice. Muriel Wood did everything for him and to further his career and aims – he was hardly allowed to cross a road unattended by her or by one of his daughters.

One of the daughters rebelled and Hubert and I were asked by Sir Henry and Lady Wood to act as intermediaries and to give her some advice and help. As I look back I feel the rebellion was inevitable. We did what we could and the rift was healed.

The last times Hubert and I dined at Appletree must have been in the summer of 1934. The second time was in the little house in the garden. The earlier time I remember as vividly as if it were yesterday. We were at the dinner table. Henry, who was on my right, had been discoursing on the amount of work he was committed to, and suddenly he looked at his wife, sitting at the end of the table opposite him; his eyes beaming, and in a voice conveying the deepest affection and emotion, said, 'I don't know *what* I would do without Muriel.' I was most moved by this and events of the subsequent years[237] only served further to impress this scene on my mind and memory.

During these years when we were so constantly visiting and being visited by the Woods, we could not but see how Sir Henry was supported constantly and in every way by his wife, and, as far as they were able, by his daughters. Some years later Sir Henry tried his hand at deck-tennis in our garden but did not like it.

169. *1931 DMF to HJF*

Avril Wood rang up and asked me to tea there. (I had written to Lady Wood to ask her to tea) so I went up and had a very pleasant afternoon. I had a piece of Constant Lambert's wedding cake!! He'd sent a big piece to Sir Henry, complete with orange blossom and a silver shoe and a silver bell – and I got full particulars of Constant's romance. 'She' is a half Chinese, half Irish girl brought up in an East End Orphanage and was the little maid of Elsa Karen.[238]

237 In January 1935, Henry Wood, aged sixty-six, left his wife Muriel (who would not allow a divorce) and a liaison ensued with a widowed former singing pupil, Jessie Linton (née Goldsack), who changed her name by deed poll to Lady Jessie Wood. Appletree Farm House was eventually sold.

238 A Russian pianist who performed at the 1929 and 1930 Promenade Concerts.

Constant came to the flat to rehearse something with her, fell in love with the maid and has now married her.

Lady Wood had sat behind Willie Walton and Edith Sitwell at the Opera and was overwhelmed at their likeness. She simply can't get over it. I told her all the mock-scandal about it and she loved it. [The mock-scandal was that Willie was the natural son of Sir George Sitwell and Dame Ethel Smyth.] She asked for Willie's life-history and said she thought or wished there was some XVIIIth century romance about it.

In 1932 life became less easy at Chorleywood on account of staff difficulties. In 1934, the staff situation at Appletree became *very* difficult. The house, though near the buses to Rickmansworth, was only reached from Chorleywood station by a climb up and across the Common, pleasant enough in high summer, but dreary and lonely in winter.

In March 1932, five years after the publication of *The Gentle Art of Singing*, Sir Henry wrote to Hubert from Appletree Farm House:

170.

Dear Mr Foss,

Many thanks for your nice long letter. I only wrote because certain students who pass up and down Bond Street daily, say they see a lot of little works, but rarely my 'Gentle Art of Singing', which they think should always be on show, if only as a sample of how the OUP can print a big work ...

I am going to ask you to release me from directing the three Bach Cantatas on October 11th [Hubert was hoping that Sir Henry would conduct one of the Bach Cantata Club's concerts at St Margaret's Westminster, and had had a half-promise that he would do so.] I am always preaching the value of historical performances and love listening to them, but loathe conducting them myself – as after all my big massive stuff (which of course may be all wrong) I don't like directing a Band of 15 and a choir [of] 20.

Further, I should have to have three chorus rehearsals, one Piano rehearsal with the solo singers, one rehearsal with the strings only, one rehearsal with solo singers and woodwind instruments (with myself at the piano) and then the full rehearsal on day of performance.

I did not realise that I should be in the thick of the 'Proms' a week before your date, and I must have a week or ten days after the 'Proms' with no music at all – and to prepare and direct three cantatas is more than I can undertake.

I am quite sure you will understand the position and release me.

As regards the Orchestral Book, I don't think I shall ever undertake it – as life (and particularly musical life) has become so complicated that there is no time left for thinking.

Sincerely yours,

Henry J. Wood

In October Sir Henry and Tania came to Hubert's and my recital at Wigmore Hall. Lady Wood had written to me some days previously to say that she could not come as she was seeing her brother for the last time before he returned to Japan. From Torquay she wrote:

'We are here for four days' rest for Henry and – imagine – when we arrived down to breakfast this morning there was "the BBC" sitting at the next table, Messrs Mase[239] and [Julian] Herbage!!'[240] Their visit was unconnected with Henry.

171. *12ᵗʰ October 1932 Lady Wood to DMF*

Appletree Farm House

My dear Mrs Foss,

Henry and Tania thoroughly enjoyed your recital and increased my regrets at not being able to go.

What a time you have had and what patience; I should have felt like saying goodbye to the guests after a weekend of it! I am keenly sympathetic about the maids; we are having a rest from them at the moment in the bungalow (which was inhabited by Mrs and Miss [Rosa] Newmarch last winter), as after being lucky for 21 years, the tide turned in May, (certainly we had rather a houseful all the summer!). So if you come up at any time, don't be put off by an unresponsive front door to Appletree Farm.

We shall love to dine with you when you are settled.

We are delighted to hear that Henry's eloquence to the powers-that-be at the BBC had some effect – or at all events it did not exercise an adverse influence!! He was very eloquent.

239 Owen Mase, BBC Assistant Director of Music 1931–33.
240 Julian Herbage, BBC Programme Planner 1927–46, better known later for the radio programme *Music Magazine* that he presented with his wife, Anna Instone.

Shall much look forward to hearing about Christopher's reaction to the dancing class.

Love and best greeting from all,

Yours ever,

Muriel E. Wood

172.   *3ʳᵈ November 1932   DMF* (Nightingale Corner) *to HJF* (Liverpool)

For the Woods we are going to have hors d'oeuvres (sardines, anchovies, Russian salad, olives, eggs, tomatoes, beetroot); fried lemon sole and tomato sauce; some sort of game in casserole (I couldn't get woodcock, so it will probably be guinea fowl or ordinary barn-door ditto). Then strawberry cream, dessert and coffee.

173.   *16ᵗʰ November 1933   Henry Wood to HJF*

Grand Hotel, Oslo

My dear Mr Foss,

I have just finished reading your splendid volume 'Music in My Time' – 'Bravo!' it held me from cover to cover, you put the matter in such a splendid logical form, & your idea of the recent distribution regarding our art, in such an interesting manner – that I must thank you <u>very</u> sincerely for the latest addition to our musical literature. It will surely have a very wide sale.

Very sincerely yours

Henry J. Wood

P. S. My concerts in Copenhagen, Oslo & Gothenburg have all been sold out – not bad think you.

174.   *30ᵗʰ June 1934   Henry Wood to HJF*

RMS *Duchess of Richmond* (Liverpool to Montreal)

My dear Mr Foss,

How very nice of you to send me a telegram; we are enjoying our trip tremendously, fine boat, very few passengers and after our London rush, most enjoyable.

Your second volume of The Heritage of Music[241] came to hand just as we were sailing, <u>many thanks</u>. I have read it with the deepest interest. Your essay

---

241 *The Heritage of Music*, collected and edited by Hubert J. Foss, OUP, 1934, twelve essays by various distinguished writers on selected composers. The first volume appeared in 1927.

on Mendelssohn is just 'fine' and how difficult. I hope in volume three you will do an essay on the sugary César Franck, it is badly needed; if only the British people would slide off Franck and slip into Berlioz, what a grateful change it would be.

> Love to you all,
> Believe me,
> Sincerely yours,
> Henry J. Wood

P. S. Your landlord, Mr Mordant Park, is on board; what a clever water colour painter.

175. *August 1934   HJF to DMF*

Tania had just come from the Hospital (a good affair!) [In August 1934 Lady Wood was injured in a car accident when Avril was driving her from Chorleywood to Queen's Hall. She was badly hurt and was taken to the Hendon Cottage Hospital where she remained for some weeks.] The girls were full of news that aged aunts and great aunts who had not seen the family for years had suddenly turned up and asked to see Mamma.

Actually, Lady Wood had been very uncomfortable, as the bed, I gather, was intolerable. Eventually she changed her bed and last night slept peacefully for the first time. Today she can see out of both eyes (I gather that is exceptional and Avril says she mustn't read or write for weeks yet – so she asked me to thank you for her letter, as she can't do it herself), and now comes the problem of keeping her quiet. Lady Wood has, I gather, to go under an x-ray yet, and have a plug removed surgically: but she was bursting to go to tonight's Proms!! The authorities say about a fortnight more in hospital, though they may let her out temporarily for a Prom if she gets extra troublesome. But I think myself it would be foolhardy of her. Anyhow, Lady Wood is going on well, reading, and beginning to eat fish, and allowed visitors.

In the programme notes for the Prom on October 5th 1929 Sir Henry Wood had the following inserted:

This superb Toccata and Fugue in D minor, one of the noblest organ works of Johann Sebastian Bach, was practically unknown in the concert world until Leopold Stokowski with his renowned Philadelphia orchestra scored it and made a gramophone record of it, since when, musical amateurs all the world

over, have been given an opportunity of becoming acquainted with one of
Bach's most noble organ compositions.

This transcription for orchestra by Paul Klenovsky of Moscow, is a remarkable
piece of work, and shows the hand of the master in every bar. In the opinion
of his teacher A. Glazunov, he was one of the greatest masters of orchestration
among the younger Russian school, and his early death was a distinct loss to
the musical world.

For the next five years this particular arrangement was played at concerts
round the world. Few realised that it was a hoax perpetrated by Sir Henry Wood
who was himself the arranger. In a note to accompany the score when he sent
it to the OUP for printing in time for the Prom on September 4 1934, he wrote:

> NB. This is my <u>original copy</u> of the scoring of Bach's Toccata and Fugue in D
> minor. I only announced it scored by Paul Klenovsky as a <u>blind to the Press</u> as I
> got <u>very fed up with them</u>, always finding fault with any arrangement or orches-
> trations I made – 'heavy Wagner handling', 'spoiling the original' etc: etc: but
> <u>directly this piece appeared, with my untrue, concocted story</u>, which of course
> I had put in all the programmes, the Press, the musicians of the orchestras, and
> the officials of the B.B.C. fell into the trap, and said the scoring was wonderful,
> Klenovsky had the real Russian flair for tone colour etc., and performance after
> performance was given and asked for. Had I put it out under my own name
> the result would have been one performance (after spending £33 on score and
> parts) slated and shelved. So for the future all my scoring will be announced
> as by Paul Klenovsky – although such a person never existed.
>
> Signed Henry J. Wood

It was then Hubert Foss's unenviable task to negotiate in double quick time
for the printing of the score in folio and miniature size. The intention was to
have the scores ready immediately after the Prom at which the hoax would
be revealed, to take full advantage of the press coverage. Humphrey Milford,
publisher to the OUP, was at first reluctant but was won round by Foss's astute
pleading. Sir Henry was very pleased with the miniature scores and took full
advantage when invited to list internationally known conductors, musicians
and friends to whom he wished to send complimentary/presentation copies.

176. *13th October 1934   Henry Wood to HJF*

Grand Central Hotel, Belfast

My dear Mr Foss,

Please forgive my not answering your kind letter of Sept 25th until now, but I have been suffering from a hectic rush. Do send the miniature scores of my BTF [Bach-'Klenovsky' Toccata and Fugue] in D minor to all the big conductors. Off hand I can only think of – here are listed 30–40 names of English, Continental and American conductors ...

Muriel is going on fairly well, hopes to leave hospital in a week or ten days and go to Osborne House, Torquay for a real rest. I am going back to Langham Hotel tomorrow (Sunday) and shall stay there until further notice. All the best –

Sincerely yours

[Henry J. Wood]

177. *14th October 1934   Henry Wood to HJF*

Langham Hotel, Portland Place, W1

My dear Mr Foss,

My joy was <u>great</u> last night, on my return from Belfast, to find the little Miniature Score. You have <u>atchieved</u> [*sic*] a fine piece of work in wonderful quick time. Shall send you a further lot of names that I should like to receive a copy and if you can be very generous, please send me here, say, 25 copies for presentation; hope I am not asking too much. Hope wife and family are very well.

Muriel is going on <u>quite well</u> and will leave, I hope, Hendon Cottage Hospital in about a week.

Sincerely yours

[Henry J. Wood]

178. *9th July 1935   HJF* **(Nightingale Corner)** *to DMF* **(Mundesley)**

Lady Wood didn't ring up till 10 to 12! She kept me over half an hour. She says that the whole HJW case has crumpled up like a pricked bubble and Henry has signed an agreement like a lamb. She is to have Appletree entire, with all the furniture, one-third of his income, all the alleged stolen money in trust for the girls, and Avril to have £3 a week as well. She says that her solicitors attribute the whole débâcle to a good counsel. They did not disclose who it was but said it was one of the men they themselves would have chosen to consult.

Lady Wood says that someone who has seen HJ and JL [Jessie Linton] together talks of her complete 'domination and proprietorship'! Rather distressing. She also said that Beecham's bon mot (so-called) on the subject was 'creditable of him but not credible'! So like TB, the cad. She's left me her address in case I hear of anything and gives no date for her return.

179.   *10th October 1937   Henry Wood to HJF*

49 Hallam Street, Portland Place, W1

Dear Mr Foss,

Did you by any chance hear the Five Handel Operatic Choruses (second set) at the 'Proms' the Handel night? I think they made a good impression and scored a success, anyhow No. 5 was encored. I am directing a concert at Stowe [School] and I feel pretty sure we shall wind up the orchestral concert with them. I have also asked for them to be put down at the second Festival Concert (Miscellaneous night) of the Three Valleys, Mountain Ash, which I direct next May – I feel this is all to the good.

The 'Proms' were a success this year and almost four nights a week the doors had to be closed at 7.40 pm. Entre nous – my next year is my Jubilee, 50 years of conducting in London. Sir John Reith has most kindly given me the BBC orchestra of 120 and the Full Chorus, the LSO of 100 and the Queen's Hall orchestra of 100, the BBC chorus of 250 and the Philharmonic Chorus of 250 – most important of all, only one soloist.

Rachmaninoff is coming specially from Switzerland to play his Second Concerto for me and he will be the one International artist.

The 16 British Solo Vocalists will sing one item with orchestra, 4 S's, 4 C's, 4 T's and 4 Basses.[242] The date will be October 5, 6 or 7 [1938],[243] the only date Rachmaninoff can manage as he leaves for a long tour in America on the 8th. Sec. Robert Mayer, Treasurer, Baron D'Erlanger.

I refused a Banquet, a Motor Car or a Portrait, and subscriptions are to go to form a Bed, Beds or a small ward in a London Hospital for Orchestral Musicians.

All the musical Knights have given it their blessing; now I desire yours.

Very sincerely yours,

Henry J. Wood

242 Vaughan Williams's *Serenade to Music*, 'composed for and dedicated to Sir Henry Wood on the occasion of his jubilee, in grateful recognition of his services to music'. The initials of the sixteen chosen soloists with whom Sir Henry had been associated throughout his career were printed against their parts in the full score.

243 5 October 1938 was the date fixed for the jubilee concert. Wood recorded the *Serenade to Music* with the same soloists ten days later.

1. Hubert Foss at Bradfield
College during WW1

2. Dora Stevens
in her teens

3. Hubert Foss in the Army

4. Dora Stevens
as a VAD nurse

5. Hubert Foss at the piano, 1920s

6. Dora Stevens,
publicity photo, 1920s

7. Dora and Hubert's wedding day, 20 July 1927

8. Dora with William Walton at Symonds Yat, September 1932

9. Hubert with William Walton at Symonds Yat, September 1932

10. Dora and Hubert with (l. to r.) Edwin Evans, Leslie Heward and William Walton in the 1930s at Nightingale Corner, Rickmansworth

11. Deck tennis at Nightingale Corner, 1930s, with H.E. Randerson, Mrs Halles, Arthur Benjamin, Hubert and Tania Wood

12. Dora, Christopher, Hubert and Diana, 1939

13. Hubert Foss
at ease, 1939

14. Hubert with
carriage clock, a
wedding present
from Henry and
Muriel Wood

15. Hubert with characteristic bow tie, 1930s

16. Dora in 1945

17. Dora with Norman Peterkin and Alan Frank at the 50th anniversary of
the Oxford University Press Music Department, 1973 © OUP

18–19. Letter from Philip Heseltine to Hubert Foss, late 1924 (see pp. 62–3)

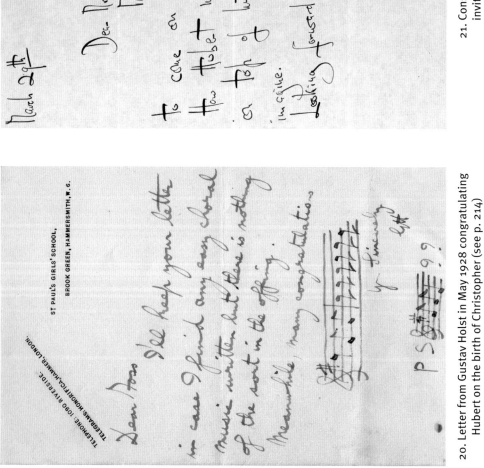

21. Constant Lambert's acceptance of an invitation, March 1932 (see p. 70)

20. Letter from Gustav Holst in May 1928 congratulating Hubert on the birth of Christopher (see p. 214)

173. Cromwell Rd.
S.W.5.

Oct. 17th 1932.

Dear Mr. Foss,

I was so sorry that I had to dash away so suddenly without being able to thank you properly for the visit.

It was most awfully good of you to have put up with me for so long, & to have given me such a very good time.

I expect that Mr. Fox told you that I caught the train, thanks to his driving like a complete John.

I hope that Christopher is progressing well with his singing and also his tin whistle. I must definitely write him a concerto for full orchestra and tin whistle in Bb (or is it A?)!

Thanking you very much again

Yours very sincerely

Benjamin Britten

My dear Hubert.

Thanks you for your letter & the copy of E.M.N. The cover is grand — & only the inside was as good! The parts are in the possession of B&D.

I don't whether they will hand. I've been here some ten days or so & have produced this or the 3rd subject, but am shivering on the brink about it. I need hardly say, quick.

Weston,
Towcester,
Northants.
July 9/35

I may be in London on the 18th for a day or two later on & Rubinstein for the week-end to discuss this ballet question with these Russian people who are coming also. I think it is almost as good an settled that I do it.

love to Dora & yourself
yrs
Willie.

What about going to the enclosed? Has the score of the first two movements arrived safely? There are still one or two things in the 2nd I've not yet made up my mind about, but will let you have it soon I'm sure, for engraving.

24–25. Letter to Hubert Foss from William Walton, July 1935, with the first sketch for the fugue in the last movement of his symphony (See p. 133)

27. Letter of sympathy from Michael Ayrton to Dora Foss, May 1953 (see p. 242) © Estate of Michael Ayrton

26. Letter from Sir Henry Wood, November 1935, asking for a copy of Walton's symphony (see p. 135)

1941

The White Gates
Nov 6

Dear Foss

This is sad news indeed — but
shall we see much of you? I do
not realize how much I care so

on you — (Ask Foss? dear? — "Ask
Foss & see." or "I'll ask Foss"
to play is over & we are home alone"
— But perhaps it is all over
& you'll own [...] any way
it is selfish & undeserved
way of looking at things —

when the foundations the OUP as
I will — came all [...]
weak for one & to you &
any [...] centuries & congratulate
to have won you for

a colleague

Yrs
R Vaughan Williams

28–29. The first and last pages of a letter from Vaughan Williams to Hubert Foss on hearing of his resignation from OUP in November 1941 (see pp. 97–8)

180. *9th October 1938   Henry Wood to HJF*

Torbay Hotel, Torquay

Dear Mr Foss,

Do accept my sincerest thanks and gratitude for all you did to make my Jubilee Concert a real triumph last Wednesday night. I know only too well the mass of detail attached to such a scheme, and all was carried through in a masterly manner.

The Press still do not understand that the Concert was given not for my own glorification, but to get money for beds in London Hospitals for orchestral musicians. Why has this generally not been mentioned or stressed, I wonder – do you know? Do you think it ought to have been mentioned more pointedly in the Programme? Many down here seem under the impression that it was for me and did not realise it was a Charity Concert. I am stony broke over it, as I spent nearly five hundred pounds over it up to date – the music bill alone is pretty stiff, and then I have given every penny from Hammond organ testimonials, De Reszke cigarettes (100 guineas) and we have received so many rude letters from strangers telling me 'how dare I descend to such a cheap advertisement'. I wonder how they feel, now they are told the truth – home on Wednesday.

With kind regards,

Sincerely yours.

[HJW]

The Wider Circle

The first part of this collection of material embraces the figures of the musical world with whom Dora and Hubert Foss had closest contact, and they are those of whom Dora wrote her memoirs. The following part shows the great variety of connections that they maintained from the 1920s to the 1950s, and how the whole breadth of musical life during this period circled round them. Indeed, the circle was wider in that it encompassed not only composers, conductors and singers but writers, publishers and stage performers. It portrays a vivid picture of cultural life between the wars and in the immediate aftermath of WW2. Dora kept a record of the musicians who had played on the family piano: Edward Bairstow, Samuel Barber, Arthur Benjamin, Benjamin Britten, Harold Craxton, John Gardner, Friedrich Gulda, Patrick Hadley, Myra Hess, Herbert Howells, John Ireland, Louis Kentner, Constant Lambert, E.J. Moeran, Gerald Moore, Herbert Murrill, Reginald Paul, Norman Peterkin, Roger Quilter, Donald Swann, Michael Tippett and William Walton.

Margery Allingham

Margery Allingham (1904–66) was a popular writer of crime fiction whose novels usually featured the aristocratic detective Albert Campion ('well bred and a trifle absent-minded'), who first appeared in *The Crime at Black Dudley* (1929). Allingham wrote over twenty novels, together with short stories and novellas. She is probably best known for the 1952 novel *Tiger in the Smoke* that was adapted in 1956 as a film, but omitting the character of Campion. Foss was a devotee of crime fiction.

181.   *8th September 1950   Margery Allingham to HJF*
                              D'Arcy House, Tolleshunt D'Arcy, nr Maldon, Essex

Dear Mr Foss,

   Many thanks for your kind letter.

   By all means see what you can do with the 'Pig'[1] and the BBC. I don't think any of my tales have been broadcast (save those written expressly for the medium) and I'd never given much thought to the idea.

---

1   Presumably *The Case of the Late Pig*, a black comedy by Margery Allingham, published in 1937. It was adapted for radio by Felix Felton and Susan Ashman, and broadcast in the BBC Home Service's *Saturday-Night Theatre* in September 1965.

Go ahead and see what happens. I fear my agents (W.P. Watt & Son) may insist on putting a finger in the pie if anything comes off but you will find us reasonable, affable and anxious to please –

Good luck,

Yours sincerely

Margery Allingham

I'm very fond of the 'Pig' and I'd love to hear it on the air.

Oswald Barrett ('Batt')

Oswald Charles Barrett (1892–1945) studied in the early twentieth century at the Camden School of Art and was a book illustrator and cartoonist, signing himself as 'BATT'. His first published drawing appeared in *The Bystander* in 1911. After service on the North West Frontier in WW1, he attended Goldsmiths' College of Art. His most widely circulated drawings were his cartoons for the *Radio Times* which continued from 1930 until the time of his death. They were so popular that the BBC issued them separately for framing. His portraits of musicians that appeared in Percy Scholes's *The Oxford Companion to Music* brought him worldwide acclaim. Batt was a droll character in word and image, and he and Foss became close friends. His cartoon of Foss (fig. 11) was painted before Foss left for the USA in 1939, with Batt predicting the supposed transformation that would overwhelm him. Batt's understanding and appreciation of music are clear from his letter.

182. *29th January 1938   Oswald Barrett to HJF*

7a Oaklands Road, Bromley, Kent

Note for Scholes Companion:

Sir Fossio (1538–3010)

The above dates of this remarkable man are given as approximate but are mentally true. He covers more than the above period & embraces all that is best within it. So much can be said of him that there is no room in which to say it. The extent of his activities can be imagined from the fact that he never wears any clothes, if he can help it, so that he is not tied to any particular period or place. Nomadic by nature he absorbs practically everything he comes across, flashing hither and thither in time & space, & has been likened to a live electric wave, a scorched pea in a frying pan, or puck, while his outsize brain, according to pathologists, is made of some material with powers of absorbtion [*sic*] some 260 times greater than blotting paper. By just turning it round in his head, with a shake, he can concentrate on a variety of things in turn, such as editing, composing, adjudicating, musicology, natural history, typography, publishing, opium-smoking, art, & many other things appertaining thereto. There is nobody else quite like him. He is very difficult to find as he is always obscured by mountains of paper, but by careful listening one can usually locate his whereabouts from the sound of his rummaging.

My dear Sir Fossio,

The two books arrived yesterday & plunged me into such a state of excitement that I missed a train. I wanted to read both at once & together in the five minutes I had to spare, which five minutes became 20! But I am really more than delighted, as the first flash of excitement in this case levels down to something of permanent value for which I am very grateful to you. These two books, with the Scholes Companion,[2] mark the beginning of a friendship which, I hope, will last at least as long as our bodies. I do not find myself in harmony with all & sundry, but at the same time I do not harbour a rabid dislike for those of different mentality. I most certainly find points of contact in you that I rarely find in others & this is something of great value, in the best sense. It is natural that this should be so as, for one thing, you are naturally made for and engaged in a series of activities in which I have the greatest interest & I do not know anyone of like kind. I doubt if there is another, anyway.

When I say interest I do not mean self-interest. Friendship based on that is never genuine and I regard a man who acts a friendship for what he can get out of it as a fraud. I firmly believe that any sort of association not governed by sound & sincere feeling is bound to crumble in the end. Purely mercenary considerations may keep it going for a time but it cannot last if there is no living root for it to thrive on. That is what is wrong with this so-called civilisation. But I mustn't dive into all that here! You are a dear fellow & that from my heart, & not only because of the 2 books you have just sent me. Naturally I have not yet had time to read them through, but I read Tovey's very able and concise analysis of the Beethoven C major[3] before we heard his performance of it last night from Edinburgh. His reading of the first & last movements was magnificent but, in my opinion, he didn't quite realise the true character of the 2nd & 3rd movements,

---

2   *The Oxford Companion to Music*, edited by Percy Scholes, OUP, 1938, including a portrait of Beethoven (oils on canvas) by BATT as a frontispiece.

3   Symphony No. 5, in Donald Tovey, *Essays in Musical Analysis: Symphonies 1*, OUP, 1935.

Fig. 11: Cartoon of Hubert Foss by BATT (Oswald Charles Barrett) anticipating Hubert's return from America in 1939

partly because of a slightly too quick tempo in the 2nd & a slightly too slow tempo in the 3rd. But it was all much more vital than Boult's Beethoven usually is. I am longing to read Closson's[4] book too & will have a talk about it one day later on, when there's an opportunity.

Of course, we enjoyed your visit enormously & Winil was sorry to be in the kitchen for so long. As usual, when there is harmony, the time went too quickly. We have few visitors, on the whole, because of the pressure of work, & often I don't see folk when they do come. I should never eat or go to bed if I could do without it. I'm afraid I'm too fond of work & always regret the hours spent in bed. Going to bed is very funny I think, when you analyse it, but a confounded nuisance all the same.

I hope your wife didn't find your absence too prolonged on Saturday as she is so unwell, but you gave us a lot of delight and interest. I want to hear more of your adventures and Winil too, & she wants to hear you laugh! She says you make yourself laugh when you laugh. It's a grand laugh anyway.

I am sending you a few notes to hand to your wife hoping they may be of some little use in her painting. By the way, it might be as well if she didn't use ordinary Flake White – I suppose she does? The smell may be harmful to her. It is, of course, carbonate of lead & poisonous. Any serious degree of poison by inhalation would take a long time & she probably doesn't use very much but all the same, in her case, it is well not to run unnecessary risk. I have suggested another white in the notes.

I saw Douglas Williams (art editor of Radio Times) the other day & asked him about that matter of copyright. He said at once that the copyright of the Radio Times portraits is mine & you are perfectly free to use them if I say so. Well, I've said so! So far as the B.B.C. is concerned the position is just as I said – they hold what they call "perpetual right of reproduction" in any of their own publications. This means that if Boult or someone gives a performance of, say, 'Israel in Egypt' next October they can, if they wish, use my Handel portrait in Radio T. for the occasion. I once did a drawing of a Hurdy-Gurdy man for R.T. & it was used at least six times & this happens to quite a number of drawings. Anyway the main thing is that everything is alright so far as the Companion is concerned & we are perfectly free to use the R.T. portraits as, of course, I always understood. I have just done a small portrait head of Mahler for R.T. & am just going to do another of Weingartner.[5] Both of these are sure to be used several

---

4   Ernest Closson, *The Fleming in Beethoven*, OUP, 1936, translated from the French by Muriel Fuller.
5   Felix Weingartner (1863–1942), Austrian composer and conductor.

times, but I shan't get a ticket for the concerts or even a packet of fags! But they pay a good price as a rule for the rights in the first place & leave it at that.

The flowers you brought are flourishing & Winil loves them. So do I. They keep your visit going, not that it will fade anyway.

Hoping to see you again soon & I'm very happy that you have come into my life. And many grateful thanks again for the books. Of these more anon, when read.

Ever yours,

Batt

Béla Bartók

Hubert Foss's first contact with Béla Bartók (1881–1945) had probably been in 1923 when the latter's *Hungarian Folk Music* was to be published by the OUP, although this did not appear until 1931, with a translation by M.D. Calvocoressi. But, with Foss's subsequent difficulty in finding a translator that satisfied Bartók for the publication of the English edition, the composer eventually withdrew the work from OUP. In March 1925 Foss gave some practical help towards a broadcast of Hungarian music that in the event had to be cancelled as Bartók was too ill to be present. (It was to have included his new piano sonata.) In February 1929 the BBC broadcast Bartók's third and fourth string quartets, and on 19 February the third quartet was performed at the Wigmore Hall.

183.   *19ᵗʰ February 1929   HJF to DMF* **(Mundesley Sanatorium)**

Well ... I sat to lunch with Bartók who was most charming, and Calvo[coressi][6] and Racz[7] of the Legation. But the last named, poor fellow, is suffering from [a] gastric ulcer and is only allowed to take milk, ever! What a game! While we ate boiled turbot and pork and claret, he drank milk! A depressing spectacle though I must say he carried it off marvellously.

After all that I tried to show Bartók the view from the top of our building but he was afraid to catch cold!

---

6   Michel Dimitri Calvocoressi (1877–1944), French-born critic with a particular interest in Russian music, and an early champion in England, with Philip Heseltine and Cecil Gray, of Bartók.

7   Dezsö Rácz, a former pupil of Bartók, later Information Officer at the Hungarian Consulate. He did much to facilitate the early contact between Bartók and the BBC.

Arnold Bax

Dora Foss included some songs by Arnold Bax (1883–1953) in her first recital, in April 1923. As she has recounted elsewhere, when her singing teacher had introduced her to Bax songs, 'They enthralled me with their atmosphere of Celtic mystery, their poignancy and sheer beauty. I bought volumes of them and literally wept as I learned them.' Bax was a prolific composer, with a large output of orchestral and chamber works and songs. After some concerts of his chamber music in 1927 Hubert wrote: 'With such a catalogue of works at 44, and one of such a quality, his magnitude must surely be accepted ... Bax's sheer ability to compose music is phenomenal, his invention of sounds never ceases. One wonders, vaguely, ... whether there could in the future be another Bax: whether, mathematically, music could stand it.'[8]

184. *13th September [1942?]   Arnold Bax to HJF*
                                      The White Horse, Storrington, Sussex
My dear Hubert,

Many thanks for your very kind and indeed lyrical words about me yesterday.[9] I was very pleased to hear the extracts from the Nonet again and am glad that you agree with me that it is one of my most characteristic works. Listening twice in one week to a radio performance of the harp & fl[ute] sonata[10] – one in the flesh and the other gramophoned, I have come to the conclusion that the bass of the harp is a very difficult affair to get over without distortion on any but a specially regulated set. There were disconcerting twangs and 'plunks' on both occasions. Otherwise everything came off well. I am really grateful to you for your delightful address.

Am suffering from some rheumatic complaint for the first time in my life – it is hell!

Best wishes from yours ever
Arnold Bax

See also the correspondence from Bax in the Walton section: letter 98, pp. 110–11.

---

8   'Some chamber music by Arnold Bax', *The Dominant*, December 1927, pp. 16–19.
9   'Music by Arnold Bax', presented by Hubert Foss with gramophone records, Home Service, 13 September 1942.
10 Fantasy Sonata for flute and harp.

Arthur Bliss

Arthur Bliss (1891–1975) had a distinguished career as composer, conductor and administrator. He studied classics and music at Cambridge, followed by a year at the Royal College of Music and, having served with distinction in WW1, he began his major compositions in 1918. His range was immense, from concertos to opera, ballet and film music. Elgar considered that in the 1920s he had become 'disconcertingly modern', but by the 1930s the music of new composers such as Walton had changed opinion of his music to 'old-fashioned'. For a short while during WW2 he was Director of Music at the BBC, and in 1953 he succeeded Arnold Bax as Master of the Queen's Music, putting the 'k' back into Musick. He had by then become a Knight Commander of the Royal Victorian Order and was knighted in 1971.

185.   *19ᵗʰ December 1928   HJF to DMF*

Then hurriedly to dine with Arthur Bliss. She[11] is so charming – dressed in a very full and floppy pink flowered silk with a complexion like a peach – quite lovely. They have the house on East Heath Road which stands just above that triangle between E Heath Rd and Willow Rd[12] – a lovely house indeed and quite beautifully arranged by them inside – a little attitudinising as usual from Arthur but all very friendly and nice and comfortable. We discussed art and books and music all the evening – a very nice light dinner beautifully served and the studio afterwards, all very decorative and jolly. Then I walked home, and now I have to write to Dyson. Then bed.

186.   *14ᵗʰ February [1933]   Arthur Bliss to HJF*
                    East Heath Lodge, One East Heath Road, Hampstead NW3
Dear Hubert,
        I have just returned to be greeted by your extremely generous article.[13] Very many thanks for it.

---

11   Trudy (Gertrude) Bliss, his American wife (née Hoffmann), whom he met in Santa Barbara, California in 1923 and married there in 1925.

12   By 1932 the Blisses had moved to St John's Wood, London NW8, and a few years later to Penselwood in Somerset.

13   Possibly 'Arthur Bliss's Clarinet Quintet', *Monthly Musical Record*, February 1933, pp. 31–32.

Anything that disappointed you in the work you have so twisted to its best advantage that I suspect more of the devil in you than I had thought.

It all makes very capable writing and good reading, which alas! my article[14] in the Telegraph did not – the Editor having altered my grammar, transposed my paragraphs and even added an opinion of his own, which is certainly staggering to one unused to being inside the office.

Gratefully yours,

Arthur B.

187. *2ⁿᵈ March 1934*   *Arthur Bliss to HJF*

East Heath Lodge, One East Heath Road, Hampstead NW3

Dear Hubert,

Thank you very much for your nice notice[15] – a good piece of writing and analysis.

I shall plunge a bit deeper and more rashly into the bones of it on the 22ⁿᵈ. I am having the MS[16] bound up as a gift to you, if you will accept it as such.

Much gratitude from Arthur Bliss

Further correspondence from Bliss, after Hubert Foss's death, is included in the Tribute section: letter 268, p. 243.

14   *Daily Telegraph*, 11 February 1933.

15   'Classicism and Arthur Bliss: his new viola sonata', *The Musical Times*, March 1934, pp. 213–17.

16   Sonata for Viola and Piano (1933), OUP, 1934.

Benjamin Britten

The early works of Benjamin Britten (1913–76) were published by OUP, and he visited Hubert Foss at his house in Rickmansworth. It is clear from correspondence that Foss admired Britten's work but felt that OUP would be unable to support the large cost of a third prolific composer who, in the early 1930s, did not have the established record of Vaughan Williams and Walton. He had considerable belief in Britten as a composer and was anxious to encourage and help him all he could. OUP did publish the Oboe Quartet and the *Simple Symphony*,[17] but Britten transferred to Boosey & Hawkes. With Britten's and Foss's differing attitudes towards the Performing Right Society regarding the management of performance royalties, it was perhaps unlikely that they were going to have a close professional relationship.

188.   *17th October 1932   Benjamin Britten to DMF*[18]

173 Cromwell Road, SW5

Dear Mrs Foss,

I was so sorry that I had to dash away so suddenly without being able to thank you properly for the visit. It was most awfully good of you to have put up with me for so long, & to have given me such a very good time.

I expect that Mr Foss told you that I caught the train, thanks to his driving like a complete Jehu.[19]

I hope that Christopher is progressing well with his singing and also his tin whistle. I must definately [*sic*] write him a concerto for full orchestra and tin whistle[20] in Bb (or is it A?)!

Thanking you very much again.

Yours very sincerely

Benjamin Britten

© Britten–Pears Foundation

---

17   See the 1934 correspondence between Milford, Whittaker, Leslie Heward and Foss re: OUP considering the publication of Britten, in particular the *Simple Symphony*, in Duncan Hinnells, *An Extraordinary Performance – Hubert Foss, Music Publishing and the Oxford University Press*, OUP, 1998, pp. 44–46.

18   See plates 22–23.

19   A reference to Jehu, son of Jehoshaphat, in II Kings 9, who drove his chariot 'furiously'.

20   This offer is recounted by Diana Sparkes (née Foss) in the CD *Hubert Foss and his friends – A recital of songs*, HJF001CD. Sadly, the concerto for tin whistle never materialised.

189. 1ˢᵗ July 1948   Benjamin Britten to HJF

as from: 295 Regent Street, London W1[21]

Dear Mr Foss,

I am sorry not to have answered your letter before this but I have been so busy that my correspondence has been shockingly neglected. But also I have been a little embarrassed to know how to answer your kind letter. Quite frankly I feel that since you have openly confessed so little sympathy with any of my recent works it is a little unfair to those works that you should be the one to introduce them to foreign audiences. Therefore I do not feel it would serve much purpose our meeting and embarrassing each other by fruitless discussion.

I hope you will understand that it is not unfriendliness which prompts this letter and I am sending a copy of it to Miss Seymour Whinyates[22] so that she will understand that it is I myself who have made this move.

With kind regards,

Yours sincerely,

Benjamin Britten

© Britten–Pears Foundation

190. 13ᵗʰ July 1948   HJF to Benjamin Britten [typed]

My dear Benjamin Britten,

I have not before replied to your letter because I sought the opportunity to discuss it with Seymour Whinyates. I take it kindly that you should have written to me as you have, but I do not feel I can subscribe to your argument. It is true that I have been critical of your works, but I hope and believe that I have been fair and frank – that is a critic's job, and it is unthinkable that any critic who expects to be read more than once or twice should write anything he does not sincerely think. On the other hand, this British Council situation is surely a little different. I write for the Council not to criticise works but to expound them, so that foreign audiences may find out, to the fullest point, the excellence of our English music. I need not, I think, tell you how keen I have always been on this work of extending the range of listeners to the works of living British composers. Now the British Council gives me a list of works to expound – a fairly long list. No one could imagine that I, as expounder, am in equal sympathy with every work on that list. Like you and all the rest of us, I have preferences. But I do not, as expositor, allow these personal views to appear. My ambition is to engage

---

21   The address of Britten's publishers, Boosey & Hawkes.

22   Seymour Whinyates, Director of the Music Department at the British Council, 1943–59.

the foreign listener's interest. I want him to judge for himself, and to have from me some material which will help him to a quicker appreciation of the music. Now as for my qualifications for this provision of material, I am not a judge. But, in the abstract, the fact that I have expressed critical judgements on certain works of yours is, I am sure, entirely irrelevant. My understanding of your scores as musical documents is in no way impaired by my personal views, and in an honest endeavour to induce more performances of your music outside England, I should probably err in my expositions on the side of over-charity, over-praise.

I can only write at some length for two reasons – your own kind letter, and a desire to establish the principle, as well as the facts of the situation, in your mind. As a matter of fact, we could go on arguing about the point for there is no need for me to tackle your works next – many others occur on the list. And, in fact, we have for a moment called a halt. But it would I feel be a pity if the exposition of your works (those on my list) were left to someone who has, perhaps, more personal sympathy but less experience in expounding or inducing people to listen. So maybe we all might think again.

Incidentally I had the pleasure of playing your Lyke-Wake Dirge on the radio the other night. It is a terrifying and excellent piece.

And, by the way, I have already done notes for the British Council on your Piano Concerto (largely based on your own note, this) and A Boy was Born.

Yours very sincerely,

Hubert Foss

191. *19th July 1948   Benjamin Britten to HJF* [typed]

295 Regent Street, London W1

My dear Hubert Foss,

Thank you for your letter which I was interested to read. I am afraid it does not make me change my point of view over this matter since I still feel that a lack of sympathy with the aims of a composer would preclude a music critic, however experienced, from being the ideal person to introduce that composer's work to the public. Your rather sinister threats of over-charity and over-praise do not make me feel any easier! I am sorry if my attitude means the non-inclusion of my works in your lists but I feel strongly that this may only be a temporary set-back for me and that the real inducement for Continental listeners to accept my music is only that the music itself should be as good as possible.

With my best wishes,

Yours sincerely,

Benjamin Britten

© Britten–Pears Foundation

192.   *23ʳᵈ July 1948   HJF to Benjamin Britten* [typed]

My dear Benjamin Britten,

Well, well, if that's how you and your publishers take the words of an honest critic, and misinterpret his intentions, so be it. I will obviously withdraw. The idea of a composer choosing his own critic is a new one in my experience, and though it may have been done in the past (as Hadow always told me it was until he broke the ring in 1897), I do not think it happened in the time of the gay Dr Pepusch.

I would like to add that I think your point of view rather limited.

Yours sincerely,

Hubert Foss

G.K. Chesterton

Hubert Foss's connections with publishing and journalism were not confined to music. Between 1922 and 1923 he wrote forty-three articles on many subjects for *The New Witness* (some of these under the pseudonym of 'Josiah Peacock'). The journal had been founded in 1911 by Hilaire Belloc (1870–1953) as *The Eye-Witness*. From 1916 to 1923 the editor was G.K. Chesterton (1874–1936), the prolific journalist and novelist whose writing covered an astonishingly wide range of subject matter. In 1925 *The New Witness* became *G.K.'s Weekly*, for which Foss wrote four articles that year. In 1923–24 he also contributed to the *Saturday Review*, a journal of politics, literature, science and art that was published between 1855 and 1938. The last letter shows Chesterton taking advice from Foss.

193.   *1ˢᵗ May 1923   Ada Chesterton[23] to HJF*
        The New Witness, **edited by G.K. Chesterton, 20–21 Essex Street, Strand**

Dear Mr Foss,

GKC has decided that the issue of May 4ᵗʰ will be the last number of the New Witness.

---

23   Ada Elizabeth Chesterton, wife of G.K. Chesterton's brother Cecil.

I want to take this opportunity of thanking you very deeply for all the help and invaluable assistance you have given me on the paper's behalf.

Yours sincerely

A.E. Chesterton

194. *13ᵗʰ December 1928   HJF to DMF*

Beaufort House, Chelsea SW3

Well I got [Percy] Scholes to lunch with me on business. GKC sprained his ankle and put me off. I was annoyed but he has since written to make another appointment next Wednesday at 4, after which I am dining with Arthur Bliss. I chased back to find Ireland and Alan Bush (the latter with a beard – not unlike your husband at this particular moment). So we argy-bargyed about money and I got rid of them about 5, worked like a maniac till 6, and then arranged the room for the party [for his office staff].

195. *19ᵗʰ December 1928   HJF to DMF*

After doing lots of things in a hurry (and I fear I shall have to bring tons away) I rushed off to see GKC. He has no teeth and is fatter than ever. We got on excellently and he defers to my judgement entirely, and wants me to suggest concrete alterations in the play[24] which he will dish up! Just what I wanted. A triumph.

John Coates

The Yorkshire-born tenor John Coates (1865–1941) was a leading singer in his day, known for his roles in opera and oratorio, especially Elgar's *The Dream of Gerontius*. He was also a familiar song recitalist. He saw four years' war service in France, and after 1921 he confined his work chiefly to concert performances and recitals. An accompanist who had a particularly close professional association with Coates was the young Gerald Moore, who in 1925 went on a tour of Canada and the United States with him and has written of Coates that he was the English singer who impressed him more than any other at the time.

---

24   Possibly Chesterton's *The Judgement of Dr Johnson* (a comedy in three acts).

196. *6ᵗʰ October 1923   John Coates to HJF* [typed]

Beaufort House, Chelsea SW3

Dear Sir,

In reply to your letter, your song 'Rioupéroux' appeals to me strongly and I certainly hope I may be able to sing it one of these days, though it does not definitely fit into the scheme of those programmes which I have immediately in prospect, but I shall certainly not overlook it, you may depend upon it, and I should be most obliged if you could be good enough to keep me posted as to anything else you may write. You can rely upon my always giving it careful attention.

Yours sincerely

John Coates

PS [in MS] I will let you know when I intend to sing Rioupéroux – with much pleasure.

Freeman Wills Crofts

Freeman Wills Crofts (1879–1957), born in Dublin and educated in Northern Ireland, held various positions in railway engineering with the Belfast Counties Railway, becoming chief assistant engineer. His writing career began in 1919 with the publication of *The Cask* (1920), the first of many crime novels which he published annually for the next thirty years. The plots centred on the intricacy of railway timetables, of which he had detailed knowledge. In 1924 he introduced his police inspector, Joseph French, a professional investigator, not a gifted amateur like many fictional detectives of that period. Wills Crofts retired in 1929 and moved to Blackheath, near Guildford, where he continued to write crime novels, short stories, and plays for stage and radio. He was a member of the Detection Club and in 1939 was elected as a member of the Royal Society of Arts. Julian Symons nominated him as 'the best representative of what may be called the Humdrum school of detective novelists' (*Bloody Murder*, 1972). Hubert Foss particularly enjoyed crime fiction (and playing patience) as a means of relaxing. He knew that Crofts was an organist at the parish church in Blackheath and hence made the gesture of offering him some scores.

197.   *13th March 1936   F.W. Crofts to HJF* [typed]
Wildern, Blackheath, Guildford, Surrey

Dear Mr Foss,

How extremely kind of you! Thank you so much for your letter.

Yes, I am very fond of music and have done a good deal of choir training, principally in connection with competative [*sic*] music festivals. I have been organist and choirmaster of four out of five parishes in which I have lived, including Coleraine in Northern Ireland. But I am not a skilful organist technically, being only able to play slow and easy music. Now I have fallen completely from grace, as in our tiny (though beautiful) church here in Blackheath, there is only an extremely ancient one-manual positive organ!

It is more than kind of you offering me some music, but for the reason given above – no pedal organ here – I could not make use of organ music. There is one thing I should like to have greatly – but I'm afraid it doesn't exist: a piano score of Vaughan Williams's 'The Shepherds of the Delectable Mountains'.[25] If there is such a thing, and if you had a copy you didn't want, and would be so kind as to let me have it, I should be very greatly obliged. Or any other single piece of music I should greatly prize as a memento of your kindness. A piano score of one of the Beethoven symphonies I should greatly appreciate, assuming such to exist.

Thanking you again,

Yours sincerely

Freeman W. Crofts

Subsequent letters dated 16–17 March thank HJF for The Shepherds. *'When I heard this work done on the radio, I immediately asked if it was set for piano.'*

---

25   Published OUP, 1925. The first work of Vaughan Williams to be published by OUP, it was later incorporated into the morality *The Pilgrim's Progress* (1951).

Henry Walford Davies

The Welsh composer, organist and broadcaster Walford Davies (1869–1941) studied (and later taught) at the Royal College of Music. He was conductor of the Bach Choir, and organist of Temple Church, London and St George's Chapel, Windsor. On the death of Elgar in 1934 he was appointed Master of the King's Music. He is best remembered for his *Solemn Melody*, the *Royal Air Force March Past* (with George Dyson), and for church music and songs, but in his day he was probably even more widely known for his series of broadcasts on music, both to children and adults.

198. *26ᵗʰ February 1937   Walford Davies to HJF*

The Athenæum, Pall Mall, SW1

King's Music[26]

Dear Foss,

I think I have that Essay nearly ready. I have based it (luckily for me) on a Dissertation[27] I prepared for the Royal Soc of Arts only last year as I have their ready permission to pilfer the pertinent parts of what I prepared for them. It seems to make just the very thing you want with the needed additions.

It will reach you, I hope, before the close of the coming week. Will that do?

O, you Nuisance of Benignant Intent!

Yours ever

Walford Davies

Walter de la Mare

After WW1, following his discharge from the Army, Hubert Foss was keen to find a job in journalism. While working for the weekly journal *Land and Water* (see p. 36), he looked for connections with more established journals. At this time Walter ('Jack') de la Mare (1873–1956) was a popular writer of novels, short stories and poems, particularly for children, and was working on his novel

26 Possibly relating to the coronation of King George VI on 11 May 1937. Walford Davies was Master of the King's Music 1934–41.

27 'One Aspect of English Music', lecture to the Royal Society of Arts, 5 June 1936.

Memoirs of a Midget (his 'new book' mentioned in the first letter), which won the James Tait Black Memorial Award for fiction the following year. It is not clear whether Foss knew if he had connections with any particular journals, but de la Mare's continued willingness to approach his contacts and keep Foss up to date speaks for the generosity of the man. De la Mare was made a Companion of Honour in 1948 and awarded the Order of Merit in 1953.

199. *10ᵗʰ October 1920   Walter de la Mare to HJF*
                                        14 Thornsett Road, Anerley, London SE20
Dear Mr Foss,

Many thanks for your letter. I will gladly do what I can, but, as I told Mrs Thomas, there are few opportunities, as for some time now all my work as a reviewer has been given up, while I have been working on a new book. I have mentioned your name to the Assistant Editor of the Westminster Gazette, but there seems to be no opening there just now. I shall be seeing Mr Hyllman of Constables on Tuesday and will speak to him; and will take advantage of any other opportunities that may come. If I hear of anything, I will let you know. On Sunday afternoons I am usually at home; but I don't like to ask you to come so far unless there's something definite to talk over.

Yours sincerely,
Walter de la Mare

200. *15ᵗʰ November 1920   Walter de la Mare to HJF*
                                        14 Thornsett Road, Anerley, London SE20
Dear Mr Foss,

You must have thought my promise had been forgotten; but as occasion has offered, I have mentioned your name when I thought it might be useful. With no very practicable results as yet, I am sorry to say. But I have just heard from Mr Middleton Murry, the Editor of the Athenaeum that he may possibly be able to give you an occasional book to review. If this would be of any service, perhaps you would let him have a word – Adelphi Terrace WC – and meanwhile I will take what further opportunities I can.

Yours sincerely
W.J. de la Mare

Edward Dent

Edward Dent (1876–1957) was a prominent figure in British music. Professor of Music at Cambridge University 1926–41, he was an authority on opera (especially Mozart), Scarlatti and Busoni, and he was much involved in the formation of the International Society for Contemporary Music and its annual festivals, becoming its first president 1923–37. He was also president of the International Musicological Society 1932–49. While he held a generally antipathetic attitude towards the music of Elgar, he showed admiration for Vaughan Williams, notably *Job* and the Sixth Symphony.

201. *4ᵗʰ April 1941   E.J. Dent to HJF*

77 Panton Street, Cambridge

Dear Foss,

Many thanks for the 2 vols of Tovey lectures,[28] with your own charming introduction and Ernest Walker's[29] excellent memoir. Talk of overlapping! I was invited myself to join both the Cramb[30] & the Alsop[31] lectures some years ago, but I didn't realize that I might have given the same lectures at each place under different titles.

I refused both invitations, and many others, including the Royal Institution, because I made up my mind not to lecture anywhere outside Cambridge during term time, as it w[oul]d have upset all my teaching here too much. There were exceptions, of course – Cornell[32] – too lucrative to throw away, besides the chance of going to America for 3 months – and Halle in 1935.

---

28   Donald Tovey, *Essays in Musical Analysis Vols 1 & II*, OUP, 1935, with an introduction by Hubert Foss. (Four more volumes followed between 1936 and 1939.) Tovey's *Musical Articles from the Encyclopaedia Britannica*, OUP, 1944, and Tovey's *Essays and Lectures on Music*, OUP, 1949, also had introductions by Foss. He had suggested publishing some of Tovey's broadcast talks, but Tovey felt that they suffered too much from the limitations imposed on him for broadcasting and that re-casting them 'would be a tiresome business' (Grierson, p. 237).

29   Ernest Walker (1870–1949), Indian-born English composer, pianist, organist (at Balliol College, Oxford) and writer, was a close friend of Tovey and co-dedicatee (with F.S. Kelly) of his *Balliol Dances*.

30   University of Glasgow.

31   Liverpool University.

32   Cornell University, Ithaca, New York.

I find the later Tovey very tedious reading: the sentences are so long-winded and pompous, and if it was not for Tovey's undoubted 'integrity' (of wh[ich] there c[oul]d never be any doubt), one might almost suspect his 'texture' of being the result of the undergraduate in examinations (and the journalist in newspapers) spinning it all out as long & wordy as possible in order to fill up paper and time!

I'm afraid my Notes on Fugue w[oul]d have annoyed him considerably! And he w[oul]d no doubt have called them 'pesky'. But I was glad to see that in his later years he did feel able to criticize some of the 'great masters' severely, even including JSB[ach]: though it was always 'pesky' of course, if anyone else criticized them.

I wish one c[oul]d perform The Bride of Dionysus[33] again, under proper conditions: it has beautiful things in it. Perhaps if John Christie captures Sadler's Wells & puts in Busch[34] as its Führer, he will attempt it!

I am still in bed, but hope it will not drag out to 4 weeks this time: it is all rather depressing, but the weather is mainly to blame. My doctor seems rather baffled: also he is very busy anyhow, and at this moment his partner is ill, so I seldom see him at all. However, I have no intention of changing him. Gerhard[35] told me the other day that Dr Kalmus[36] was in Cambridge, and on hearing of my illness, at once produced an uncle from Vienna in Hampstead who was the greatest dietician in the world. I certainly shan't call him in, for his theory is that milk & fish etc. are pernicious, & that the only thing to eat is game: venison & hare and wild boar & all that (only obtainable in the Wiener Wald) – I sh[oul]d write a second Freischütz instead of motets.

Yours

Edward Dent

Further correspondence from Dent, after Hubert Foss's death, is included in the Tribute section: letter 269, p. 244.

---

33 *The Bride of Dionysus*, opera by Donald Tovey, composed 1907–18 and performed in Edinburgh, 25 April 1932. Substantial excerpts were recorded in May 2009 by George Vass and the Ulster Orchestra and issued on Dutton Epoch CDLX7241.

34 Fritz Busch (1890–1951), German conductor associated with Glyndebourne Opera 1934–39 (founded by John Christie) and briefly after the war.

35 Roberto Gerhard (1896–1970), Catalan composer who moved to England during the Spanish Civil War, settling in Cambridge in 1940.

36 Alfred Kalmus (1889–1972), Austrian-born music publisher who emigrated to England, establishing the Universal Edition London in 1936.

The Dominant

The Dominant[37] was a short-lived house periodical of the Music Department of Oxford University Press, lasting from November 1927 until November 1929. Edited by Edwin Evans, it generally appeared monthly and there were in total seventeen issues. Many well-known musicians and critics contributed occasional articles and reviews, including M.D. Calvocoressi, Percy Scholes, Basil Maine, Wanda Landowska, W.G. Whittaker and Constant Lambert. Hubert Foss made three contributions, one significantly being on 'The printed page in music'.

202. *2ⁿᵈ November 1927   John Johnson to HJF* [typed]

> I must not forget to send you a note of admiration for your new Periodical. You go from strength to strength and there is no more to be said.
>   Yours ever,
>   John Johnson[38]

The Dominant Dining Club

In 1924 Hubert Foss, who was skilled in book design and typography, co-founded the Double Crown Club, a dining society exclusively for expert typographers.[39] Humphrey Milford and John Johnson were among its members. Then in 1929 Foss was involved in the formation of the Dominant Dining Club which was for musicians.

203. *17ᵗʰ December 1928   HJF to DMF*

> I went off to my dinner about Berlioz. Darling one, it was a great success! I never expected such reasonableness from such a mixed crowd. And Scholes showed

---

37   Simon Wright, '*The Dominant*: a note on a short-lived periodical', *Brio* Vol. 41 No. 2 (Autumn–Winter 2004), pp. 36–39.

38   John Johnson (1882–1956) was Printer to the University of Oxford (1925–46).

39   For further reference, see James Moran's *The Double Crown Club, a history of fifty years*, London, Westerham Press, 1974, a limited edition of five hundred copies.

up so well. We really got at least half-way to a conclusion when I had expected a mere bicker! Excellent. Harty was so pleased he suggested making this into a dining-club of small dimensions so as to ventilate other vexed questions, and Evans and I, in view of the general enthusiasm shown at the idea, are going to try and form it. It might be a really historic thing in English music, even if it only lasts for a time. We have last night established a tradition of English musicians quarrelling in mind and not in temperament – literally without the personal coming in more than it always must in the formation of critical views.

I worked like a slave – Evans being rather effete, and ended up with Harty and van Dieren alone – rather amusing though I was far too tired to enjoy it. I got back, quite sleepless and incapable of bed, at 1.30, and sat up before the fire reading musical magazines till 3!

204. *8ᵗʰ January 1929   HJF to DMF* **(Mundesley)**

Then I went to lunch with Alec Robertson and Eleanor Farjeon. Eleanor was very nice and I find that Alec Robertson, who is an old Bradfield man, is also, he thinks, vaguely related to me on my father's side! He will let me know how. It all came through Uncle Hugh [Foss], the Japanese Bishop I gather!

Norman [Peterkin] spent much time choosing songs this morning. In talking to me of mine he said he wanted to put in Rioupéroux and She sauntered. I parried the latter, but on second thoughts gave way on the grounds that it was dedicated to you. I then found that he's already chosen If I were living in Eirinn for the same reason! So is music chosen. You may be a commercial asset to me yet!

Then I saw Clement Spurling [of Oundle] and Edwin Evans and did the Dominant afterwards. Then I pushed off to the RCM to see [Henry] Ley. He says that Harris[40] has followed Ponsonby at the House [Christ's Church College, Oxford] and that New College will be vacant for a bit (no rumours even). I bicycled to and from Wimpole Street and got back (uphill and all and the mist included) in 10 minutes. Pretty good. I have greatly enjoyed my bike today.

Then came the Dining Club. I will tell you most about it when I come up. But I do think it may be a very important meeting. We formed the Club – The Dominant Dining Club, [Hamilton] Harty Chairman (how nice he is!), [Edwin] Evans Vice Chairman and me Secretary. (We are the Committee.)

---

40 (Sir) William Harris (1883–1973), English composer and organist at New College 1919–28 and Christ's Church 1928–33.

Numbers at present us and Norman P[eterkin], van Dieren, Calvocoressi, [Percy] Buck, Bliss, Bax, Howells, Steuart Wilson, Dyson, C[harles] K[ennedy] Scott, [Harvey] Grace, H[arry] Plunket Greene.

Honorary members: Scholes, [Harold] Samuel,[41] Bairstow, Tovey, Hadow, Bantock (why?), Whittaker, Herbert Thompson, C S Terry, Percy Hull, Dent. Pretty good crowd. It was really a most excellent evening and we all got to discussing the BBC with dire results to that worthy organisation. We may well alter it I feel. All very good and excellent work for the cause and no one yet afraid to speak his mind. Greene called Elgar a liar and I excluded Samuel from full membership as a Jew!

This may mean much, not only to us but to music.

205. *11ᵗʰ February 1929   HJF to DMF* **(Mundesley)**

A very enjoyable dinner last night. Harty, Evans, HJF, Buck, Bliss (whom a very little wine roused to a most talkative pitch, to be suppressed by Harty and others!!), Calvo[coressi] and Norman. We discussed 'Artists and Critics' and arranged to discuss at the next meeting 'The present state of composition in England'. Three members having fallen out, we decided to bring as guests to the next dinner Henry Wood, Ernest Bullock and Lord Berners, to stand for membership.

Ruth Draper[42]

Ruth Draper (1884–1956) was born into a well-to-do family in New York. She became a popular actress and 'diseuse', noted for her monologues in which with very few props she created a variety of characters. She toured the USA and the continent, on one occasion playing before King George V and Queen Mary. She was made an honorary CBE in 1953. Her many recordings, which preserve her approach and technique, have continued to inspire a multitude of actors and actresses, of whom Joyce Grenfell is a direct example. It is not known what prompted her to elevate Foss.

---

41   Harold Samuel (1879–1937), English pianist of note.
42   See p. 22.

206. *19th January 1933   Ruth Draper to HJF*

Dear Sir Hubert,[43]

I shall be very happy to take supper with you and Lady Foss on Friday after my performance. Thank you so much

Sincerely yours

Ruth Draper

Edward Elgar

Hubert Foss had no professional relationship with Elgar (1857–1934), and while he admired his music, from what he wrote in 1933 it is clear that he was not in complete sympathy with it: 'Elgar has given the world a store of musical treasure … His music is like a national monument. It is full of aspirations and ideals; and today the world, I fear, is not … His sheer musical merit has won the respect of those who differ from him. But there will never be a really close affinity between the style of Elgar and the style of the future.'[44]

There is only one letter from Elgar and I am quite unaware to what it refers! [DMF]

207. *24th October 1923   Edward Elgar to HJF*

The Athenæum, Pall Mall, SW1

Dear Sir,

Please do not publish any anecdotes concerning me: I detest publicity.

Yours very truly,

Edward Elgar

Hubert J. Foss Esq

43   Hubert Foss was in fact never knighted.

44   *Music in my Time*, pp. 167 & 80.

John Gardner

The composer John Gardner (1917–2011) was born in Manchester but brought up in North Devon, his father having been killed in the last months of WW1. He studied at Wellington College and Exeter College, Oxford. As the John Gardner homepage states: 'An important figure in his early career was Hubert Foss of Oxford University Press, who published the *Intermezzo for Organ* in 1936 and introduced him to the composer Arthur Benjamin', who gave him much encouragement and advice. Gardner regarded Foss as 'possibly the most active protagonist of modern English composers amongst the whole publishing fraternity'.[45] He taught at Morley College and the Royal Academy of Music, and was director of music at St Paul's Girls' School. His own works, though numerous and approachable, have sadly not been as widely performed as they deserve, apart, that is, from the popular carol *Tomorrow shall be my dancing day*.

208. *6th February 1934   John Gardner to HJF*

Combermere, Wellington College, Berks.

Dear Mr Foss,

I am writing to ask your permission to dedicate my overture to you, in recognition of all that you have done for me and my career.

It isn't yet completed but it is all more or less down in rough form and about 2/3 of the scoring is finished. Since you heard it, I have altered it almost entirely and although the themes are the same I have cut down on the amount of thematic materials. I found that I had more than enough for a piece of that length. I showed it to Mr [Gordon] Jacob who gave me one or two hints concerning the orchestration. He says that he doesn't know of anyone else who is going in for the competition.

If there is time I will send it you to have a look at before I finally send it up to the *Daily Telegraph*.[46]

Yours very sincerely

John L. Gardner

---

45   Emily Gardner, 'John Gardner: a portrait of a composer as a young man', *British Music* (Journal of the British Music Society) vol. 39, 2017/1, p. 23.

46   The *Daily Telegraph* overture competition in 1934 was won by Cyril Scott's *Festival Overture*, with Frank Tapp second and Arnold Cooke third. Contributions from William Alwyn, Grace Williams and Eric Fogg all received commendations. Gardner's overture *Orpheus*, a juvenile work which is extant, was unsuccessful in the competition.

209. *26ᵗʰ May 1934   John Gardner to HJF*

Wellington College

Dear Mr Foss,

Your letter was indeed a windfall! I am delighted about the sonata[47] and so is Mr Timberley to whom I am now teaching it.

There is a chance of my being able to come up too if I can get round Mr Malin, our headmaster, but his heart takes some softening.

I have just embarked on a setting of Manasses' Prayer from the Apocrypha for unaccompanied voices. This is to act as a compensating balance for my Back to Barnby Harmony Exercises.

My work for the ARCO is progressing satisfactorily and is on the whole quite interesting.

Well, thank you again for your kindness in giving my sonata a chance.

Yours ever

John L. Gardner

210. *13ᵗʰ January 1936   HJF* **(OUP)** *to DMF* **(Mundesley)**

The most interesting caller was John Gardner who is growing up a nice young man.

211. *11ᵗʰ July 1951   John Gardner to HJF*

4 South Close, Morden, Surrey

Dear Hubert,

Thank you for your letter. To receive it gave me particular pleasure since I owe as much to your interest and encouragement as to anything else that I entered upon a career of composition. There is lots more to come: lots already written since 1947 (when I completed the symphony).[48] I shall go right ahead now, I know.

Yours ever,

John Gardner

Further correspondence from John Gardner, after Hubert Foss's death, is included in the Tribute section: letter 270, p. 245.

---

47   One of Gardner's early performances was of the Second Piano Sonata, in London in 1934.

48   Gardner's First Symphony was given its first performance, conducted by Barbirolli, at the 1951 Cheltenham Festival.

212. *2ⁿᵈ January 1996   Diana Sparkes to John Gardner* [typed]
16 Leigh Road, Highfield, Southampton SO17 1EF

Dear John (if I may),

I must apologize first for the shock you will receive after reading this letter from someone you don't know at all! Cast your mind back to 1934 when you were at school composing. You wrote to the OUP Music Department, I believe, and asked for help/advice – and you received it, from my father Hubert Foss. He and my mother always talked most affectionately of you and I know that my father admired your work immensely. That is all a very long time ago: he died in 1953 and she in 1978. On our mother's death, my brother and I inherited a vast archive,[49] which we have divided between us, but much of his part (the numerous, huge, commonplace/scrap books) is now mine. The problem was always going to be what to do with it, and in this respect, you will be interested to know that we have been saved by a really splendid post-graduate Duncan Hinnells, who is writing his thesis on RVW but who will now include a great many references to HJF because of the latter's influence etc. on RVW. Duncan is like an answer to prayer. He is a very bright young man and 'lovely' with it!! Naturally, I am thrilled about this interest in my father after so many years, as my brother and I have always felt that he was totally undervalued.

My husband, Brian Sparkes, lately retired (early) as Professor of Classical Archaeology at Southampton University, and I have been cataloguing the contents of the commonplace books and have, at last, nearly finished. They are full of letters, programmes, press-cuttings etc. and continuously emphasise the enormous part my father played in the 1920s and 1930s when he was only in his 20s and 30s (being born in 1899), in shaping the future of British music in this century. The OUP Music Department is to celebrate 75 years in 1998 and Duncan is to write a booklet for this event,[50] much of which will support my father up to the hilt. Do you yourself have any letters or memories which might be of use to Duncan? He is also planning to write a much bigger book once he has his doctorate, which will include a great deal more about my father. Just as we are pleased with Duncan, so he is thrilled with our untapped archive, an answer to every researcher's prayer.

So why did I think of you just now? Partly, of course, because your name and letters crop up in the archive, and partly because you came to mind when I was singing (alto now) in a choir before Christmas and we performed your brilliant

49   Hubert Foss Archive. See pp. xv–xvi.
50   Duncan Hinnells, see fn. 17, p. 187.

'Tomorrow shall be my dancing day'. (I remember our son twenty years ago performing your magnificent 'Fight the good fight'.) I didn't study music, but read Classics instead, and kept music as a hobby. So now I play the organ in church, piano too and sing in Southampton Philharmonic! I retired 2 years ago after teaching Latin in the Comprehensive system – a challenge every day! I am also, in my 'spare time' doing some archive work in connection with the 150th birthday of Queen's College Harley Street in 1998. I was there at the centenary in 1948! Tempus fugit, doesn't it? Correct me, if I am mistaken, but didn't you marry a fellow student of mine, Jane Abercrombie? It's 45 years ago and a lot of water has flowed under the bridge since then!

I do hope you keep well and are not too amazed by this sudden letter!

Very best wishes, sincerely,

Diana [Sparkes, née Foss]

213. *4th January 1997   John Gardner to Diana Sparkes* **[typed]**
                                                    20 Firswood Avenue, Epsom, Surrey

Dear Diana,

You are mistaken. By my reckoning we've met twice at least. In 1932 (or it may have been 3) my mother and I lunched with your parents in Rickmansworth and met Christopher, a post-toddler, I suppose and you a babe-in-arms. My main memory is that your garden backed on to the old Great Central main line and at one point an express went by and your father counted the passengers aboard it. 'Three in that one; five in that one; two in that one, none in that one ... and so on. Roaring trade!'

Then on 21 November 1953 Jane and I dined with your mother in Golders Green, and she gave me a book from Hubert's library and showed me his priceless (literally) collection of Lambert postcards. What has happened to those?[51] An archive of great value. I only remember one of them. A picture of Burnley – a collection of factory chimneys. On the message side he'd written 'Only three coronas between me and the gas oven'. And there was another I've just remembered. The Monarch at Bay (or is it Monarch of the Glen) on which he said 'A wee, sleekit, timorous cowering beastie' – I guess I've that Burns quote a bit wrong. No matter, the point's made.

Your father's archives sound important and eminently keepable and maybe publishable. He wrote a very good Music in My Time book, and I have copies of one or two of his songs, which I must look out some time.

---

51   The Lambert postcards are now in the British Library, Deposit 2009/03.

He is somebody I look upon as being absolutely crucial in getting me into a musical career. He was endlessly kind to me and it was a great tragedy for OUP when he left. It has never been the same since, and now, though still in existence as a music house, it is a shadow of itself. This is possibly due to the fact that the printing of music has become almost a cottage industry. We have a Sibelius 7 and on that Jane prints my music in the dining-room much more quickly than it takes a publisher to do so with all that wearisome to-ing and fro-ing by post and slow fulfilling of publishing plans and all that. Of course a publisher can market, I can't. But for most of the things I write there isn't a market in the full sense of the word.

It was Edith Sitwell, a friend of my mother, who put me in touch with your father. That would have been in 1932 or 3, probably the former.

The upshot of all this is that I have many memories that I could contribute to Duncan Hinnells, many more of which would be prompted by his questions. So please put him in touch with me, because I'd love to help in any way I can.

When I taught at the Academy I was a frequent visitor at Christopher's in Baker Street. He did several nice printing jobs for me and we used to chat now and then. He has now retired, I believe, and I never see him. I suppose your father, who knew all about printing, was an inspiration to him. When you next see him, please give him my regards.

I'm the world's worst typist, but [I] find writing letters a pain when forced to use a pen. Jane, of course, has two computers and all that, but I'm not allowed to use them. Don't know how to, anyway.

All the best

John Gardner

214. *13ᵗʰ January 1997   Diana Sparkes to John Gardner* [typed]

Dear John,

I was absolutely delighted to receive your kind letter. It must have been 1933 (late) when you came to Rickmansworth, since I wasn't born until September that year. Christopher would have been 5½. You remember the railway very clearly as does Christopher, but I was only three when we moved to London, so I can't recollect it at all!

However, I looked up Nov 21 1953 in my engagement diary of that date, and sure enough, it said 'Jane and John to dinner'. How did you remember the date? Did you write it in the book Mama gave you? What book was it? You mentioned the Lambert postcards. I have these,[52] and many letters of his too, and Duncan has borrowed them just now. He rang up last night having found both the cards you mentioned. The one with the Burns quotation had a picture of a hairy Highland ox on it. You quoted correctly. What a fantastic memory you have!

Brian and I have very nearly finished cataloguing onto disc my father's common-place books. It has been hard going, especially when an ... [the remainder of the letter has faded].

John Goss

John Goss (1894–1953) was a singer and friend of Foss's from the early 1920s when he was invited down to Eynsford, where 'The Warlock Gang' gathered for their riotous weekends (see pp. 64–7). Myfanwy Thomas, in recalling that period in *One of These Fine Days* (1982, p. 141), remembers Goss as 'a delightful singer'. Throughout the 1920s Foss accompanied Goss at his recitals, in which he championed Heseltine's songs. He was noted for his volumes *An Anthology of Song* (1929) and *Ballads of Britain* (1937).

215.   *Sunday [early 1920s]   John Goss to HJF*

176a Kings Road, Chelsea

Dear Mr Foss,

I left London [too] early on Saturday morning to 'phone you, and I've had no chance to write while I've been away. If I am free, I shall be very pleased to sing for you at Eynsford. I don't know what to say about fee. Perhaps you could let me know what the concert will stand and I will endeavour to fit in. You will let me know the date as soon as you can, won't you?

I was sorry not to be able to accept your kind invitation to Harold Samuel's recital. Thanks for asking me.

Do you mind my saying how much I admire your critical writings? Your remarks on 'The Immortal Hour'[53] – particularly the performance of the

---

52   See previous footnote.

53   *The Immortal Hour*, opera by Rutland Boughton (1878–1960) that had two successful runs in London in 1922 and 1923.

Ffrangcon-Davies girl [Gwen] pleased me considerably. I am amazed that such a performance doesn't take musical and dramatic London by storm.

Yours sincerely,

John Goss

216. *17th April 1924   John Goss to HJF*

176a Kings Road, Chelsea

Dear Hubert,

I have fixed with Stolls for a fortnight from April 28th with options week by week for a period not exceeding ten weeks. I should like you to play for me if you would, but I doubt very much whether it will be worth your while. I can only afford a fiver a week.

This will be for 12 shows and until the show gets on its feet and we know a pretty good repertory backwards, it will be too nervous a business to put up with substitutes. Let me know what you think! We shall be on sometime between 3.25 and 4.15 and 9.25 and 10.15. Perhaps you might consider doing it for the fortnight, and then retiring if Stolls insist on their option to continue. I would like three or four rehearsals next week.

Yours

John

217. *28th April 1927   John Goss to DMS*

47 Cleveland Square, W2

Dear Miss Stevens,

Many thanks for your letter. I think it would be great fun to do the Wolf Italian songs with you some time in the manner the composer suggests. I shall be away from London for most of the next fortnight. I'll ring you up as soon as I return and probably we can fix a meeting.

Yours sincerely,

John Goss

Percy Grainger

In August 1931 Percy Grainger (1882–1961) had written from Pevensey Bay, Sussex to Hubert Foss, enquiring about the possible publication of some of his choral works.[54] The two had already met ('It was so nice seeing you again in Oxford,' Grainger had written). But as Foss did not have the same enthusiasm for Grainger's music as he did for his OUP composers, nothing progressed. However, many years later he invited Grainger to contribute a memoir to the reprint he was editing of Heseltine's book on Delius.[55]

218.   *27th September 1950   Percy Grainger to HJF*

RMS *Caronia* (Cunard White Star)

Dear Hubert Foss,

My wife & I were in England for a few days – just between boats – but those days were taken up with elaborate preparations, amongst which getting a visa for my wife's neice [*sic*], who is paying us a visit in USA. There was not a free moment, alas, & that is why you did not hear from me.

It was a great disappointment not to see you, but I hope we will do so on our next visit to England, which I hope will be soon, or that we meet in USA or somewhere.

I find what you write always so thrilling & bull's-eye-hitting & I look forward to your edition of the Delius book most eagerly.

The below address will always find me.

Yours ever admiringly,

Percy Grainger

Percy Grainger, 7 Cromwell Place, White Plains, NY

---

54   *The All-Round Man – Selected Letters of Percy Grainger 1914–1961*, ed. Malcolm Gillies and David Pear, OUP, 1994, pp. 108–10.

55   *Frederick Delius* by Peter Warlock (Philip Heseltine), reprinted with additions, annotations and comments by Hubert Foss, The Bodley Head, 1952. Grainger contributed a memoir, as did Roger Quilter and Charles Kennedy Scott.

Harry Plunket Greene

The Irish bass-baritone Harry Plunket Greene (1865–1936) was a leading singer in his day and known particularly for his interpretations of Vaughan Williams, Parry and Stanford. He was a close friend and biographer of the latter (*Charles Villiers Stanford*, Edward Arnold, 1935). At his recital at the Aeolian Hall in June 1930, Plunket Greene sang a group of contemporary English songs and included Foss's settings of *Fear no more the heat o' the sun* and *O Mistress Mine*.

219. *18th May 1930   Harry Plunket Greene to HJF*

65 Holland Park Road, Kensington, W14

My dear Foss,

I'm doing the two little songs on June 13th[56] and I want to know if you'd mind writing two or three bars leading up to the voice opening in Fear no more. The other one doesn't need it. It fits on capitally but the mood of the [Walford] Davies (When Childher plays) is so gentle and so tender that I feel you want quite a few seconds to give that mood to the audience before the blinking singer butts in. What about it? Not, of course, any idea of putting it into your own version – simply for me.

Yours ever

HPG

Key C# min-maj.

220. *16th June 1930   Harry Plunket Greene to HJF*

65 Holland Park Road, Kensington, W14

My dear Foss,

I'm frightfully glad you were pleased with the two songs – more touched than I can say. You must have thought me an ungracious dog never to have asked you to hear them beforehand, but when I get something I've really got my heart in (like these two little ducks) I get scared that I'll be asked to change my readings maybe, so I put my manners in the fire & trust to luck that they'll be all right with the 'Principal' – & thank heavens, they were. They're a topping

---

56   In the Aeolian Hall.

pair & I'd have liked the first one over again too. I didn't feel anything wrong with the piano part. However you're the judge & [...]. Three cheers that you were pleased.

Yours ever

H.P. Greene

Patrick Hadley

The Cambridge-born composer Patrick ('Paddy') Hadley (1899–1973) served as a gunner in the last stages of WW1 and was wounded, the amputation of his right leg giving him pain for the rest of his life. He studied at the Royal College of Music in the 1920s under Vaughan Williams and afterwards taught composition there until 1962. In 1946 he succeeded to the Chair of Music in Cambridge, where he was a much-loved figure as a teacher and conductor, noted for his sometimes bawdy sense of humour. His relatively small output of compositions, influenced by folk song, are chiefly for chorus or voices and orchestra, his most significant large-scale works being the symphonic ballad *The Trees So High* (1931) for baritone, chorus and full orchestra, and *The Hills* (1944) for soli, chorus and orchestra, both published by OUP.

221. *23rd September 1950   Patrick Hadley to HJF* [postcard]

Heacham, King's Lynn

Emerging from my bath this morning & dallying with my toilet (a lucid period of the day I always think, one of my few) I recalled for certain how the tortuous rectitude tale reached me. It was EJD[ent] quoting E[dwin] E[vans], and chuckling a good deal over it, who had recently made the crack at the meeting. I am only saying that's how it originally reached me. My less absolutely certain recollection is that the crack was anent VW saying he didn't want his own works recommended for the ISCM; that sort of thing was for the young, and so forth.

[Patrick Hadley]

Thomas Hardy

Hubert Foss had a particular love for the poems of Thomas Hardy (1840–1928), whose poetic gifts are now rated by many at a higher level than his novels. Foss's copy of Lascelles Abercrombie's *Thomas Hardy: A Critical Study* (1919) has numerous pencil markings in the margins. The poems Foss set to music as a song-cycle (for baritone, male-voice chorus and piano) are taken from the first three volumes of poems that Hardy published. 'The Sergeant's Song' (No. 2), 'Hap' (No. 4) and 'Friends Beyond' (No. 7) are from *Wessex Poems and Other Verses* (1898), 'The Sleep-Worker' (No. 1) and 'To Life' (No. 6) from *Poems of the Past and the Present* (1901), and 'Night in the Old Home' (No. 3) and 'The Dark-Eyed Gentleman' (No. 5) from *Time's Laughingstocks and Other Verses* (1909). The song-cycle was first performed at the Wigmore Hall on 13 June 1925 by John Goss and Hubert Foss. At the time of its composition, Hubert received the following letter from Hardy:

222. *8th November 1925   Thomas Hardy to HJF* [typed]

Max Gate, Dorchester

Dear Mr Foss:

The music-setting to the seven poems has arrived, for which I must thank you, and for the inscription. I have not been able to investigate your compositions as yet, but later on I shall find means to get them played over and, I hope, sung. I wish every success to the melodies and harmonies you have had the power to create.

Very truly yours,

Th: Hardy

Some years later, after a performance of the song-cycle, Hubert received the following letter from his friend, the choral conductor Charles Kennedy Scott:

223. *14th March 1934   Charles Kennedy Scott to HJF*

My dear Foss,

It was practically your concert last night in spirit and in truth, for you inspired it and gave it its character, and I want to say 'thank you' for it. The main fact is always the composer and don't let's forget it. And what a pessimist Hardy is, and how you brought it out in your music – rightly so, of course. Is life quite as dreadful – could we indeed live if it were so? I can stand Hardy and be invigorated in some hard salty way by him alone, but Hardy-cum-Foss is almost more than my frail spirit can bear – anyway 'bravo' to you and to [Sydney] Northcote[57] too.

Yours ever
CKS

Myra Hess

The pianist Myra Hess (1890–1965) is especially remembered as the founder and director of the morale-boosting series of 1,600 lunchtime recitals given during WW2 in the National Gallery (its paintings having been stored safely in a disused slate mine in Wales) and for her Bach transcriptions, notably *Jesu, Joy of Man's Desiring* (BWV147) and *Sleepers Awake* (BWV645).

224. *26ᵗʰ August 1940*   *Myra Hess to HJF* [typed]

48 Wildwood Road, London NW11

National Gallery Concerts

Dear Hubert,

Wonders will never cease! Here, contrary to all probability and expectation, is the MS of my arrangement of Sleepers Awake. If I was a 'swell guy' to say I'd do it in the first place, I can't imagine what I shall be now ... even your vocabulary will be put to the test!

Seriously, if you can let me have the proofs fairly soon it should be possible to get it out in time for the autumn list.

Yours virtuously,
Myra

Gustav Holst

Gustav Holst (1874–1934) was not a composer with whose music Foss had a great affinity. Referring to him as 'Holst: the bringer of paradox' in an article for *The Listener*, 17 September 1942, he offered this assessment: 'He was an

57   Sydney Northcote (1897–1968), Welsh-born composer, singer (tenor), editor and adjudicator.

explorer by type, an experimenter, for whom the writing of each new work was a process of discovery ... This is music of reaction, not of action, music that will not charm, will not delight, will not be comfortable, lest it should be suspect.'

225. *18ᵗʰ July [1927]   Gustav Holst to HJF*
                                        St Paul's Girls' School, Brook Green, Hammersmith, W6
Dear Foss,

Please accept my warmest congratulations on your marriage [20 July 1927].

[Ralph] Greaves told me that you had mentioned it to me before and I cannot think how I could have been so silly as to forget it. I hope you'll get a real honeymoon during which you will forget all about the OUP, British Music and

Yrs sincerely

Gustav Holst

The following was written after the birth of HJF's son, Christopher, on 21 May 1928:

226. *[May 1928]   Gustav Holst to HJF*[58]
                                        St Paul's Girls' School, Brook Green, Hammersmith W6
Dear Foss,

I'll keep your letter in case I find any easy choral music written but there is nothing of the sort in the offing.

Meanwhile, many congratulations.

[MS quotation from Handel's *Messiah* 'For unto us a child is born']

Yrs sincerely

GH

[Another very brief MS quotation from 'For unto us a child is born']

227. *18ᵗʰ May [1934] Gustav Holst to HJF* **[in pencil]**
                                                          Beaufort House, Ealing W6
Dear Foss,

Thank you for all the trouble you have taken. If I had known the circum-stances I should not have bothered you.

As for me, I am having rather a thin time – only three weeks out of a bedroom since Xmas. But things are improving at last and I hope to be strong enough

58   See plate 20.

for an operation within the next fortnight. I shall be at this nursing home for at least another six weeks but school address will always find me.

> Yours sincerely
>
> Gustav Holst[59]

PS Since writing, Kennedy Scott has been to see me and among other nice things he has promised to lend me 'Music in My Time'.

Gordon Jacob

Gordon Jacob (1895–1984) was a composer, conductor and teacher especially known for his textbooks on orchestration. Born in London, he saw service in WW1 in the infantry and was taken PoW. After the war he studied under Stanford at the Royal College of Music, where he later taught for forty years until his retirement in 1966. He married his first wife Sidney Gray in 1924, and after her death in 1958 he married his wife's niece Margaret Gray the following year. His output of over four hundred works includes some well-known transcriptions of pieces by Vaughan Williams and Elgar, and the frequently used harmonisation of the National Anthem.

228. *6th November [1951]*   **Sidney Jacob to HJF**

Pine Cottage, Brockenhurst, Hants.

My dear Hubert,

Gordon & I did not see your article in the Listener[60] till yesterday, owing to the move. He has gone to town today, & I feel I must send you a line of thanks for a really wonderful bit of writing. The article had a great emotional effect on us both – perhaps even more on me than on him. In fact it made me weep, to find out that someone, besides myself, really understood at last. I can honestly say that for over a quarter of a century my whole devotion has been to Gordon's music; & your appreciation of it brings a very rich reward. I say 'reward' because being married to a genius is not always easy! There have been times, quite often, when he has said he would 'never write another note' & that his 'ideas'

---

59   In April 1934 Holst entered the Beaufort House nursing home at Ealing. On 23 May he underwent an operation for the removal of a duodenal ulcer, but died two days later of heart failure.

60   'The Music of Gordon Jacob', *The Listener*, 1 November 1951, p. 764.

were 'second rate' or something of that sort, & it has been up to me to cheer him on, & assure him that all he did was worth while. Your article seems to me quite amazing.

A few months ago, I had occasion, (when Gordon was away from home) to write to him entirely about his music, & one of the things I said was: – 'I think the chief characteristics of your music are Purity, Beauty, & Gaiety' – & now you say – 'with the warmth of Constable, he combines the classic line of Gainsborough & the humour of Rowlandson'. Of course your way of saying the same thing is much better!

May I quote a few more things you say which especially appeal to me?

1) Jacob's mind is a rare example of reasoned simplicity – – – [*sic*].
2) He characterises his instruments.
3) Here we meet music distilled from sound, not audible impressions of a state of mind.
4) He thinks in instruments & finds music in them.
5) He can laugh in his music with the genuine ring of pleasure.

– And so on & so on.

I do hope I haven't taken up too much of your time, but I feel very deeply, all I have said, & all you have written. Gordon does too, I know.

This is a sweet peaceful spot: be sure & let us know if ever you can come & see us.

Yours very gratefully

Sidney Jacob

PS Of course no answer needed or expected!

The Joyce Book

The Joyce Book consisted of settings by various composers of thirteen poems from the collection *Pomes Penyeach* by James Joyce (1882–1941). Edited by Herbert Hughes and designed by Hubert Foss with a frontispiece by Augustus John, it was published in 1933 by the Sylvan Press. In large format on special paper and bound in hand-woven silk, only five hundred copies were printed and the proceeds were to be given to James Joyce, who was suffering from poverty following the scandal caused by the publication of *Ulysses*. However, it was not a financial success and Joyce received nothing ('un nettissimo niente', in his letter to his son on 24 December 1934).

From Herbert Hughes

229. *5th February 1933*

125 Church St., Chelsea SW3

I confess to experiencing a real thrill when the Joyce Book turned up. It is indeed lovely, surely the loveliest thing that has ever come out of an English Press. I feel that without your masterly collaboration, such a book would have been impossible and you have my deepest thanks for all the trouble you have taken.

Yours always

Herbert Hughes

From Bernard van Dieren

230. *6th February 1933* [typed]

68 Clifton Hill, St John's Wood, NW8

... I received my copy of the Joyce Book. It certainly does look very swell although I do not know that I entirely approve of silver edges. But I suppose that is neither here nor there.

As regards the paper and the cover, the type and the proportions, my heart swells with fulsome praise. No, really, it does look most attractive.

From Holbrook Jackson[61]

231. *28th February 1933* [typed]

Drury House, Russell St., Covent Garden WC2

It is an admirable tribute to a great writer and most excellently carried out. Such a musical tribute has never been paid to a writer before so far as I know and you as typographer have risen to the occasion most nobly.

From James Joyce

232. *24th February 1933*

42 Rue Galilée, Paris VIII e

Dear Sir,

I have now received from you two copies of the Joyce Book which you have published and presented to me in the name of many artists.

---

61   Holbrook Jackson (1874–1948), a journalist, writer and publisher.

It is a tribute of which I am very proud and the gift itself is a splendid one. I can easily understand what trouble it cost you in the production and by your painstaking zeal you have laid me under a deep obligation.

Allow me to thank you also for the kind expression concerning my daughter's health[62] for the facsimiles [...] of the text. It gave us both great pleasure to be able to offer you the book.

Sincerely yours

James Joyce

From John Johnson

233. 28ᵗʰ February 1933

... the handsome 'Joyce' book. Courage was always your dominant note – and here again is courage.

Yours ever

JJ

D.H. Lawrence

While he was assistant editor of *Land and Water*, Hubert Foss wrote to D.H. Lawrence (1885–1930), and the following two letters from Lawrence[63] would appear to be their only extant correspondence. In April 1920 Lawrence's short story 'You touched me' was printed in *Land and Water*. It seems likely that in subsequent correspondence Hubert had suggested that the novel *The Lost Girl*, begun in 1913 and completed in May 1920, be serialised in *Land and Water*. However, Lawrence clearly had other intentions. It was published by Martin Secker that same year. A few years later, Hubert wrote an article entitled 'Music and Mr D.H. Lawrence' that appeared in the *Musical News and Herald*, 21 June 1924.

---

62   Joyce's daughter Lucia (1907–82) had shown signs of mental illness. She was diagnosed with schizophrenia and in 1935 was put in an institution in France.

63   *The Letters of D.H. Lawrence Vol. VIII Previously Uncollected Letters*, edited and compiled by James T. Boulton, Cambridge University Press, 2000, Nos 2020a and 2048a.

234. *24th May 1920   D.H. Lawrence to HJF*

Fontana Vecchia, Taormina, Sicily

Dear Mr Foss,

Thank you for your letter. I should really like to be serialised in <u>The Queen</u>: such a relief after English Reviews, highbrow and Nash.[64] But is it just a random suggestion?

Anyhow I send the MS of <u>The Lost Girl</u>. I am under contract with Secker – he will publish it in book form. If within the next ten days or so I cable you 'Send MS. Secker', will you be so good as to post it across to [him]? It will be at least 8 days coming to you, I [sup]pose. If you have no word from me, do [let] <u>The Queen</u> see the book. Secker has already written to me for this carbon copy MS. But he has the original, so don't know why he wants this. Anyhow I should like the Queen to see it: would be fun if she printed it. So I send it to you. You will be so good as to send it across to Secker, 5 John Street, Adelphi, if I cable you – won't you. – And if ever you should want to cable me, <u>Lawrence, Taormina, Sicily</u> is enough.

Yours sincerely,

D.H. Lawrence

235. *23rd July 1920   D.H. Lawrence to HJF* [postcard]

Fontana Vecchia, Taormina, Sicily

Dear Mr Foss

Have you received the MS. of my novel <u>The Lost Girl</u> which I posted to you exactly a month ago, on the 23rd June, by registered manuscript post[?] I should be glad to know.

If you have this MS., and Secker wants it to make corrections in his uncorrected copy, please let him have it. But if <u>The Queen</u> would like to see the book, and if 'She' could read it in a week or so, perhaps let her have it <u>first</u>, because if once Secker gets it there is no knowing when he will part from it again: he would only <u>need</u> to keep it a few days.

Hope it has arrived.

Yrs

D.H. Lawrence

---

64 *Nash's Pall Mall Magazine*, a monthly literary magazine formed by the merger in 1914 of two publications.

Francis Meynell

Francis Meynell (1891–1975), poet and typographer, was a conscientious objector in WW1. In 1922 his second wife, Vera Mendel, and David Garnett joined Meynell in the creation of the Nonesuch Press, which issued high-quality editions of poets such as William Blake and John Donne, and dramatists such as William Congreve. Their aim was to produce fine press editions at a lower price than was customary. A more popular publication was *The Week-End Book* (1924), which contained poems, music, plays, suggestions for food and drink, etc.; Vera and Francis were the general editors, with John Goss (see p. 207) the music editor. It was hugely successful, ran through annual impressions, and was revised and enlarged with a new edition in 1928. Meynell was knighted in 1946, and in 1947 married Alix Kilroy, a pacifist and important civil servant. Meynell had been a frequent visitor to Hubert Foss's musical parties at Eynsford, and as can be seen from his letter, he approved of Foss's typographic design.

236. *2ⁿᵈ December 1929   Francis Meynell to HJF*

                                                            16 Great James St., London WC1

My dear Hubert,

  I cannot read, I cannot play, I cannot sing your songs (or anyone else's).

  But I can – and do – admire the admirable Shakespeare pattern of the wrapper. It is fine in the vague mass and good in the detail and there's no nasty sharp break between its general and its particular effects.

  Many thanks to you

  Francis

Napier Miles

The Bristol-born Philip Napier Miles (1865–1935) was a wealthy landowner, amateur composer and generous supporter of local opera. He studied both abroad and in England, privately under Parry. He founded the Avenmouth Choral Society and gave financial assistance to Rutland Boughton's Glastonbury players. His own compositions, now generally neglected, included the operas *Westward Ho!* and *Markheim* that received first performances respectively in London in 1913 and Bristol in 1924.

237. *24th April 1933   Napier Miles to HJF* [typed]
                                   King's Weston, Shirehampton, Bristol

... it has been a real pleasure to have the business put through with such
courtesy and interest as you have always shown ...

Sir Humphrey Milford[65]

Humphrey S. Milford (1877–1952) studied at Oxford and became a senior editor
and publisher to Oxford University Press from 1913 to 1945. When only twenty-
three he was appointed Assistant Secretary to the Delegates who were responsible for OUP policy. He enjoyed a close working relationship with Hubert Parry,
Henry Hadow and Thomas Strong. The formation of the Music Department was
one of Milford's initiatives, and in 1923 he appointed Hubert Foss head of this
new department. He was succeeded by Geoffrey Cumberlege. Knighted in 1936,
he was father of the composer Robin Milford.

238. *20th December 1948   Humphrey Milford to DMF*
                                   The White House, Drayton St Leonard, Oxford

I was delighted to receive a Christmas card from you both – as always, one of
the most beautiful of all one's cards. Many thanks and best wishes for Christmas
and 1949.
   Yours
   HSM

Oxford University Press Dramatic Society

Another of Hubert Foss's interests was amateur dramatics, and he produced
a number of plays for the Oxford University Press Dramatic Society, including
George Bernard Shaw's *The Devil's Disciple* (January 1933), and Stanley
Houghton's *The Dear Departed* and Monkton Hoffe's *Many Waters* (November
1933). In February 1934 they performed *Many Waters* at the British Drama
League Community Theatre Festival.

65   See pp. 1–2.

239. *December 1933*

Dear Mr Producer,

'Many Waters' is over and the cast dispersed. Happy memories alone are left, unless we can count the eager anticipation of 'next time' among the feelings which have been created by our efforts during the past few weeks.

All of us have been so happy during this time that we feel that an expression of very real thanks from us all will not come amiss, and is indeed whole-heartedly offered to you.

Your skill in production, your extreme kindness to us – yes, <u>and</u> your sound ratings at rehearsals – have not only helped us but have created, from nothing, at least something which was appreciated by a large number of people at G[uildhall] S[chool] of M[usic], at Oxford and the Scrubs [Wormwood Prison]. You have thanked us for our efforts, but we all feel that the thanks of everybody – cast and 'supers' alike – are especially due to you, without whom we should never have been a company.

Whatever qualities you have found in us are of your creation, aided by your enthusiasm and determination. Your gamble in casting was a big one, but the result has shown how successful it was.

We trust that the inadequacy of this letter will be – partially at any rate – remedied by its sincerity. Thank you very much indeed.

[Thirty-five signatures]

Roger Quilter

Roger Quilter (1877–1953), one of the so-called Frankfurt Gang who studied abroad in Germany, is remembered especially for the incidental music he wrote for the children's play *Where the rainbow ends* and his delightful *Children's Overture*. But his output consists mainly of a number of fastidiously crafted songs, with settings of Herrick, Shakespeare and Shelley prominent among them. When Dora sang in the all-Quilter recital referred to in the following letter, as she has recounted elsewhere, the composer first came to her home to go through the songs with her.

240. *25ᵗʰ July 1939   Roger Quilter to DMF*

23 Acacia Road, NW8

Dear Mrs Foss,

  Thank you so much for your charming letter. It gave me so much pleasure to take part in your recital[66] – and to feel that you sang my music (and so beautifully and so sympathetically too). In fact I was more touched than I can say at the generous and delightful thought of you and your husband, and at the immense trouble and 'tender care' you both of you took over the affair.

  I wish you every success with your singing and I hope many many people may have the pleasure of hearing you sing, for many, many years.

  Best of wishes to you and Mr Foss – also, please, to your delightful children.

  Gratefully and sincerely yours,

  Roger Quilter

Further correspondence from Quilter, after Hubert Foss's death, is included in the Tribute section: letter 271, p. 245.

E.L. Richardson

Ernest Lamont Richardson (1858–1937) was a master at Bradfield from 1908 to 1921 and taught Hubert Foss.

241. *29ᵗʰ August 1914   E.L. Richardson to HJF*

20 Sion Hill, Clifton, Bristol

I was very glad of the opportunity of having a brief chat with you last term – and very glad you welcomed it. I remember the days when we had orchestra practice up here – and I was always ragging you – and you took it so well and never got cross. I am ready to repeat all that I said to you last term, and am also sure that you have much 'raw' musical ability. Forgive the epithet, but you will understand it.

---

66   See p. 78, fn. 92.

242. *December 1917   E.L. Richardson to HJF*

I am awfully sorry you should have to join up as I know you hate service under arms – but perhaps it will not be as bad as you anticipate and you may find it possible to find a job you like ... Anyway, I know you will do it cheerfully as you have trained yourself to all sorts ... think of us as kindly as you can, in spite of our faults. For my own part, I do not find myself conscious of your faults, if you have any as I suppose must be the case – but I am very much alive to your attractions, as I think you well know and shall always remember you with affection. You will be missed by the school – as well as by your special friends – and a source of life and movement will be gone from us.

Bruce Rogers

Bruce Rogers (1870–1957), known to his friends as 'BR', was a highly esteemed American typographer and type designer, noted for his adherence to classical designs. He asserted that 'the first requisite of all book design is orderliness'. Initially he worked at the Riverside Press in Boston and then at New York Dyke Mill. He came to England in 1916 with the hope of founding a high-class press, but WW1 sabotaged his chances. He stayed for a few years working for the Cambridge University Press. His second visit was in 1928 to work on a new edition of Homer's *Odyssey* translated by T.E. Lawrence, which was printed as a limited edition by the Oxford University Press in 1932. Foss's interest in book design made for a close friendship and led to Rogers's membership of the Double Crown Club (see p. 198). Rogers returned to the States in 1932, where he was much in demand as a freelance designer.

243. *17ᵗʰ May 1929   HJF to DMF* (Mundesley)

I had a most enjoyable lunch, but suffered sadly afterwards from indigestion, sleepiness and general debility of will! Bruce Rogers was really delightful. Full of reminiscence and talk, and we had long discussions about printing. I showed him round the place, and he was most excited about our lovely view of St Paul's. Also about H[umphrey] S M[ilford's] room. He has been in close touch with Colonel Lawrence, or Aircraftsman Shaw as he is now called. He says he's a most likeable modest intelligent person, with much more eye for design and much less blarney than his namesake G B Shaw. Lawrence has, I gather, no means at all, except a cottage which is mortgaged! And so his army exploits in

Mes[o]pot[amia] are the real thing, a real earning business. I suppose he was really doing secret service work, but the change of name is caused, I gather, by the dislike of the publicity he got as Colonel Lawrence. He apparently will not use the name, not even to make a living. Any paper would of course pay for the name, but I gather he sends a lot of stuff round to papers under other names only to get it rejected! So he now goes into camp as Shaw again and resents having to work 8 hours a day instead of the 4 hours of Mes[o]pot[amia].

A most interesting talk. Bruce Rogers is a great man.

Incidentally, one thing Bruce said last night amazed me. His grandfather, he tells me, learnt the organ from a pupil of Bach's! Isn't that odd?

244. *17th May 1929   HJF to Bruce Rogers* [typed]

OUP, Amen House, EC4

Dear Bruce Rogers,

I have quite unintentionally insulted you. I am so sorry. I had quite forgotten that we had the honour of having you as an ordinary member of the Club. We shall meet there anyhow.

Yours sincerely,

Hubert J Foss

Bruce Rogers returned the letter with handwritten additions. He added an exclamation mark after 'sorry', crossed out 'quite' and added up the side a finger pointing at 'ordinary' which he underlined with three exclamation marks and 'Perhaps you mean "ornery"'. At the bottom he wrote:

Dear Hubert Foss,

I like to be insulted by invitations to dinner. You've insulted me again! Coffee & cocktails for two – B.R.

Malcolm Sargent

Foss's letter below concerns an ongoing battle between Malcolm Sargent (1895–1967) and Dame Ethel Smyth (see p. 228) that had come to a head during rehearsals of her *Mass in D* with the Royal Choral Society. Smyth had a reputation for interfering with rehearsals of her works in the hope of taking over the conducting herself. This had happened at the rehearsals for the 29-year-old Sargent's first concert with the RCS in January 1925. When she couldn't get her way, she instructed a reluctant switchboard operator to connect her with the Palace to invite an aged Queen Alexandra to the concert – and she came. At rehearsals for a repeat performance in November 1928, Dame Ethel once more pressed her wish to conduct, and after Sargent's insistence that he had been invited to conduct, the matter was left to the Council of the RCS to decide. At the Council meeting the following day, first a note from Smyth was read out aloud: 'Sargent is a cad.'[67]

245. *26ᵗʰ October 1928   HJF to DMF*

> Then on to Nottingham. Alas, I ran into Malcolm Sargent and had to talk to him all the way. He's had a superb row with Ethel Smyth who had complained of him to the Queen! I'm all on Ethel's side as I dislike MS very much. However he brought me an amusing experience. He has apparently known the attendant in the Restaurant Car pretty well for some time and discovered he was a mouth organ expert. The attendant passed and noticed Sargent and took us up to the Guard's van and gave us a really first rate recital on his little instrument! He's a marvellous technician and a very amusing fellow.

Percy Scholes[68]

Percy Scholes (1877–1958), English musician and critic, was author of *The Listener's Guide to Music* (OUP, 1919) and editor of *The Oxford Companion to Music* (1938), the two volumes of *The Mirror of Music 1844–1944* (1947) and *The Concise Oxford Dictionary of Music* (1952). He also frequently contributed pieces on music to *The Observer* and *Radio Times*.

246. *19ᵗʰ September [1928]   Percy Scholes to HJF*

> This is just a line to thank you for the trouble you have taken to make it so attractive in appearance[69] – a notable example of the combination of seduc-tiveness with dignity – like yourself – and (of course) myself too.

---

67   Charles Reid, *Malcolm Sargent: a biography*, Hamish Hamilton, 1968, pp. 126–29.
68   Further correspondence from Scholes, letter 264, p. 241.
69   Percy Scholes, *Miniature History of Music*, OUP, 1928.

247. *15ᵗʰ September 1937   Percy Scholes to HJF*
                                  Cornaux, près Chamby sur Montreux, Switzerland

My dear Foss,

I often write to you on particular points concerning the Encyclopedia. This time I write on a more general subject – & no reply is necessary.

As a Northcountryman I don't gush – perhaps I go to the other extreme, so probably I have never said what it now comes into my head to say – that I recognise the immense gain to my book[70] of your personal interest in it, your visits here, your reading of the proofs (tho' I protest against this as too much for you to undertake) & your organisation of the illustrations.

It will be a great day when the book at last appears (would that day had dawned!) & it will be a day of relief for you as much as for me, for you have thrown yourself so heartily & thoroughly into the labour of preparing it that it has been partly yours.

We both sincerely hope that the family holidays have been a great success &, above all, that Mrs Hubert J Foss feels herself to be reaching her old level of well-being.

Yours ever

P Scholes

Evelyn Sharp

Evelyn Sharp (1869–1955) was sister to Cecil Sharp, the leading figure in the English folk song and dance movement. Born in London, Evelyn was a journalist and author, writing books for children and adults. She was also a prominent activist in the women's suffrage movement and she edited their journal *Votes for Women*. She was twice arrested and even once went on a hunger strike. In 1933 she married her long-time friend and lover, the campaigning journalist Henry Nevinson (father of the artist Christopher Nevinson), after the death of his wife. Evelyn had been the librettist of Vaughan Williams's light opera *The Poisoned Kiss* (1927–9) and Hubert wrote to her, asking if she would dramatise Chesterton's 1914 satirical novel *The Flying Inn*.[71] In her reply she wrote:

---

70   *Oxford Companion to Music*, OUP, 1938.

71   It was reported in *John O'London's Weekly*, 10 November 1928, that Hubert Foss and G.K. Chesterton were collaborating on an opera based on Chesterton's 1914 satirical novel *The Flying Inn*.

248. *24ᵗʰ April 1933   Evelyn Sharp to HJF*

4 Downside Crescent, Hampstead NW3

... I have now read the book and as the whole point of it seems to turn on a joke against temperance reformers, I don't feel I could approach it with enthusiasm. I never can make jokes about temperance reformers, however absurd they may be and often are, because at least they are trying to stop what I think one of the greatest social evils, and as everybody knows I feel like this they would think I had suddenly gone mad if I were to dramatise Chesterton's book, delightful as it is as a fantasy.

Ethel Smyth

Described by Hubert as 'that wonderful, if somewhat formidable, woman', the ebullient, indomitable Ethel Smyth (1858–1944) was the composer of, among other works, six operas, most notably *The Wreckers*. For a while she was a prominent member of the suffragette movement, for which she composed the *March of the Women*. In 1911 she was jailed for her militant activities and Beecham famously visited her in Holloway Prison. She was created a Dame in 1922. The author of several volumes of autobiography, in her last years she suffered from deafness. Among her finest works are the Concerto for Horn, Violin and Orchestra and the comic opera *The Boatswain's Mate*.

249. *11ᵗʰ May 1923   Ethel Smyth to HJF*

Coign, Woking

Dear Sir,

I am obliged for your offer which I am unable to accept through consciousness of a lack of gift for the sort of thing required. Also I am sworn off all literary work just now.

As to Fête Galante[72] which is to be produced in Birm[in]g[ham] on June 4ᵗʰ (not 2ⁿᵈ) all I can say is that Curwen's have the Vocal Score but I fear not yet the text books. The libretto is a dramatisation by myself of a story of Maurice Baring's which fascinated me when first I read it (name Fête Galante) and the

---

72   A one-act opera presented by the Birmingham Repertory Theatre in June 1923 and later arranged as a ballet.

poetic vesture, so to speak, is by another friend, Edward Shanks. I wanted lyrics and lyrical words here and there and didn't feel equal to it myself tho' I don't mind comic lyrics (see Bosun[73] and a forthcoming opera not yet finished). It's entirely fantastic yet might have happened – no doubt <u>has</u> happened, and though it's tragic, I think it not at all sad, because the fool, who adores the Queen secretly, has, and takes, the chance of saving her good name at the cost of his own life – and he knows that she knows! – This is the best thing that could happen in such circumstances.

Yours truly

Ethel Smyth

I'm thrilled to see P. Shelving's[74] decoration!

Mr Barry Jackson says I shall love it.

250. *14ᵗʰ January 1929   HJF to DMF* **(Mundesley)**

Then the dear Dame (Ethel) came to lunch. What a charming creature she is! She was most witty and entertaining and ate a huge lunch (cod and mayonnaise sauce, duck, and mince pies (2) and two large glasses of claret!) and was full of schemes for downing the BBC and upping Henry Wood with a letter in The Times to follow! Eventually we got to musical business and so called in Greaves [Ralph Greaves – one of Hubert's assistants at the OUP]. After that she yarned again, and told us a long tale of her latest sheep dog aged 9 months, apparently a prize beast and all that – she said that he had only one failing, and that he would visit her while she was in the bath, and drink her bath water which made him sick!

I hope I shall be as young as that at her age [seventy-one] – but I doubt it.

251. *14ᵗʰ March 1929   Ethel Smyth to DMF*

Coign, Woking

Dear Mrs Foss,

I was so sorry to hurry away before the end – but ... I got train panic as I always do! I enjoyed some of the music so much – your <u>quick</u> songs (No. 2 and

---

73 *The Boatswain's Mate*, a comic opera in two scenes, first performed 1916. Together with *Fête Galante*, it ran for a fortnight at Birmingham in 1923, produced by Barry Jackson.

74 Paul Shelving, a British theatre designer who worked at the Birmingham Repertory Theatre.

another later on) and the 2 first pieces of Mr Randerson.[75] The next I rather doubt my ever being able to really appreciate – but ... it may be that I lack practice in listening to that sort of music. Anyhow I make no merit of it! Nor am I ashamed! To feel <u>sincerely</u> is what a listener should try to do – It was so good of you to ask me to listen ... how beautifully you and your friend both play!

I have just got the MS score and the wind parts of the Interlinked Melodies[76] back – I am going away till either March 23rd or 25th. I don't know how nearly the engraving is ready, but if worth sending, my address is 13 Cliff Avenue Cromer.

<u>L. Goossens is back</u>. I sh[oul]d love a record to be made of these Oboe Trios as Chamber Music. Have you links with either HVM [*sic*] or Columbia?

Yours sincerely

Ethel Smyth

Ethel Snowden

Ethel Snowden, née Anniken (1881–1951), in 1905 married the Labour Party politician Philip Snowden, who became Chancellor of the Exchequer in 1924. A human rights activist and supporter of women's suffrage, in 1926 she was appointed a governor of the BBC (a position she held for six years) and later a director of the Royal Opera House. In 1931 she became Viscountess Snowden when her husband entered the House of Lords.

252. *[n.d. 1928/9] HJF to DMF* (Mundesley)

I'm eating biscuits all the time I write having had no food beyond a sandwich at 7.15. The world is pretty busy, having been much occupied with the fact that the Russian Bessel[77] has seized our copies of B[oris] G[odunov][78] and caused thereby a situation. I've had to send Calvo[coressi] to Paris and may go anytime myself. It's all very worrying and I hate equally the names Mussorgsky, Calvocoressi, R[imsky]-Korsakov, Bessel and Boris Godunov. In fact I wish it were all buried, and all the people with it. Ugghum!! I shudder.

---

75   Horace Randerson (1892–1992), an employee at OUP.
76   *Two Interlinked French Folk Melodies* for flute, oboe and orchestra.
77   V. Bessel & Co., publishers of the first edition of Mussorgsky's opera *Boris Godunov*, St Petersburg, 1873.
78   In 1929 OUP published an edition of *Boris Godunov* in a translation by M.D. Calvocoressi.

The BBC stunt (the anti that is) progresses and the scheme has gone into the editor at the M[orning] P[ost]. I may progress, but at least I've found another way in, PAS[choles] brought Mrs Snowden [later Viscountess] to see me today. She's awfully nice and very able and took in all I and Milford and Scholes said about the BBC. Something may happen I hope – no gain to me but at least a thing done!

I cannot give her her due in this letter, but it would need an eloquent pen. We got on well at once and I thought very well of her.

253. *8ᵗʰ November 1932   The Viscountess Snowden to HJF* [typed]

72 Carlisle Mansions, SW1

Dear Mr Foss:

The newspaper reference must be to a sentence in a letter of recommendation of Landon Ronald's new MUSIC FOR THE HOME book, about which the NEWS-CHRONICLE asked for my opinion. At the end of my letter to them, I said that if they should publish a companion volume of valuable contemporary music they would be astonished how large a part of it would bear the names of English composers.

There is a Board meeting of the B.B.C. to-morrow, and I will try to get in touch with the people who make the programmes and give them a hint about your admirable suggestion, but they grow restive, I fear, under my continual exhortations to duty! I must use tact.

I so enjoyed your wife's concert. I told her so in the ante-room. And your accompaniment was no small part of the pleasure both Miss Picton-Turbervilee [*sic*] and I felt.

With sincere regards,

Ethel Snowden

Leopold Stokowski

Of Polish and Irish descent, Leopold Stokowski (1882–1977) became a student at the Royal College of Music in 1896. He moved to New York in 1905 as an organist and choirmaster but soon made his name as director of a number of American orchestras, most notably the Philadelphia Orchestra. He gained international fame for his appearance in Walt Disney's animated film *Fantasia*. He was a flamboyant character with an unrestrained manner of conducting.

254. *15th March 1930   Leopold Stokowski to HJF* [typed]

Packard Building, Philadelphia

Dear Mr Foss –

I am so delighted at the prospect of seeing you when you come back from the West.

I too remember with so much pleasure our day together in London.

Sincerely your friend,

LEOPOLD STOKOWSKI

255. *28th April 1930   HJF (Washington) to DMF*

To go back to Friday, I lunched with Stokowski. He was very full of things although rather tired after a heavy season, and most communicative. He's going to be a father again soon it seems – no. 3 is expected. We got on splendidly as usual, and formed a real basis for interchange of ideas, although we both adopted the convention that he is not English. He glibly says to me 'In your country'! We lunched at his club and he said he was coming to England for a few days and wanted a quiet country holiday. I suggested various places, like Thame and Pangbourne and Abbotsbury, and asked him to come and stay with us. I think he probably will – I hope so because he's most exciting as a person and you'd be thrilled I am sure. Also I shouldn't feel such a pig meeting all these people without you. I'm seeing him again in New York next week I hope. I'm determined to make him play more British music – only one thing last year's season – the Enigma Variations and then he didn't conduct it himself!

I went to his concert in his private box – a request performance. The orchestra was magnificent but very tired, it was clear. This is their last pair of concerts (they always give two of the same programme, Friday afternoon and Saturday evening). They did César Franck's Symphony, a good performance which made the work no less detestable to me! Meistersinger Overture, gloriously played, a stupid piece of orchestral burlesque by Coppola,[79] and a piece that has got the States running this season, the new Bolero by Ravel, which is nothing but a highly skilful nerve-tickler. Sto (or Stokey as Philadelphia calls him!) made a speech (in broken English as usual!) and then I went to his room. He's got it furnished in highly modernistic style, most amusingly and has a valet whom he bullies rather prettily!

79   Piero Coppola (1888–1971), Italian conductor and composer.

Christopher Stone

Christopher Stone (1882–1965) was editor of the *Gramophone* magazine founded in 1923 by his brother-in-law Compton Mackenzie, and from 1927 a regular broadcaster on the BBC, presenting programmes of gramophone records, earning him the title of the first disc jockey in the United Kingdom.

256. *4ᵗʰ February 1933* **Christopher Stone to HJF**
Weston Old Rectory, Steyning, Sussex

... Just a word of appreciation for your broadcast talk the other evening,[80] the first of the series that I have had the luck to hear and just what one wanted to be told. Many thanks.

Lionel Tertis

Lionel Tertis (1876–1975), the son of Polish-Jewish immigrants in West Hartlepool, Teesside, was brought up in the East End of London. Having learnt to play the violin, he moved quickly to the viola and became the outstanding soloist on the instrument. In 1900, when only in his mid-twenties, he was made Professor of Viola at the Royal Academy of Music. He was himself a composer, adapting pieces for the viola originally written for cello, violin or piano, and many others composed works for him, including William Walton, whose Viola Concerto Tertis famously rejected but quickly realised his mistake and took up the work with great success. In 1936, at the age of sixty, he retired from performing in public and concentrated on teaching. He was awarded a CBE in 1950, and shortly after his death an International Viola Competition (1980) was inaugurated in his memory. More than anyone else, Tertis rehabilitated the viola, which was once regarded as the 'Cinderella' of string instruments.

80 Introductory talk to a concert of music by Schubert, Vaughan Williams, Bax and Delius, 1 February 1933.

257. *10ᵗʰ April 1938   Lionel Tertis to DMF*

The Westbourne Hotel, Bath

Dear Mrs Foss

Thank you so much. The little book[81] has been really <u>mostly</u> artistically produced, for which I thank Hubert with all my heart. It is a delight to look at.

Would you give him my love.

With kindest greetings

Yours sincerely

Lionel Tertis

Oh dear – do forgive this hand. I am in a <u>tearing</u>! hurry to catch post.

Michael Tippett

Michael Tippett (1905–98) was born in London and studied at the Royal College of Music. He was music director of Morley College from 1940 to 1951. A conscientious objector during WW2, he was briefly imprisoned in 1943 for failing to follow the conditions of his exemption. Although a slow developer, two works in particular helped establish his name: the Concerto for Double String Orchestra (that received a performance by amateur forces in April 1940 and its first professional performance in July 1943) and the oratorio *A Child of Our Time* (first performed in March 1944). These were followed much later, in January 1955, by the opera *The Midsummer Marriage*. In the 1980s and '90s his was to be one of the most significant names in British music.

258. *14ᵗʰ November [1937?]   Michael Tippett to HJF*

Whitegates Cottage, Oxted, Surrey

Personal

Dear Foss,

What you said on last Sunday as to 'better philosophy than music', has come to seem to me a very just criticism. I am very drawn to the boundaries between art and philosophy, or psychology even perhaps, & the price paid for the one is at the expense of the other – I can see clearly enough that in the

---

81   Lionel Tertis, *Beauty of Tone in String Playing*, with Foreword by Fritz Kreisler, OUP, 1938.

'Song of Liberty'[82] the balance is overweighted to the philosophical side, and Sunday's try-out accentuated this, because of the technical inexperience of the performers – they sang rather from 'elation' than technique! However it's got to stand on that disadvantageous ground, tho [sic] there are certain passages which I shall have to put straight and clarify.

As you might expect, even before the 'Song of Liberty' was finished, I was already living in the other mood – that of being closer to purely musical consid-erations – I got considerable profit from Vincent d'Indy's book on composition. So that for some months I have been at work on a piano solo work of a simple and more formal kind, and have no intention of leaving the earth for philo-sophical speculation again for some time to come! But your remark made this process much more conscious and clear to me & I am grateful to you for it.

Incidentally I hope I haven't been a nuisance to Alan Frank by first promising (in a sort of way) to let him have the piano work to see, by Xmas, and now letting him down. I found that the effort to drive myself to time worked the wrong way – the result was restlessness & exactly not the music I am wanting.

I have written to you in this personal way because I have felt you would be interested to know how your criticism was taken. It has come across to me eventually as helpful advice for further work. I think I feel that the 'Song of Liberty' will find its own place, but you made [me] more aware of its inherent weakness of approach & what is needed to redress the balance.[83]

With kind regards
& to your wife
Yrs sincerely
Michael Tippett

82   A Song of Liberty: The Marriage of Heaven and Hell, for chorus and orchestra to a text by William Blake (1937, unpublished).
83   This letter, read by Diana Sparkes (née Foss), was included in the CD Hubert Foss and his friends – A recital of songs, HJF001CD.

William Gillies Whittaker

William Whittaker (1876–1944), born in Newcastle upon Tyne, was mainly associated with the northeast: at the Armstrong College, Newcastle, and as conductor of the Newcastle Bach Choir (which he formed in 1915), and the Scottish National Academy of Music in Glasgow, where he became Professor of Music at the University. 'W.G.' was noted both as a composer (solo songs, unison and part songs, and choral works) and scholar, especially for his studies of Bach. He was general editor of the Oxford Choral Songs series that was launched by the OUP in 1923. Holst, a very close friend, was a major influence on his career. Whittaker's 1924 letter to Foss shows that they too became close friends soon after Foss had been made head of the OUP Music Department.

259. *28th November 1924   William Gillies Whittaker to HJF* [typed]
4 Granville Road, Jesmond, Newcastle-upon-Tyne

My dear Foss,

I feel I must write and thank you warmheartedly for all your splendid arrangements this week end.[84] You are an ideal 'manager'. You seemed to think of everything, nothing was omitted, there was no worry, and you are always smiling and ready to do services in every possible direction.

All the choir is singing your praises, but they do not sing as many as I do. It has been a wonderful experience. I shall never forget it. The memory of that music in the wonderful church, together with the appreciative and still audiences, and the enthusiasm of everyone, will be a precious dream.

With gratitude,

Yours ever

WGW

260. *Wednesday 14th November 1938   HJF to DMF*

You don't know how I hate staying at Whittaker's house, except for the personalities concerned. The food's messy and the table always cluttered up with nut cutlets and bananas: I hate W's awful anthracite stove which gives me a sleepy kind of headache, there's nothing of what I call comfort anywhere. Yet

---

84   Byrd's Great Service at St Margaret's, Westminster, 25 and 26 November 1924.

they are so nice and kind, and mean so frightfully well. Oh the bathroom! And never any hot water.

Well, I caught my train and had lunch (I knew it would be necessary!) at the Station Hotel in Newcastle. Then I went to WGW's only to find that he had a ½ holiday, so we got to business at once and chattered till he had to go to the Bach Choir rehearsal. I went with him, for cigarettes and (I don't mind telling you quietly) a whisky and soda on the q.t. I had arranged for a typist to come in at 6.30 and I solemnly dictated letters until 9.15 and then wrote some more till 10.15! After which I was tired! We'd had high tea at 5.0 (fish and cutlets on the same dish!) and then at 10 we had supper and after that W and I talked till 12. Then I struck and went to bed and the undisturbed quiet of my detective stories!

Tributes to Hubert Foss

From Herbert Howells

261. ***28ᵗʰ May 1953   Herbert Howells to DMF***

Royal Hotel, Bristol

My dear Dora:

Here in Bristol this morning I have read with great concern and very real regret of Hubert's death, and it has come not only with disturbing unexpectedness but with added poignancy in this week of general colour and happiness.[1] I send you and your son and daughter the very genuine sympathy of a fellow-musician to whom Hubert shewed unfailing and most heartening kindness and encouragement right through the years.

My last news of him had been so reassuring. He was, I know, destined for new and important editorial work[2] in a post he w[oul]d have filled brilliantly: and he must have been looking forward to it keenly.

We will all be so sorry it was not to be.

And among countless others I shall bear him in mind with admiration and affection.

You yourself will be much in our sympathetic thoughts.

I beg you not to attempt any acknowledgement of this note.

Yours very sincerely

Herbert Howells

From Gordon Jacob

262. ***28ᵗʰ May 1953   Gordon Jacob to DMF***

Pine Cottage, Brockenhurst, Hants.

My dear Dora,

Sidney and I were much shocked to see the announcement of Hubert's death in the Times today.

It seems impossible that such a vital personality should have passed away at such an early age. We quite thought that he had recovered from his illness in a remarkable way. He will be very much missed by the wide circle of friends he made in the course of his varied interests to each of which he brought his always youthful and vivid enthusiasm.

Please accept our deepest sympathy,

Yrs sincerely,

Gordon Jacob

---

1   The week prior to the coronation of Queen Elizabeth II.
2   *The Musical Times.*

From Dora Powell[3]

263. *28th May 1953* Dora Powell to DMF

Poels, East Grinstead, Sussex

Dear Mrs. Foss

I was so shocked and sad to see today's Times. I am so very sorry – & so sorry for you and all the trouble & anxiety that you must have been through. I have known Mr. Foss for so many years and shall never forget his kindness & encouragement over the 1st edition of my Elgar book by the Oxford Press in 1937.

I doubt if I should have got on so well as I have without his help.

With every sympathy

Yours sincerely

Dora M Powell

From Percy Scholes

264. *28th May 1953* Percy Scholes to DMF

Rutland House, 41 Davenant Road, Oxford

Dear Mrs Foss,

I wish to express my very deep sympathy with you and your children in the trying period through which you have been passing and the sad termination of it.

I was for long years much associated with your Husband and often had occasion to admire his outstanding ability and unceasing energy.

I remain,

Ever yours sincerely

Percy A Scholes

(Please do not think any acknowledgment to be necessary. You have enough to do at such a moment)

---

3   Dora Powell (1874–1964) was 'Dorabella', one of 'the friends pictured within' in Elgar's *Variations on an Original Theme (Enigma)* and, as Mrs Richard Powell, author of *Edward Elgar – Memories of a Variation*, OUP, 1937.

From Ralph Vaughan Williams

265.   *28th May 1953   Ralph Vaughan Williams to DMF*

The White Gates, Dorking

My dear Dora

It was dear of you to telephone – I was so glad I saw Hubert such a short time ago. He was always such a good and helpful friend to me. If there is to be any kind of memorial service, could someone let me know. I want to come if at all possible.[4]

Yours R Vaughan Williams

P.S. No answer of course.

From Michael Ayrton[5]

266.   *29th May 1953   Michael Ayrton to DMF*[6]

Bradfields, Toppesfield, Essex

Dear Mrs Foss,

I write to send my very deepest sympathy to you at the loss of my old friend Hubert whom I shall bitterly miss. I know that there is little or no comfort to be derived from such letters as this but nevertheless I should like both you and your son and daughter to know how much I valued Hubert's friendship and that I share therefore some fraction of your own loss.

Yours sincerely,

Michael Ayrton

© Estate of Michael Ayrton

---

4   Vaughan Williams attended the memorial service which was held at St John's Church, St John's Wood on 24 June 1953.
5   Michael Ayrton (1921–75), English painter and sculptor, and friend of Lambert (with whom he shared a house) and Walton, both of whom he sketched and painted. A frequent broadcaster for the BBC, in the Third Programme and on television, and an occasional member of the *Brains Trust* panel.
6   See plate 27.

From William Walton

267. ***29th May 1953   William Walton to DMF***

Lowndes Cottage, Lowndes Place, London SW1

My dear Dora.

I am dreadfully upset to read of the death of poor Hubert. I'd only just heard that he had been so ill & I was looking forward to coming to see him as soon as the Coronation was past.

He was always such a staunch supporter & I can never forget what a help he was to me in the early days or for that matter always.

The only small comfort would appear that his death was sudden & that he didn't suffer any lingering agony.

Susana[7] & I send you all our deepest sympathy in your sad loss.

As ever

William

From Arthur Bliss

268. ***30th May 1953   Arthur Bliss to DMF***

15 Cottesmore Gardens, W8

Dear Mrs Foss,

It was with great sorrow that I heard of Hubert's sudden death. I had known him for a great number of years and shall always remember many instances of his generosity to me and my music. One of the most characteristic things about him was that he was incapable of small gestures or petty actions. I feel the musical world has suffered a great loss by the death of so vital and generous a spirit. Please accept my deep and sincere sympathy.

Arthur Bliss

---

7   Susana Gil Passo, Walton's Argentinian wife whom he married in January 1949.

From Edward Dent

269. 1st June 1953   E.J. Dent to DMF

17 Cromwell Place, SW7

Dear Mrs Foss

Hubert's creation of the musical department of the Oxford Press was nothing short of epoch-making in English music. Before that, the young English composer met with no encouragement from the old-established music publishers who were interested only in oratorios, church & organ music of the conventional kind, or in drawing-room ballads and military band music.

Vaughan Williams, up to 1924, was published mainly by Breitkopf & Härtel in Leipzig, and some of the other composers had to rely on German firms. Hubert was the only music publisher who was a real musician himself as well as being young, energetic and enterprising. Apart from the modest help of the Carnegie Trust, the OUP was the only hope for young composers, and for a good many young composers in foreign countries too. The modern English School could never have made headway without Hubert's understanding, encouragement & practical help.

I can't tell you how much I feel indebted to him myself, as a writer & translator, and for his continual support and for the stimulus he always gave me towards future work. Only a few days before his death I got a letter from him asking me about the projected publication of my collected essays – a plan that I should never have thought of myself at all if he had not originally suggested it. It is unfortunate that he was not able to take up the editorship of The Musical Times, as he would certainly have put new life into that very orthodox and conventional periodical.

With all sympathy,

Yours sincerely,

Edward Dent

From John Gardner

270.   *11ᵗʰ June 1953   John Gardner to DMF*

4 South Close, Morden, Surrey

My dear Dora,

I was greatly shocked and saddened to learn of Hubert's death since, apart from being so fond of him as a person and friend, I suppose I owe what little success I have achieved as a composer to his enthusiasm and drive in the nineteen-thirties when, alone among the big wigs of the profession, did he consider it worthwhile to encourage my writing of music as something more than the spare-time composition of anthems and glees to which my professors thought I should relegate it.

English music has lost one of its greatest benefactors (in the spiritual sense) and I hope that greater names in the profession than mine (who owe just as much as I do to Hubert) will recognise that fact.

With all sympathy and kindness to you and your family in their sorrow,

Y[our]s ever

John Gardner

From Roger Quilter

271.   *12ᵗʰ June [1953]   Roger Quilter to DMF*

Dear Mrs Foss,

Please forgive me for not writing before this. I have been ill ever since my birthday party on Nov 1ˢᵗ. I felt so grieved for you, and he was always so good to me.

I am sure you know you have my very deepest sympathies.

Believe me, dear Mrs Foss

Always very sincerely yours,

Roger Quilter

[Roger Quilter died on 21 September 1953.]

Hubert James Foss 1899–1953

by Herbert Howells
An address delivered at St John's Church, St John's Wood,
on 24 June 1953

In a mood of gratitude and affection we are here to honour the memory of
Hubert Foss: not in cold judicial terms, but as men and women eager to mark,
in a lost friend and artist, attributes of impulsive generosity any of us might
envy, and all of us would wish to acquire.

A Johnsonian epigram reminds us that in paying tribute to a departed friend
we are not on oath. But whether on oath or otherwise, we need not fear to see a
man whole. To have any value at all, tribute is best offered against a background
of courageous sincerity, and with a wide-eyed view of all the circumstances
surrounding and shaping its subject.

It is customary to set bounds to a man's life by dates of birth and death and
the sum of years. In the eyes of government the method has its uses. It is tidy
– but it is unimaginative. It lays stress upon a numerical quantity rather than
upon the tempo and intensity of a career. It will have been remarked in most of
the obituaries of Hubert Foss that his life was comparatively short. But the true
measure of the span of life – and it is particularly true of the man we honour
today – is the intensity, scope, contacts and enterprises, and (even more) the
temper of that life.

Today, so soon after his going, we have a vivid impression of his bounding
vitality, of his sometimes reckless passion for kaleidoscopic activity, of a
physical exuberance that was the counterpart of a restless energy of mind, of
an insatiable interest in things and causes and people. Almost the impression
is of a man caught up in a series of days whose hours numbered themselves
beyond the appointed two dozen; a man whose calendar would appear to have
acquired unconventional and unaccepted extensions. In the years to come that
impression will be adjusted and clarified. It will permit a less confused estimate
of the unsparing profusion of his interests. It will rid us of the concern we may
at the moment feel as to the possible wastage of a brilliant energy – energy so
often devoted to tasks he may have suspected of being ephemeral. In any later
and steadier view the hard core of solid achievement will be acknowledged. In
a clearer light than even his own brilliance could throw upon his enterprises,
we shall come to see the nature and value of what was permanent.

But today, in our affectionate memory of him, it is no business of ours to take time by the forelock, or to anticipate a verdict that cannot yet be arrived at. In the meantime we who knew the mastery of his dialectic might wish it were possible to ask him what *he* would have accounted the permanencies and the ephemera to which he set his hand. One may suspect his answers would be Foss-like – unexpected, unpredictable; almost certainly excluding from the catalogue of ephemera things commonly rated as such. The journalistic element, for example: that class of products so perishable as to be unable to outlive the day of birth. Most likely he would have said, 'I wrote this article, and that notice, reviewed X's book and Y's symphony, with eager interest, white-hot indignation, or excited admiration. The things I set down in the one and the other were the product of my heart and mind. They may soon be lost, forgotten. But they were at the time a living part of me. Were they, in essence, ephemeral?' So might he have spoken.

The singer, the actor, the lecturer can all perish with the breath of their works and so pass into a swift oblivion. As for lectures, I think he would have claimed the power of survival. He would have numbered some of his own as by no means among the vanished assets.

Those of us who from time to time have passed through the inescapable studios of the BBC, delivering talks, may with a humility not untouched by pessimism think only of the swift mortality of words addressed to a microphone. But I believe he himself, who so often graced 'Music Magazine', or in old days spoke to the Ordinary Listener, or on occasions of prime importance was entrusted with authoritative pronouncements of grave matter and high import – I think he would have scorned the common assumption that such utterances died with the breath that launched them. Even now, and without effort, we can catch again and retain in memory the inflections of a beautifully-modulated voice saying things of utmost grace of style, and (so often) of permanent value.

We must be wary in our too-glib assessment of the supposed ephemera of brilliant men and women. The wastage in human achievement is often critically linked with our own refusal to attempt an intelligent salvage. Foss was a salutary rebuke to us: to those of us, for instance, who, for so long, had entertained an almost pitying admiration for an odd electrifying man called Donald Tovey, who seemingly was galloping to certain oblivion in a chariot of his own eloquence. We all knew the majestic sweep of Tovey's knowledge. Willingly we were ready to sit at his feet, listening to his convoluted but penetrating commentary upon music and musical analysis. There was a ready lip-service to the man who in his own life-time had become an Oracle, almost a Legend. There were concert programmes, containing notes. But these we generally lost on the way home from the concert. We did not worry. But Hubert Foss did. With irrepressible zeal he saw to it that Tovey should not be allowed to become the archetype of the ephemeral. The fruits of Tovey's knowledge and Hubert's tact and patience now adorn the shelves of every serious student in the land.

We might well see to it that our late friend's own Programme Notes shall not be lost. For indeed they are the reflection not merely of a rich mind but of a warm humanity. *The Times* did well, in its notice of the Coronation Concert on the very night of his death, to remind us how in his programme-note on Vaughan Williams's 'Sea Symphony' Hubert declared his 'inability to write about it judicially and without deep affection'.

That phrase is worth remembering. It touches and reveals a heart that was often disputing a mind. Disputing sometimes, perhaps, to a point imperilling critical balance. I have often pondered the struggles between heart and mind that must have torn him in the exercise and responsibilities of his chief enterprise – the building of the Music Department of the Oxford University Press. For that task, the most enduring of all his works, he enjoyed the liberal, far-seeing support of Sir Humphrey Milford. But the editorial and managerial hand, the bias, emphasis and direction were, from its birth in 1924 onwards for eighteen or nineteen years, Hubert's own.

The fruits of that work have been rich and abundant. He brought to his task an infallible ear for the significant and vital in the work of younger men. Not only the warm heart but also the cooler mind was admitted to the choice and publication of the works of Walton and Lambert in the days of their still-unproven mastery. The early Rawsthorne was brought in; so, too, was Moeran, at a critical stage. Warlock was passed on to us; and under Foss's hand Gurney's lovely songs ended their wanderings. Finzi knocked at the door of Amen House and was with many another made welcome. More than all else, Vaughan Williams became identified with the Oxford University Press in Foss's day; and with that identity went the promise and ultimate fulfilment of authoritative biography of that illustrious composer.

The heart and mind of a man governing the accumulation of an extensive catalogue ought, under Providence, to be inhumanly poised and balanced. If the catalogue came to include some dusty items among its shining riches, need one wonder? If what we now recognise as dead-weight seemed, in its springtime, to deserve the first opportunity for young-eyed creative effort, need we complain? Shall we criticize the generous spirit of the man who took a risk? It is precisely that generosity of his that now so moves us to admiration and affection. And there went with it two other qualities – courage and loyalty. Out of direct experience of these qualities I could myself so easily speak. So could anyone in the wide community of his friends. I could, for example, in imagination, take you with him, as I in fact took him many times, to visit a grievously afflicted fellow-composer spending the slow grim days of mental decline in a remote asylum. More even than the victim's own ruin and misery I recall the signs of Hubert's compassion and his dread of the ordeal of those visits. He went again and again, seeking with exemplary tact and persistence for any means by which he might mitigate another man's misery.

Those who best know the merciful workings of the Musicians' Benevolent Fund could relate how in the stern and recent time of his own physical suffering he was still the irrepressible optimist in the sight and hearing of those about him whose misfortune seemed to trouble him more than his own. Courage of compassion he certainly had. Courage of opinion, too. That brand of his courage held decisive results for many of us. Without permission (but, I hope, without offence) I will quote from a letter written a few days ago by a composer[8] now widely known and established. He wrote:

'Apart from being so fond of him as a companion, I suppose I owe what little success I have achieved as composer to his enthusiasm and drive in the nineteen-thirties when, alone among the big-wigs of the profession, did he consider it worthwhile to encourage my writing of music as something more than the spare-time composition of anthems and glees to which my professors thought I should relegate it. English music has lost one of its greatest benefactors (in the spiritual sense) and I hope that greater names in the profession than mine (who owe just as much as I do to Hubert) will recognize that fact.'

There are in this gathering of his friends so many who could speak with direct authority on other of his activities and cherished causes. Those who were for five or six years his leading collaborators in the Bach Cantata Club have told me of his selfless work for the important music-making of that society. There are discerning musicians who think of him first as the man whose settings of Thomas Hardy revealed the sensitive creative gift that was in him. A series of Christmas Cards signed 'Dora and Hubert' are of the kind one keeps and

---

8   John Gardner, writing to Dora Foss on 11 June 1953. See letter 270, p. 245.

treasures, for to their choice and printing and whole presentation went the grace and exquisite taste that marked his influence in many a distinguished product of the Oxford Press. His heart and mind were attuned to the beauty of sound; his eye to the beauty of the printed page. To the excitement of writing a poem he could add that of printing it with all the experienced skill of a born typographer. On small and great things he lavished an equal care and discernment. For him, the appearance of things in print and the message they contained were indissoluble.

The current of his life ran swiftly. There were perils. He survived them. There were excitements, exhilaration. He turned them to profit. He reached journey's end on the full tide of the admiration and sympathy of countless friends. His courage remained, his optimism defied disasters when these threatened. In his home most of all, and but little less abroad among his colleagues and fellow-musicians, he found a rare devotion. In the tempo and zest of his days he outpaced many of us who, to his swift gaze, must have seemed as men stuck fast in yesterday. That is why the impression remains not of our looking back to him, but forwards.

If now his tireless and driven spirit is at last still, we pray it may rest in deep tranquillity and peace.[9]

---

9   Extracts from this address are read by Diana Sparkes (née Foss) on the CD *Hubert Foss and his friends – A recital of songs*, HJF001CD.

From J. McKay Martin[10]

The Musical Times, August 1953, p. 371

I want to write about Hubert Foss the man, not Hubert Foss the musician, publisher or writer. Others more capable than I have dealt with that side of his life. I want to write about him as a friend. I have not known him as long as some people, but during the past eleven or twelve years we have been very closely associated in all sorts of ways. I have stacks of letters and notes – his bits of paper were famous – asking for my comments on articles, scripts and the like, on which he was engaged.

Sometimes I wondered why he did this, because I have great difficulty in putting my thoughts on paper and have none of those enviable capacities by which some seem to get to the heart of a problem almost before the problem is propounded. I can only think he did it because he always valued a candid and genuine opinion even if he disagreed with it. What he could not stand was pretension, and he was capable of being almost brutally rude to those who put up a façade of knowledge.

All this brings me to the first great point about him: his very real humility. His was an endless search for knowledge and understanding. And with this went a capacity for giving help to others. About a year ago he gave three talks on music to a very small group of people at a South East London Settlement. I know at first hand of the great trouble he took to prepare his talks, a trouble out of all proportion to their seeming importance. The organizer of these meetings will bear me out when I say that not only did he do this; he made himself available to her at almost any hour to give advice and assistance in the planning and arrangements. I remember when it was over he said to me, 'I hope it is what you wanted. I hope it was useful to them.'

Then there was his keen and very lively appreciation of natural beauty. I remember walking with him one day on the outskirts of Epping Forest hammering away at some project which was taking shape in his mind. In the middle of a most involved discussion he suddenly called my attention to some little flowers growing on the bank. Over and over again he did that kind of

---

10   James McKay Martin was a close friend of Hubert Foss. It was he who suggested the conva-lescence subscriptions for Hubert on his illness in 1950 (see list of contributors in letter 7, p. 43).

thing: clouds scurrying across the sky; a vista, perhaps unnoticed by many; some unexpected architectural beauty; to such things he was instantaneously responsive. To the resilience of his mind and the strength and courage of his convictions his whole life and work bear witness. In friendship it was the same. He was quick to sense a mood, quick to understand and appreciate a difficulty, and even quicker to give help and comfort. For he moved among the great with distinction and amongst the less famous with rare courtesy and never-failing kindness. He never patronized a single human being. To him the paper-seller who played the cornet in his spare moments was as worthy of his notice as the world-famous performer.

His whole life was a never-ceasing search for the truth of things, the truth of art, the truth of living, the truth, as far as he could get at it, about himself. To that truth he got a good deal nearer than most of us.

With this awareness went the courage that carried him forward in all his undertakings and sustained him during his long and serious illnesses. Even during these difficult periods he was always looking forward with characteristic clear thought and determination. He never repined. There was nothing negative or backward-looking about his thinking. When events failed him, he quickly moved on to something else. If anyone carried thought and action into realms of present accomplishment, and future hope, it was Hubert Foss. His example is a shining one.

J. McKay Martin

From Ralph Vaughan Williams

272. 25th July 1953   Ralph Vaughan Williams to DMF

The White Gates, Dorking

My dear Dora,

I am so glad to have a copy of the Vesper Hymn.[11] Thank you so much for sending it.

With love from us both,

Love

Ralph

---

11   Hubert Foss's last composition, OUP, 1953. It was performed at his memorial service.

VESPER HYMN

Words and music by Hubert Foss

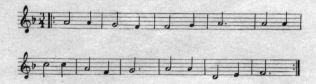

Now the end of day is near,
Lord, we ask thy presence here;
    Guard us through the night.

Evil dreams, we pray, avert,
Sin, temptation, thoughts that hurt;
    Keep us pure till light.

Pray we to Thine only Son;
Thou, the Spirit, He are one;
    Save us by Thy might.

Amen.

Fig. 12: Hubert Foss's *Vesper Hymn*, 1953

At the Memorial Service, in St John's Church, St John's Wood on
24 June 1953, Hubert Foss's *Come, sleep* and *Vesper Hymn* were sung
with RVW's motet *O taste and see* and Bach's *Come, sweetest Death!*

Selected Poetry of Hubert Foss

Hubert was an avid reader of English literature and particularly of English poetry, and he composed poems from childhood. Many were occasional poems, for births, birthdays and anniversaries; others were linked to places and events. Most are clever, light and humorous, and reflect the musical talent which he possessed in abundance. While in the 1920s he contributed a few poems to such journals as *The New Witness* and *New Age*, they were generally written for private enjoyment. This small selection is devoted to the poems he dedicated to his beloved Dora. Some carry a date and/or the occasion.

TO DORA, FOR MUSIC
18–19 February 1939, Toronto

The swan sings again,
Firm-necked, courage-eyed:
It was not her last song.

She sails, through thickening rushes
Into the open water
Splendid as strong men swimming,
Or quiet, like a cat in a corner
Whose avenues none can follow.

The sound of her breath, her voice renewed,
A low note, a high note –
She is the one singing swan,
She will sing at my death,
And joy my mourners.

DORA
Christmas [undated]

When Christmas time is coming round,
    I feel my view is wrong,
For everyone is all a-bound,
      Their hearts are full of song,
      They yearn and itch and long!
While I would rather go to ground
Till all the glories have been found.

Here is a little extra thing
    That might assist your nose,
It's black, and therefore does not ring
      'gainst bag or winter/summer clothes.
(I scorned the peach and rose!)
If it encourages you to sing,
that will be, once more, everything.

It's rightly called (I'm told) compact
    (of what I have no notion),
I learnt at school Latin and tact,
      All about land and ocean,
      Deportment and free motion.
      Assisted by more lotion!
Your use will prove the name a fact;
I'll learn on seeing how you act.

It seems to me a curious toy,
As swift to pass as water,
But as you have a strapping boy,
    An enviable daughter,
I offer it in hope some joy
    will follow in its train some time
(I've had to change the scheme of rhyme)
And ask you to believe that I'm
    Affectionately Hubert.

TO DORA – MY AMBITION
Easter [undated]

I want to write
      Thousands of words,
Words about music
      Not mathematics,
      Nor logorithms
      cosines or surds.
Can we do something at Easter?

Uninterrupted by
      Flanders or slanders,
News of superlative
      feats of commanders:
Just my silly old book,
      One day you'll all have a look!

Five days away from it –
      Days clear of office – then
Days don't matter a bit!
      (save to an earner
      who still is a learner!)
Let's get a scheme going when.

Dictionary troubles me
      more than my mood –
more than a family,
more than your views of me,
      far more than food.
Maybe it'll be quite good!

Under a new régime
Things won't be what they seem
      (Gilbertian rhyme)
Tell me it's not so bad
So many words a day
Saying his silly say,
Then Father won't look so mad.

I'll wake at 6 o'clock
      start work at seven,
         write all the day

Till when the syllables block
   flow of the pen
      I shall sleep then.
     P'raps at 11.
That w'd be heaven!

RONDEL
28 February 1944

When Dora sang, I heard the poet's word,
   His flexions ordered to our English tongue.
Each nature's sweet disorder that occurred
   Tamed to our music, in our music sung,
And yet with voice as simple as a bird,
   When Dora sang.

Many our English singers: who among
   Them, with vowels Italian, has not erred,
Nor with German accent? Few have stirred
   our hearts so simply, richly. There was rung
A bell in English music to be heard,
   When Dora sang.

FOR DORA – MOTHERING SUNDAY
27 March 1949
(with suitable acknowledgements to the *Oxford Book of Carols*)[1]

'It is the day of all the year,
of all the year the one day,
when I shall see my Mother dear,
And bring her cheer.
A-Mothering on Sunday.'

The Pope should bless the golden rose,
The son go to the baker
To fetch a cake, and as he goes

---

1   First published OUP, 1928, edited by Percy Dearmer, R. Vaughan Williams and Martin Shaw.

The daughter mind the household close,
A-resting time to make her.

Of old we should have brought to you
Caraway, cinnamon, spice,
To make your dishes pleasant.
We'd hope your taste would find them nice
To flavour bread and cakes and rice;
we can't do that at present!
There is no baker, nor no wheat,
No simnel cake to offer;
Little we get, but what we eat
Is fetched by Mother's nimble feet,
Is all provided, trim and neat,
From your unfathomed coffer.

Others may testify in kind
with presents on this one day:
my verse I hope you will not mind –
At best, it's just the crusty rind
of what I feel this Sunday.

'He who will go a-Mothering
Finds violets in the lane.'
May I find violets burgeoning,
Blessings once and again,
From those whom you sustain!

'It is the day of all the year.'
The washing hangs on Monday.
Tuesday, there's 'Binding' on the air,[2]
And Music Club is very near;
By Friday night, the week's a year,
And grocer's goods are shocking dear,
The lack of meat's a horrid fear.
But 'here come I, our Mother dear'
(Long in the trotter, antique and sere)
'To bring you cheer
A-Mothering on Sunday.'

2   The popular comedy radio programme *Much-Binding-in-the-Marsh*.

BIRTHDAY GREETING TO DORA
[undated]

I'm sorry my plans went all astray,
    I tried (and failed) to keep to the day,
But that is the play of the world and its way,
    And not a thing will I try to say.

However, I found that I had a book strewn
    In a certain place where you would never look –
Maybe it's a spectre, perhaps it's a spook.
    But something, in some of the papers, caught me on a hook,
I fought – perhaps I was 'took'?

So I add my little dedication
with love and respects
And all admiration,
Knowing you're doing the work of a nation,
without a reward or remuneration.

Happy birthday, may you live
To gain reward for all you give.
    Love – Hubert

FOR DORA – A LOVING TRIBUTE
20 July 1947 [wedding anniversary]
Two Decades – A Ballade

My wave-length made touch with some fine protozoa,
    A larva, bacillus, and heterodyme.
The contact was clear, and though nothing much lower
    Has ever been known since man grew from the slime,
They answer my question, unlike the Brain's Trusters
    When I asked of their process of 'blood, sweat and tears,'
They replied on the dot, without hiccoughs or blusters,
    'The difficult time is the first million years.'

I argued with Schoolmen, those scholars Erasmic
    Who rose from the mud of the ignorant age.
The men who dug learning from minds almost plasmic,
    Forgotten old mouths whom their cells had made sage.

The amplified voice scarcely roused their attention,
      Their minds were intent, so they'd closed up their ears:
But one time, they answered, in Latin declension,
      'The <u>difficult</u> time is the first thousand years.'

I put up a query in Hampton Court Gardens,
      A plantain, a grass-tuft, responded at once.
They bawled out in concert, 'of course, the soil hardens.
      If a thousand fools stride on the lawn like a dance.'
The plantain was violent, expecting the hoer,
      The grass was more kindly, said almost in tears,
'If you give me some water, a roller and mower,
      The <u>difficult</u> time is the first hundred years.'

Methuselah groaned, with a fine flow of curses,
      For I was disturbing his elderly sleep,
And Old Father William was mumbling his verses
      As he brought in his crony, the elderly sheep.
Politely, I asked about eldermen's knowledge;
      Is it boredom, or deafness, or stiffness that sears?
They jointly replied 'We have not been to college,
      But the <u>difficult</u> time is the first fifty years.'

At Dartmoor, one morning, I spoke to a lifer,
      An old lag if ever one lived on this earth,
A burglar, recidivist, bag-snatcher, knifer,
      Who knew just exactly what prison was worth.
I asked him to talk about years long before us,
      When no doubt he was gay with his 'buds' and his 'dears';
He answered, backed up with a faint, cell-like chorus,
      'The <u>difficult</u> time is the first seven years.'

ENVOI
Princess, in traditional manner, I greet you
      (I'm not a royal consort – you stand with your peers)
With inadequate rhymes, for no words can complete you,
      The <u>difficult</u> time is the first twenty years.

TO DORA
19th December 1949 [her 56th birthday]

Nineteen from twenty-five is six,
And what a fix it puts me in!
Christmas and birthday do not mix,
And jam today must be spread thin!

There isn't anything of value
That writer's pockets can achieve.
A single gift (one thinks) or shall you
In preference spread out what you give?

Nothing I have could do you honour,
Nor can I find a fitting gift.
Take from me, with voluntas bona,
What came to me as a last shift.
It is hardly beautiful, not precious,
No great achievement of the hands,
Not of a quality to mesh us
In 'amorous nets' or 'beauty's bands'.

Rather, it is a humble token
That I know it's your natal day.
And here, I'm sure, you're glad I've spoken
This last word that my verse can say
(Except to wish your birthday could be more exciting, full and gay.)

Dora Foss: A Eulogy

Avril Wood

Dora lived to the age of eighty-four, an amazing feat considering how many times she had been ill with TB during her life. Christopher and Diana decided that Avril Wood should be asked to give the eulogy at her service of thanksgiving, which was full of English music. She had known Dora since the 1930s. Her father was Sir Henry Wood, with Robert Newman founder of the Promenade Concerts; her mother, Lady (Muriel) Wood, was Diana's godmother. Avril herself had worked for the music section of the British Council and was very 'au fait' with the musical world. She was a perfect choice, and we feel proud to print the eulogy here in Dora's memory.

DORA FOSS WAS THE MOST WARM, vital and lovable person, and to me, of course, above all, a wonderful friend, and it is as a friend of nearly fifty years' standing that I have been asked to say these few words about her.

I was a school girl in the early 1930s when I first remember her and Hubert coming to lunch with my parents at their house in Chorleywood where we used to spend the summers. Dora often told me of the first time she met Henry and Muriel Wood, my parents, for Hubert took her to meet them on the Sunday before their marriage in July 1927, and apparently my father and Hubert never stopped talking musical 'shop' from the second they arrived until the second they left, and I remember Dora saying that it served as a wonderfully useful introduction and warning as to what her future life, married to Hubert, would be. A little later on, Dora and Hubert moved to Rickmansworth and became fairly close neighbours, and there was much coming and going between the two households.

My father was a great friend and ardent admirer of the Fosses, and used to describe Hubert as 'the liveliest of live wires'. Dora fulfilled wonderfully the role as conductor of all that electricity that Hubert generated. Of him as Head of the Music Department of the Oxford University Press, Professor Edward Dent wrote: 'His work was nothing short of epoch-making in English Music.' Dora can claim a large share of the credit for that description, for behind that epoch-making work was the wife whose sympathetic enthusiasm and knowledge went far to match her husband's, and whose whole life was devoted to supporting him and to furthering his career and interests.

The two of them were in the forefront of all the exciting things that were happening in music here in the thirties. They were familiar figures at concerts, parties and all sorts of social musical gatherings. They knew everyone, and everyone knew them, and they were in the thick of everything at the start of what could be called the English musical renaissance, a re-birth in which Hubert played so large and vital a part, and Dora was the ideal companion for such a man at such a time. She was herself a very gifted singer with a warm, musical and very pleasing voice – and she could certainly have made a full-time career as a professional singer had she not devoted so much of her energies to furthering Hubert's cause and to bringing up their two children. But those were indeed labours of love, and what a joy those two children, Diana and Christopher, and her son- and daughter-in-law, Brian and Norah, were to her all her life, and how proud and devoted she was to her two grandchildren, Philip and Catherine. She followed their every doing with intense interest and keen pleasure, and whenever she and I were in touch, she would regale me with the latest news of their progress, but never boringly, never in the tedious detail of which some fond grandmothers are guilty.

She had over twenty years of widowhood, and when Hubert died, a very bright light went out for her, but she never allowed her interests, enthusiasms and humour to wane. They continued to flourish and she kept in close touch with all that was going on in the profession. I spent many delightful evenings with her at Corringham Road when we indulged in what I can only describe as a 'gorgeous gossip' – and I shall miss these sadly. She seemed to me no older on that wonderfully happy and lively occasion of her 80th birthday party in Christopher's and Norah's house, than when I first remember her all those years ago at those lunch parties in Chorleywood. She never let her mind grow old and her humour was as fresh and vigorous when we had our last 'gorgeous gossip' on the telephone some weeks ago, as it had ever been.

Dora was, to use a modern expression, a 'life-enhancer'. Her family and all her friends are more the poorer for her loss, but I for one am more than grateful than I can ever say, for having had so many years of the joyous and generous companionship of this loving and much-loved friend.

February 1978

Discography

Unless otherwise stated the following recordings are issued on CD.

1. Dora Stevens

Haydn Wood: *Bird of Love Divine* (1912)
Robert Coningsby Clarke: *Loving is so sweet* (1912)
Beatrice Parkyns: *There is dew for the flow'ret* (1902)
    Dora Stevens (accompanist uncredited)
    Recorded at The Hayes Gallery, 19 May 1914 (private recordings)

Walton: *Three Songs* – *Daphne*, *Through Gilded Trellises* and *Old Sir Faulk*
(Edith Sitwell)
    Dora Stevens,[1] Hubert Foss
    Recorded 20 March 1940
    Decca M489–90 (78), Dutton CDAX8003 and HJF002CD

Warlock: *Rest, sweet nymph*
    Dora Stevens, Hubert Foss
    Date unknown (private recording)

2. Hubert Foss as accompanist

Schumann: *Du bist wie eine Blume*
Brahms: *Auf dem Schiffe*
    Dorothea Helmrich, Hubert Foss
    Recorded c. 1931
    Columbia 'History of Music by Ear and Eye' Vol. 4 DB1233 (78)

---

1   These are the only commercial recordings of Dora singing.

Schumann: *An den Abendstern*
Brahms: *Die Schwestern*
   Victoria Anderson and Viola Morris, Hubert Foss
   Recorded c. 1931
   Columbia 'History of Music by Ear and Eye' Vol. 4 DB1233 (78)

Falla: *Siete canciones populares españolas*
   No. 1 *El paño moruno*
   No. 2 *Seguidilla murciana*
   No. 3 *Asturiana*
   No. 4 *Jota*
   No. 5 *Nana*
   No. 6 *Canción*
   No. 7 *Polo*
      Nancy Evans, Hubert Foss
      Recorded 13 July 1937, Thames Street Studios, London
      Decca X197–8 (78s), Dutton CDBP9723

Ivor Gurney:
   The Scribe **(de la Mare)**
   Nine of the Clock **(John Doyle = Robert Graves)**
   All Night under the Moon **(W.W. Gibson)**
   Blaweary **(W.W. Gibson)**
   You are my Sky **(J.C. Squire)**
   Latmian Shepherd **(Edward Shanks)**
      Nancy Evans, Hubert Foss
      Recorded 20 April 1938, Thames Street Studios, London
      Decca K889–90 (78s), Dutton CDBP9723

The Lord is my Shepherd **(arr. Jacob)**
   Margaret Donnington, Mary Datchelor School Choir, Hubert Foss
   Columbia, National Sound Archive (British Library)

3. Hubert Foss as composer

She walks in beauty as the night (Lord Byron)
As I walked forth one May morning (William Blake)
The trees they do grow high (Hertfordshire folk song arr. Foss)
The new mistress (A.E. Housman)
Rioupéroux (James Elroy Flecker)
The Sergeant's song (Thomas Hardy)
If I had but two little wings (Samuel Taylor Coleridge)
Auprès de ma Blonde (French trad. arr Foss)
    Gordon Pullin, Charles Macdonald
    Recorded November 1998, Roedean School, Brighton
    HJF001CD

Agincourt Song (arr. Foss)
Three Ravens (arr. Foss)
Here's a health unto his majesty (arr. Foss)
L'amour de moi (arr. Foss)
    Goss Male Quartet
    Divine Art DDA25048

Bach Cantata BWV85 *Ich bin ein guter Hirt* movement 5 transcr. Foss *See what his love can do*
    Jonathan Plowright (piano)
    Hyperion CDA67767

4. Hubert Foss as speaker

1. Talk by Hubert Foss, reviewing E. Walter White's 'The Rise of English Opera', broadcast on the BBC Third Programme on 12 October 1951.
2. BBC talk by Hubert Foss on Herbert Hughes, broadcast on the BBC Northern Ireland Home Service, 4 June 1952.
3. 'Ralph Vaughan Williams, OM', a talk by Hubert Foss originally heard on the BBC North of England Home Service, 14 January 1953 after the broadcast of the first performance of *Sinfonia Antartica*, and repeated in *Music Magazine*, Home Service, on 8 March 1953.

[These recordings, in private hands, are the only ones known to exist of Hubert Foss talking.]

Select Bibliography

A Book of Instructions about Printing, intended to define the Style of the House of Henderson & Spalding Limited, Camberwell, Henderson & Spalding[1] by Hubert J. Foss, 1926

The Heritage of Music collected and edited by Hubert J. Foss, OUP, 1927

Music in My Time by Hubert J. Foss, Rich & Cowan, 1933

The Heritage of Music (Vol. 2) collected and edited by Hubert J. Foss, OUP, 1934

The Concertgoer's Handbook by Hubert J. Foss, Sylvan Press, 1946 (paperback 1951)

Ralph Vaughan Williams: A Study by Hubert Foss, George Harrap, 1950 (corrected reprint 1952)

Frederick Delius by Peter Warlock (Philip Heseltine), reprinted with additions, annotations and comments by Hubert Foss, The Bodley Head, 1952

London Symphony – Portrait of an Orchestra by Hubert Foss and Noel Goodwin, The Naldrett Press, 1954

Asmussen, Kirstie, *Hubert Foss and the Politics of Musical Progress: Modernism and British Music Publishing,* DPhil thesis, University of Queensland School of Music, 2016

Cobbe, Hugh (ed.), *Letters of Ralph Vaughan Williams 1895–1958,* OUP, 2008

Dibble, Jeremy, *Hamilton Harty – Musical Polymath,* Boydell Press, 2013

Foden, Peter and Nash, Paul W., 'The Wet Grass of Bookishness: Hubert J. Foss as Book Designer', *Matrix* 14, 1992, pp. 139–47

Geller, Eleanor, *'A Musician Talks' – Hubert Foss's broadcasts (1933–1953),* M.Mus. dissertation, University of Southampton, 2010, 321579482

Hayes, Malcolm (ed.), *The Selected Letters of William Walton,* Faber & Faber, 2002

---

1   Foss was typographical adviser to and later a director of Henderson & Spalding, Music and Lithographic and Letterpress Printers.

Hinnells, Duncan, *An Extraordinary Performance – Hubert Foss, Music Publishing, and the Oxford University Press*, OUP, 1998

Lloyd, Stephen, *William Walton: Muse of Fire*, Boydell Press, 2001

Lloyd, Stephen, *Constant Lambert: Beyond The Rio Grande*, Boydell Press, 2014

Moran, James, *The Double Crown Club, a history of fifty years*, London, Westerham Press, 1974 (limited edition)

Wright, Simon, '"Willie Comes to Tea with Symphony": Hubert Foss as Walton's Publisher', *Brio* Vol. 37 No. 2, 2000, pp. 2–14

Wright, Simon, '*The Dominant*: a note on a short-lived periodical', *Brio* Vol. 41 No. 2 Autumn–Winter 2004, pp. 36–39

Wright, Simon, 'Vaughan Williams and Oxford University Press', *Ralph Vaughan Williams Society Journal* 56, February 2013, pp. 3–15

Wright, Simon, 'Music Publishing', ch. 16 in Wm Roger Louis (ed.), *The History of Oxford University Press Vol. III 1896–1970*, OUP, 2013

Wright, Simon, '"Vaughan Williams and the Orchestra": an article by Hubert Foss introduced and edited by Simon Wright', *Ralph Vaughan Williams Society Journal* 72, June 2018, pp. 3–8

Correspondents

This list includes the writers, not the recipients, of letters included in this book. The number of letters sent by each correspondent is in square brackets, followed by the number assigned to each letter.

Allingham, Margery [1]   181
Armstrong, Thomas [1]   7
Ayrton, Michael [1]   266 (plate 27)

Barrett, Oswald [1]   182
Bax, Arnold [3]   7, 98, 184
Bliss, Arthur [4]   7, 186–7, 268
Brian, Havergal [1]   26
Bridge, Frank [1]   14
Britten, Benjamin [3]   188 (plates 22–3), 189, 191

Chesterton, Ada [1]   193
Coates, John [1]   196
Craxton, Harold [1]   1
Crofts, Freeman Wills [1]   197

Davies, Walford [1]   198
Dent, E.J. [3]   7, 201, 269
Dieren, Bernard van [3]   13, 16, 230
Draper, Ruth [1]   206

Elgar, Edward [1]   207

Foss, Dora [DMF] [12]   12, 43, 45, 74, 117, 153–7, 169, 172
Foss, Hubert [HJF] [83]   fig. 5, 8–11, 18–19, 28, 31, 37–40, 44, 46–57, 60–4, 69, 71, 75, 92–6, 113–16, 118–19, 124, 127–31, 134–7, 139–45, 166–7, 175, 178, 183, 185, 190, 192, 194–5, 203–5, 210, 243–5, 250, 252, 255, 260

Gardner, John [5]   208–9, 211, 213, 270
Goossens, Leon [1]   3
Goss, John [3]   215–17

Grainger, Percy [1]   218
Greene, Harry Plunket [2]   219–20

Hadley, Patrick [4]   4–5, 7, 221
Hadow, W.H. [8]   17, 20–5, 163
Hardy, Thomas [1]   222
Harty, Hamilton [8]   27, 29–30, 32, 111, 121–3
Heseltine, Philip [1]   33 (plates 18–19)
Hess, Myra [1]   224
Holst, Gustav [3]   225, 226 (plate 20), 227
Howells, Herbert [1]   261
Hughes, Herbert [1]   229

Ireland, John [2]   34–5

Jackson, Holbrook [1]   231
Jacob, Gordon [2]   7, 262
Jacob, Sidney [1]   228
Johnson, John [2]   202, 233
Joyce, James [1]   232

Karpeles, Maud [1]   7

Lambert, Constant [1]   36 (plate 21)
Lawrence, D.H. [2]   234–5

Mare, Walter de la [2]   199–200
Martin, J. McKay [1]   7
Meynell, Francis [1]   236
Miles, Napier [1]   237
Milford, Humphrey [1]   238
Moeran, E.J. [1]   41

Northcote, Sydney [1]   7

OUP Dramatic Society [1]   239

Index